A FAMILY CHRISTMAS

A FAMILY
Christmas

THE READER'S DIGEST ASSOCIATION
PLEASANTVILLE, NEW YORK
CAPE TOWN, HONG KONG, LONDON, MONTREAL, SYDNEY

READER'S DIGEST CONDENSED BOOKS
Editor: Joseph W. Hotchkiss
Executive Editor: John S. Zinsser, Jr.
Managing Editor: Barbara J. Morgan
Assistant Managing Editors: Anne H. Atwater, Ann Berryman,
Tanis H. Erdmann, Thomas Froncek, Marjorie Palmer
Senior Staff Editors: Jean E. Aptakin, Fredrica S. Friedman, Angela Weldon
Senior Editors: Barbara Bradshaw, Olive Farmer,
Angela C. Gibbs, Alice Murtha, Virginia Rice (Rights), Margery D. Thorndike
Associate Editors: Linn Carl, Thomas S. Clemmons, Estelle T. Dashman,
Joseph P. McGrath, Maureen A. Mackey, James J. Menick
Senior Copy Editors: Claire A. Bedolis, Jeane Garment
Associate Copy Editors: Rosalind H. Campbell, Jean S. Friedman, Jane F. Neighbors
Assistant Copy Editors: Maxine Bartow, Jean G. Cornell, Diana Marsh
Art Director: William Gregory
Executive Art Editors: Marion Davis, Soren Noring
Senior Art Editors: Angelo Perrone, Thomas Von Der Linn
Associate Art Editors, Research: George Calas, Jr., Katherine Kelleher

CB PROJECTS
Executive Editor: Herbert H. Lieberman
Senior Staff Editors: Sherwood Harris, John E. Walsh
Senior Editors: Catherine T. Brown, John R. Roberson, Ray Sipherd
Associate Editor: Dana Adkins

CB INTERNATIONAL EDITIONS
Senior Staff Editor: Francis Schell
Senior Staff Editor: Sigrid MacRae   *Senior Editor:* Istar H. Dole
Associate Editor: Gary Q. Arpin

The following appear in condensed form:
"The Legend of the Christmas Rose," *Miracle on 34th Street,*
"Old Applejoy's Ghost," "Christmas Every Day,"
"Little Jesus, wast Thou shy"

Library of Congress Cataloging in Publication Data
Main entry under title:
A Family Christmas.
Includes index.
1. Christmas—United States. 2. Christmas stories.
3. Christmas decorations—United States. 4. Christmas
cookery. I. Reader's Digest Association.
GT4986.A1F35 1984   394.2'68282   84–8343
ISBN 0-89577-193-4

Printed in the United States of America

CONTENTS

99 Christmas in the Kitchen

139 A Christmas Storybook

Grandma Mollie and Grandpa in front of their home

A Family Christmas

by Jessamyn West

The magazines lie side by side on the coffee table. One has given its space to an examination of the possibility of a nuclear holocaust. The second, this being the season when Christmas is celebrated, is filled with the memories of those who entered this world before such words had come into use.

I am such a one. Not only to a world that had no use for these words, but to a region, southern Indiana, that loved words and knew how to use them.

Near the farm where I was born were towns with names like "Gnaw Bone," "Bean Blossom," "Stony Lonesome," "Maple Grove." Writers Booth Tarkington and Lew Wallace, who wrote *Ben Hur*, grew up in nearby counties. Christmas celebrations in one-room schoolhouses from the Atlantic to the Pacific heard the recitation of Christmas verse written by Indiana poet James Whitcomb Riley.

There was less poetry heard in my grandparents' farmhouse, where I spent my first five Christmases; but the Christmases celebrated there were not quiet, either. There were reasons this was so.

First, those meeting for the celebration, though frequently related, often lived far apart. Some had not seen each other for years. They came from as far away as Kansas or Kentucky. They arrived by spring-wagon or surrey as there was no train into town. Since they were celebrating not only the birth of their Savior but the meeting after long absence of brothers and sisters, of mothers and sons, the shouts of cousins from Kansas and the softer greetings of brothers-in-law from Kentucky could be heard. Family ties had brought them to that one white farmhouse.

Children, of course, were the chief source of Christmas sounds. In later years one of those farmhouse children, remembering his earliest Christmases, wrote of his father:

> Pa, he's good to all of us
> All the time; but when
> Ever' time it's Christmas,
> He's as good again!
>
> 'Side our toys and candy,
> Ever' Christmas he
> Gives us all a quarter,
> Certain as can be!

Candy and toys and quarters! Christmas has changed, and in many ways the Christmases of my childhood were unlike the ones we celebrate now. Much that characterizes a Christmas today had not yet reached Jennings County, Indiana, during the first decade of this century. Christmas trees were not popular there as they were in England where Queen Victoria had brought them from the dark German forests of her bridegroom. Why should they be? The pioneers had spent two centuries cutting down similar trees that impeded their passage across the continent. Why should they now fill a parlor with brothers of the departed? At my grandparents' home it was certainly not done. The birth of Christ was not celebrated by the death of a tree.

This was the least of that household's peculiarities. My grandfather, a Quaker of long standing, played the accordion. His mother, a widow who shared his home, was a Quaker minister. Female preachers were not novelties to the Quakers; but a preacher whose son played the accordion was.

In addition to this, Grandpa had married an Irish girl. "Marrying out of Meeting" was not approved in those days. Quaker married Quaker. Marrying a non-Quaker Irish girl was as unconventional as accordion playing. Members of that sect believed that music stirred up the baser passion. But one look at Mary Frances Cavanagh was so stirring music was unnecessary. One look at the black hair, blue eyes, pink cheeks, made marriage, "in Meeting" or out, desirable.

Known as "Mollie" to her husband's family, and later "Grandma" to us, she seemed to have brought Christmas with her into that farmhouse. Grandma didn't transport trees from Ireland, but she did transform the house with loops of crinkled crepe paper. Pictures still remain of the long Christmas dinner table under a pagoda-like conical roof of Grandma's crepe paper attached to the kerosene lamp suspended from the ceiling.

Before the food was set forth under Grandma's crepe paper pagoda, the Christmas gifts were distributed. This was at an early hour, without the benefit of trees or stockings hung at the fireplace. The hour was early to keep the children quiet. Once the toys, the candy, and possibly the quarters were in the children's hands, there was nothing more for them to scream about.

The gifts were homemade, not store-bought, and often they were the same year after year. Aunt Allie, for example, always made bib aprons for the girls. For the boys, she knitted mittens. Grown women received pot holders, large and fancy with appliqués of farm vegetables or animals. No one complained of the monotony. There was none. Calico for aprons came in innumerable colors and designs. Mittens sometimes had fingers, sometimes did not. Christmas cards were not yet used. People still wrote letters.

It was easy in those days to give children something they didn't have. Almost any toy was magical then—clothespin dolls and balls made by winding string around a core of rubber. And a thread spool rigged up so that you could knit with it; or a homemade Indian suit of fringed khaki with an Indian bonnet, likewise homemade, of mixed Rhode Island Red and Plymouth Rock feathers.

My own mother liked to cook, and the best gift you could give her was to eat a lot of what she had provided. She often made a fondant at Christmas that she called "heavenly hash." She made it by the dishpanful, Papa pouring the hot syrup over the beaten whites of eggs while she stirred.

She made plum puddings that she steamed in one-pound Hills Brothers coffee cans; and while others may think of Christmas red as the red of holly berries, I think of it as the red of Hills Brothers coffee cans. She made plum puddings as she made everything—in bulk—so that if you were starved for plum pudding, you could sit down and eat a whole one without worrying about being selfish.

She made candied orange peel—crisp, sweet-bitter—by the crockful. She candied big English walnut halves, and fried others in butter and salted them in such quantities that by December twenty-seventh or twenty-eighth no one wanted to see another English walnut.

It was better for her to concoct her Christmas sweets about the day before Christmas. Once, trying to be forehanded (which didn't come naturally to her), she bought a five-pound bucket of store candy a couple of weeks before Christmas. Immediately after that she began saying, "Oh, children, shut your eyes. I think I hear Santa Claus's reindeer on the roof." We would close our eyes, and sure enough, when we opened them Santa had been there, leaving double handfuls of gumdrops and peppermint sticks and licorice whips. Santa just couldn't resist these premature visits—and by the time Christmas arrived he had run out of candy.

After the presents had been distributed, the dinner, which was Grandma's Christmas contribution, was put on the table. Dinner alone of our Christmas ritual differed from that of the neighboring farms where chicken was the meat dish. This was the result of the presence at the table of two women who had learned their cooking miles away in Kansas and Ireland. In Ireland a meat pie in which chicken might be included was served. Kansas brought to the feast what was portable: ham. Grandma prepared what was accepted as the ideal accompaniment of ham: candied sweet potatoes. Grandpa's mother's contribution was the result of fifty years of practice in making: a fruitcake the size of the washbowl that held the pitcher of water in each bedroom.

Christmas afternoons at Grandma Mollie's were well organized. While the young women cleared the tables, the children and older women examined the presents—their own and those of others. My cousin Ben who, along with my sister Lydia, said he liked the Fourth of July more than Christmas, demonstrated this by swinging the rag doll I had been given so close to the base-burner that you could smell her petticoats scorching. He said she was a Tory. After a trip to the woodshed with his father, Ben came back, like my doll, a hundred percent Yankee.

For Grandma Mollie, however, the purpose of Christmas had little to do with eating and gift giving. Such activities were in no way evil, but they were no more particularly suited for December twenty-fifth than for May first.

The word for Christmas was love. There were many acts of love, and gift giving could be one of them. The toys, the candy, even the quarters, made their appearance, but we were never permitted to forget that the purpose of Christmas was to celebrate the birth of Jesus in the hearts of those who loved Him.

Love comes from the heart and can best be made known by language. Grandma Mollie, with an Irishwoman's belief that we exist more fully when we let others know by the words we use what lies at our heart's core, initiated Christmas afternoons of talk. The talk could be spontaneous; could be the repetition of a poet's words; could be one's memory of words spoken by a forebear long departed the world.

My mother was always the first to be called on. She always repeated the same verse: a reminder to herself, I always felt, of our human limitations in the sight of God.

> I know not where His islands lift
> Their fronded palms in air;
> I only know I cannot drift
> Beyond His love and care.

Grandpa knew an accordion piece sufficiently religious to justify its being played on Christmas Day. It was funny, too—called "The Preacher and the Bear." The preacher's presence made the song suitable for the occasion; and the bear, who chased the preacher up a tree but never caught him, provided the excitement.

Could a child who had a mother and a grandmother and a great-grandmother, a rag doll (petticoat slightly scorched), a grandfather who knew a song about a preacher who was chased by a bear, want anything more? This one could. She wanted snow. Nothing was so Christmassy as snow. She had experienced one Christmas when the corncrib was whiter than an Eskimo igloo, when an uncle's whisker had gone from cinnamon to salt and pepper.

Most of the objects, songs, poems, associated with Christmas mentioned snow: reindeer and Santa Claus and stockings before the fireplace and sleds and holly seemed materially to belong to snow country. Did Jesus ever see snow? Southern Indiana was not always snowless, of course. But the Christmas I remember best at Grandma's was.

William Dean Howells characterized the four seasons thus: "We speak of the 'fullness of spring, the height of summer, the heart of autumn and the dead of winter.'" To my mind, there is no "dead of winter" when the ground sparkles with a covering of snow, but it really did exist the Christmases I spent at Grandma's. A sky the color of a cast-iron skillet; leafless trees; a steady fire in the kitchen stove and living-room grate.

Before the journeys home were started, the mittens Aunt Allie had knitted were pulled onto hands already turning blue. Those who lived not too far distant drank their cider and ate their fruitcake early so that their journey wouldn't keep them traveling all night. Those who did live at a distance spent the night, either at Grandma Mollie's or with relatives nearby.

After the travelers had departed, the food had been eaten and Grandma Mollie's program had been completed, those who were spending the night talked on quietly; first of the day that was ending, then of former Christmases

12

when those we did not know had been present. Grandpa's mother, the preacher, told us that when she was young, the birth of the little Jewish child who saved us was remembered with more prayer than was the custom nowadays.

"Why," said she, "there's so much hullabaloo now you can't tell whether it's July fourth or December twenty-fifth that's being celebrated."

No one was sure whether her words were directed to her son with his accordion or to Ben and Lydia, their red faces betraying their preference.

"Grandmother," her daughter-in-law said, "We haven't come to firecrackers yet for the twenty-fifth."

"Praise be," said Grandmother. "Nor hard cider."

Maybe Ben and Lydia really did prefer the Fourth of July; but for everyone else celebrating Christmas at Grandma Mollie's, there was a heart-warmth no other holiday ever produced. And the heart-warmth for Ben and Lydia has increased with the years. I know. We talk of it often.

No, no other holiday, especially not the Fourth of July with its firecracker imitation of gunfire, is comparable to the day when wise men and shepherds followed the shine of a star which led them to a crib where they learned that God is love.

We still believe it. And on Christmas Day we try to practice it.

Jessamyn West at lower left, aged five

Christmas Customs and Crafts

The Christmas Tree

Every year North Americans buy thirty-four million Christmas trees: shapely Scotch pines, elegant Douglas firs, fragrant balsams, graceful white pines, prickly cedars and even a few Norwegian blue spruce trees. In thirty-four million homes parents and grandparents, youngsters and newlyweds decorate these evergreens in thirty-four million ways, so that each is an individual, distinctive tribute to the holiday spirit.

Schoolchildren labor for hours making chains from loops of red and green construction paper. Aunts make their fingers fly crocheting a blizzard of white snowflakes for the tree of the newest niece or nephew. Even teenagers breach their carefully built blasé attitude toward life to protest the substitution of a new tree-top ornament, usurping the place of the star, now terribly battered, they have seen there "since I was a child."

Not all Christmas trees stand in homes, of course. When Skylab was circling the earth in December 1973, the three astronauts living inside fashioned a tree from odds and ends of space life—the world's first weightless tree. At office parties workers pause in their everyday pursuits to pay tribute, and maybe drink a toast, to the Christmas tree. In women's clubs committees debate for hours the choice of an appropriate theme for the tree for their club's Christmas celebrations.

Some trees are small. Sometimes by choice—a tree no more than a foot high can be exquisite, with decorations in scale. Sometimes by necessity—when it's for a small apartment or when generous-hearted gift shopping has left insufficient funds for a ceiling-scraping tree. One family spent all their

*Bring forth
  the fir tree,
The box,
  and the bay,
Deck out
  our cottage
For glad
  Christmas Day.*

ANONYMOUS, OLD ENGLISH

available cash on a tree, leaving none to buy ornaments. They improvised, beautifully decorating it with silver knives, forks and spoons.

Some trees are huge. The Nation's Christmas Tree in Kings Canyon National Park in California is a giant sequoia 267 feet tall, decorated in place. The tree for Rockefeller Center in New York City, always several stories high, is chosen only after months of searching each year. The huge tree in Trafalgar Square in London is a gift from the people of Oslo, in continuing remembrance of the days of World War II when the Norwegian royal family found refuge in Britain. Each Christmas their subjects smuggled a Norwegian tree past the Germans for them.

The tree enjoyed by the most people in the United States, thanks to television, is the one on the Ellipse, to the south of the White House, in Washington. The President of the United States takes time from his busy schedule to light this tree. The first to perform this happy task was Calvin Coolidge in 1923. But the White House has had trees indoors since 1856, when Franklin Pierce joined in a new wave of enthusiasm for Christmas trees then sweeping the country.

Not every President has approved of the custom. Theodore Roosevelt was an ardent conservationist who worried about the depletion of the nation's forests. In 1901, his first year in office, he announced there would be no White House Christmas tree. Presidential edicts made little impression on his young son, Archie, however. The President described what happened on Christmas Day in 1902:

> Yesterday morning at quarter of seven all the children were up and dressed and began to hammer at the door of their mother's and my room, in which their six stockings, all bulging out with queer angles and rotundities, were

Douglas Fir

White Pine

Red Pine

hanging from the fireplace. So their mother and I got up, . . . put on our wrappers, and prepared to admit the children. But first there was a surprise for me, also for their good mother, for Archie had a little Christmas tree of his own, which he had rigged up with the help of one of the carpenters in a big closet; and we all had to look at the tree and each of us got a present off of it.

Roosevelt asked an even greater conservationist, Gifford Pinchot, Chief of the Bureau of Forestry, to explain matters to Archie and Archie's co-conspirator, his brother Quentin. Pinchot surprised the President by telling the boys that proper harvesting of Christmas trees could actually help the timberland, by thinning it out. Archie had his tree every year after that.

In most families, unchanging ritual governs the annual selection of the tree. First, there is the trip to the lot where trees are sold, to search for the perfect tree. Since each member of the family has a different criterion of perfection, the selection is never made easily. One child may want the largest tree in sight. Another may plead for the one shaped most like the Christmas trees in picture books. The littlest child often identifies with the littlest tree. The father may notice the high prices, remember how many things are still to be bought, and wonder how to say something about money that doesn't sound Scrooge-like. Usually it is the mother who calmly observes that the big tree is too tall for the ceiling, the little tree would not have room for all the family's ornaments, and there is no use paying a lot for a classic shape when one side will not be seen. "Just picture how *this* tree will look in our corner," she says, holding one at arm's length.

The family votes: "Maybe." "I guess so." "Well, all right," and after the tree is decorated, the usual verdict is "It's the best ever."

Scotch Pine

Spruce

Balsam Fir

White Christmas by Grandma Moses, 1954

Decorating the tree is another occasion for the whole family. The collection of lights and ornaments is brought from the safe place where it stays eleven months in the year. Dad checks the wires for fire hazards and puts the lights on, the object being to distribute the lights evenly over the tree and to hide the wires in the greenery so they do not show. Other members of the family watch and offer suggestions. Then everyone has a share in putting on ornaments. Finally it is time to put a star or angel on the very top of the tree. That honor goes to the tallest family member, whoever that may be. The lights in the room are turned off, to get the full effect of the lights on the tree. By then, all present are tired enough to sit down for at least a few minutes and look at the beauty they have created together.

"It wouldn't seem like Christmas without a tree" is a sentiment that echoes and re-echoes. Actually, December's tree ritual is much older than Christmas itself. Long before Jesus was born, men and women were gathering around evergreen trees in the month of the shortest days in the year. No matter how brown and dead the rest of nature seemed, the evergreens testified that life would continue. In some regions people cut branches, or whole trees, and took them inside as symbols of life.

Christianity has its own symbols, and the church tried in its early centuries to suppress veneration of a tree, considered a relic of paganism. It seems likely that the conversion of pagan tree to Christian symbol came about by way of the legends of various trees that blossomed miraculously in the dead of winter, at Christmas. The thorn tree at Glastonbury in England is one of the most famous of these. Not every town was favored with such a miracle tree, of course, but it was a simple matter to make a representation of one by fastening handmade flowers to an evergreen tree. The earliest record we have of this practice dates from 1510. It tells how a merchants' guild in Riga, Latvia, decked a tree with flowers on Christmas Eve. In the next hundred years, similar observances were recorded in other parts of Central Europe. Other symbolic decorations soon joined the flowers.

The people who developed the most skill in decorating trees were the Germans. They excelled in making candies and cookies in beautiful shapes. By the seventeenth century, decorations that provided food for both spirit and body covered the German tree, called the *Christbaum*, the "Christ tree." It is not surprising that sometimes German children valued the tree more for its taste than for its message. In any case, the combination was irresistible.

The *Christbaum* custom spread rapidly throughout all the German states and wherever the Germans went. Legend has it that the first Christmas tree in America was set up at Trenton, New Jersey, by those Hessian soldiers

Paper angel to hang on a tree

Resplendent stands the glitt'ring tree Weighted with gifts for all to see.

ANNE P. L. FIELD

21

Antique ornaments, clockwise from left: springerle cookie made with an old wooden mold; delicate cherub made by blowing glass into a mold, a technique that originated in Lauscha, Germany; Charlie Chaplin ornament, made in the same way; Christmas tree candle in a clip-on holder counterweighted for stability; silver embossed cardboard trolley car, a type of ornament made in Dresden from 1880 to 1910.

George Washington crossed the Delaware to attack on Christmas night, 1776. While there is no firm evidence that this actually happened, there are records of Christmas trees in the homes of peaceful German immigrants who settled in Pennsylvania in the next fifty years.

In England Queen Charlotte, the German wife of King George III, introduced a Christmas tree at Windsor Castle in 1800. However, it was Prince Albert, Queen Victoria's German husband, who did the most to popularize the custom in the middle of that century. He gave decorated trees to English schools and army barracks, and in 1848 the *Illustrated London News* printed an engraving of Victoria and Albert and their children standing by a tree. Two years later in the United States, *Godey's Lady's Book* published a similar engraving. On both sides of the Atlantic fond parents were quick to copy the royal example.

Another mid-nineteenth-century picture that had a far-reaching influence involved the sixteenth-century religious reformer Martin Luther. It was said

that as Luther walked home one Christmas Eve, the stars in the night sky inspired him to put candles on the tree as a reminder that the Christ Child is the light of the world. Over three hundred years later in 1845, C. A. Schwerdgeburth painted a picture showing Luther and his family with a candlelit tree. The painting was widely reproduced, and the tree in it widely imitated. If any historian pointed out that the first known mention of a candlelit tree is dated 114 years after Luther's death in 1546, few people paid attention. The story was lovely, as were trees decorated with candles.

Most old-timers who remember candlelit trees swear that they were much more beautiful than the trees we have now. If their grandchildren today quite rightly object that those candles presented a terrible fire hazard, they are likely to hear, "We never had a problem. The tree was absolutely green and fresh, cut the day before. Our parents supervised the candle lighting and the candles never burned more than a few minutes." That was what made the tree so special—all that beauty concentrated into so short a time.

23

To give even more splendor to a candlelit tree, shiny ornaments stamped from tin were added which reflected and multiplied the candles' glow. Some were in the shapes of stars and crosses, showing the religious origins of tree decoration; others took shapes more difficult to link to the Christ Child—butterflies, for instance. Tin ornaments were produced in great quantities from about 1870 to 1900.

At about the same time, even more fanciful shapes were created in the German city of Dresden, made of silver and gold embossed cardboard. These three-dimensional Dresden ornaments are particular favorites of Phillip V. Snyder, collector and author of *The Christmas Tree Book*, who describes their appeal:

> [They] came in a seemingly endless variety of shapes: dogs, cats, suns, moons, every animal of the barnyard, frogs, turtles and even alligators. There was a whole sea full of fish, including the European carp, a German Christmas delicacy, and a virtual zoo of exotic creatures, including polar bears, camels, storks, eagles and peacocks. . . .
>
> An astonishing amount of detail could be pressed into these tiny ornaments. . . . One gold carriage was complete with horses, harnesses and all, a coachman on the coach box keeping his feet warm in a sack, and a lady in the carriage, not quite an inch high, with a chenille collar around her neck.

Neither tin nor cardboard ornaments achieved the lasting popularity of those made from a third material—glass blown almost to the thinness of a soap bubble. Glass ornaments silvered on the inside, as we know them today, were long the specialty of the German village of Lauscha, sixty miles north of Nuremburg. Lauscha became a center for glassblowing in the 1590s. The people of the village made drinking glasses, bull's-eye glass for windows and, later, glass beads for jewelry. They sometimes amused themselves by blowing glass bubbles. In the nineteenth century they added a technique of swirling a solution of silver nitrate around on the inside of the bubbles, giving them a mirror-like finish. Soon these silvery bubbles from Lauscha were hanging on Christmas trees all over Germany, and then in other countries as well. Eventually the whole village had to work the year around just to meet the demand. Some glassblowers painted the glass on the outside, or frosted it, or added crinkled wire of silver or gold. They learned to blow the glass into molds to make many shapes. Hot air balloons, and later airships and automobiles, joined the ornaments on the tree. Lauscha was the ornament capital of the world until World War II.

The latest lasting addition to tree decoration is electric lights. Only three years after Thomas Alva Edison first demonstrated his electric light bulb in 1879, Edward H. Johnson, a vice-president of the Edison Electric Company had a custom-made string of eighty little colored bulbs on the Christmas tree in his New York City mansion. Soon electric trees were outshining each other in splendor—but only in the homes of the wealthy. Author Phillip Snyder estimates that the total cost—for bulbs and an electrician to wire the tree—was the equivalent of one or two thousand dollars today. Even when the Ever-Ready Company and General Electric collaborated in 1903 to market ready-made strings of twenty-eight lights, they cost twelve dollars, "an average man's weekly wages."

The new lights were much less of a fire hazard than the candles they replaced, especially after Underwriters' Laboratories established safety requirements for them in 1921. But they had a characteristic that often endangered if not the house at least the domestic tranquility: When one bulb burned out, the whole string of lights went out. In order to find which one needed to be replaced, it was necessary to test each bulb on the string. And no matter where on the string one started the tests, it seemed always to be the final bulb that had failed.

In 1927 General Electric developed lights without this problem. They had, however, other problems. They were more expensive and the bulbs, as necessitated by the technology of the time, were much bigger—much less like stars or candles. It wasn't until the 1960s that the lighting industry came up with strings of tiny lights that stay lit when one bulb burns out.

Smart tree, to steal betimes away/From fields where glory cannot stay, to change A. E. Housman's words a bit. The end of a Christmas tree is sad, but sadder still is the sight of a tree, once the center of attraction of a glorious festival, standing forlorn while the stores fill up with Valentines. What to do? Listen to the son of a Virginia clergyman:

"My father loved the Christmas tree too much to leave it on a trash heap, all brown and neglected. So every year, after Twelfth Night, he would cut the tree into pieces and burn it in the fireplace, piece by piece. Fire purifies, you know. I always went to bed before he finished, but I still remember him there, gazing into the fire, thinking about Christmas."

Wood Shavings Ornaments

These graceful ornaments are simply the curled shavings of pinewood, shaped by hand and glued together at key points.

Materials and tools: Pine boards 1 inch thick and 6 to 12 inches long; white glue; toothpicks or similar glue applicators; plastic-coated bobby pins or paper clips (the coating is important; uncoated metal can stain damp wood); spool of strong cotton or nylon thread; woodworking vise; wood plane; scissors (or single-edge razor blade or utility knife); metal-edged ruler.

Ready-made wood veneer may be substituted for pine shavings. Rolls of veneer are available in a variety of lengths, widths and thicknesses at lumber yards, hardware stores and hobby shops that specialize in woodworking supplies.

Wood preparation: Soak the boards in water overnight. This will make the wood more pliable and result in fewer split shavings. Be sure that the blade of the plane is sharp and free from nicks or burrs. Plane along the length of the board until you have accumulated an adequate supply of long, even shavings (Step 1). Further soften the wood strips (or rolls of wood veneer) by soaking in water about 15 minutes prior to shaping them. Gently blot off any excess water.

Individual designs: After soaking the shavings, cut them to approximate length and form them as shown at right (Step 2). After you have glued the separate pieces and removed the clips (Step 3), reglue or reclip any loose joints before gluing the shapes together. For identical shapes and sizes, cut the shavings to equal lengths. The circles and whorls may be any size you wish, as long as they are in the correct proportion to each other. Hang finished ornaments with a loop of heavy thread at the top.

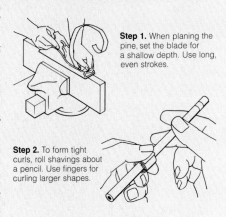

Step 1. When planing the pine, set the blade for a shallow depth. Use long, even strokes.

Step 2. To form tight curls, roll shavings about a pencil. Use fingers for curling larger shapes.

Step 3. Apply thin coat of glue to points where segments join. Clip them together. Remove clips when glue is dry.

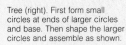

Tree (right). First form small circles at ends of larger circles and base. Then shape the larger circles and assemble as shown.

Star (left). Glue the four star points to inner circle. Form and glue smaller circles to fit snugly between points.

Fancy heart (right). Make top shape with fingers, bottom one with pencil. Glue halves together. Form and attach base.

Snowflake (left). This easy ornament consists of decreasingly smaller circles. The form shown uses three sizes, but you could use many more.

Bell (right). Make small curls at top, then bend the strip and glue and clamp the curls together. Add the other parts as shown.

2

3(A)

1(B)

1(A)

3(B)

1(C)

1(D)

Ecuadorian Stars

Though these colorful ornaments stem from an Ecuadorian folk tradition, you make them with the most modern (and inexpensive) materials.

Materials and tools: Embroidery cotton, or 3-strand crewel yarn. (Yarn is easier to work with, but cotton has brighter colors.) Cardboard, $\frac{1}{16}$-inch to $\frac{1}{8}$-inch thick; craft or dressmaker pins, at least $\frac{1}{2}$-inch long; foil paper; white glue; ruler; pencil; scissors; utility knife; tape; large-eyed needle or small crochet hook.

General directions: Using utility knife, cut two 2-inch squares of cardboard for each ornament. (You can always use larger squares for variety.) Glue foil to both sides, then glue squares together to form an 8-pointed star. Insert pin into each point, leaving $\frac{1}{16}$-inch extended. Tape end of thread to center of star. Glue another piece of foil, or place a foil sticker over the taped thread.

The thread is wound around the star in a sequence starting either from one point to another or from one joint (the "V" between the points) to another. Keep threads taut and close together. The ornaments may revolve after they are hung, so be sure that the back pattern is also correct.

Before starting a new color, make sure the line count of previous color is equal all around. Then tie end of last color to starting end of new color. With pin, tuck knot into the wound threads. Resume winding.

Weave end of final color under threads at one corner. Knot close to

work and trim. Push pins all the way in after winding is completed.

To make a hanging loop, cut an 8-inch length from final color. Fold in half. Pull folded end through threads at a point or joint. Knot the cut ends and conceal the knot under threads. You may, if you wish, add a foil seal to the front for a special, finishing touch.

Winding patterns: The technique for all patterns is basically the same. The thread is started from the front, wound around a point or joint, passes to the back and continues to alternate front and back (see diagrams below). With pattern 1, the second and subsequent threads are laid to the left of the previous one, except for 1 (C), below, which is wound to the right. With patterns 2 and 3, the threads are laid to the right.

Variations on opposite page are due to differing winding patterns, colors and number of thread rows. Pictures are numbered according to winding patterns and color sequences.

The four stars numbered "1" are point-to-point designs based on diagram 1 below. From point A, skip two points forward to B, skip one point backward to C, two forward to D, etc. Work from points, moving toward joints, laying threads to the left, except for 1 (C).

1 (A) has 6 rows blue, 6 rows yellow, 6 rows copper. Note seal.

1 (B) has 2 rows green, 6 rows yellow, 4 rows light blue.

1 (C) has 6 rows yellow, 4 rows

red, with threads laid to the right.

1 (D) has 5 rows russet, 2 rows yellow, 5 rows navy.

Star "2" in the photograph is a joint-to-joint design based on diagram 2 below. From joint A, skip two points to B, then back three points to C, then forward 2 points to D, etc. Work from joints, moving toward points, laying threads to the right. The star shown alternates 5 rows light blue, 2 rows red, 6 rows green.

The number "3" stars are also joint-to-joint designs, but are based on diagram 3 below, with all rows laid to the right.

3 (A) has 4 rows green, 2 rows fuchsia, 3 rows purple.

3 (B) has 4 rows light blue, 2 rows navy, 4 rows red.

Winding patterns   1   2   3

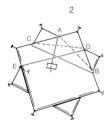

Pin
Foil-covered cardboard
Tape

Wind from point to point.
Dotted lines show thread in back.

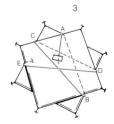

Wind patterns 2 and 3 from joint to joint

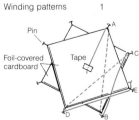

Winding pattern 1

Alternate
7 rows gold,
4 rows red

Star in photograph (top) is based on this diagram

Eighteenth-century Neapolitan crèche figure

And this will be a sign for you:
you will find a babe wrapped in swaddling cloths and lying in a manger. LUKE 2:12

The Crèche

The figures may be made of wood or stone or any material close at hand. They may be elaborate life-sized statues bedecked in jewels or simple paper models made by children. They may even be real people acting out the pageant of Christ's birth in native costumes. But whether it is the Italian *presepio*, the Spanish *nacimiento*, or the simple Christmas crib, the re-creation of the Nativity scene is one of the oldest and most sacred of all Christmas traditions.

While most people visualize the Nativity as having taken place in a stable behind an inn, the actual location of Christ's birth in Bethlehem is not known. There is no mention of a stable in the Gospels, and early popular tradition was that He was born in a small grotto, or cave, which would have been more likely than our present-day idea of a stable. In the year 326 A.D. Constantine the Great, the first Christian emperor of Rome, built the Church of the Nativity over the accepted spot of Christ's birth in Bethlehem, replacing a temple previously built by Hadrian. Sometime later a fourteen-pointed silver star was set in the jasper floor to mark the birthplace. Today that silver has been almost worn away by pilgrims who have come to touch the spot.

Although there were re-creations of the Nativity scene as far back as the fourth century, the popularization of the crèche tradition as we know it is attributed to St. Francis of Assisi in the thirteenth century. Francis sought to remind people of the joyful, humble origins of Christmas. In his own words: "I desire to represent the birth of that Child in Bethlehem in such a way that with our bodily eyes we may see all that He suffered for lack of the necessities for a newborn babe, and how He lay in the manger between the ox and the ass."

Greccio, in the Umbrian hills, was one of Francis's favorite mountain retreats. It was in the woods near the church there that a friend arranged at his request for a manger to be filled with hay and an ox and an ass to be placed beside it. The place was brightly lit with candles, and as Francis celebrated mass there on Christmas Eve, 1223, the forest was filled with light and singing. St. Bonaventure, in describing the scene, wrote: "Greccio was transformed almost into a second Bethlehem and that wonderful night seemed like the fullest day to both man and beast for the joy they felt at the renewing of the mystery."

In one form or another this first crèche became the model for crèches in all the centuries to follow. Families began to make miniature manger scenes for their homes, and the tradition quickly spread from Italy to France (where it is said to have been introduced by Pope John XXII in 1316) and to other parts of Europe. The figures generally included the Holy Family, the traditional ox and ass, the shepherds and the Magi, sometimes even the occupants of the entire city of Bethlehem. Usually these figures resembled the people who made them more than those they were supposed to represent, a characteristic still true of modern crèches. In every country and at every time people came to identify the Nativity scene in their own terms, re-creating the event in a way personally meaningful to them.

The living reenactment of the Nativity can be traced to before Francis's time. In England the crèche, watched over by the Virgin Mary, would be placed behind the altar where a choirboy dressed as an angel sang carols while clergymen dressed as shepherds came to the altar. In Germany altar boys would even rock the cradle to comfort the Baby Jesus, a custom that became known as "cradle rocking." Such church performances would soon evolve into part of the mystery and miracle plays of the Middle Ages. These were elaborate productions that included all the characters of the Nativity as well as contemporary additions, and the roles were often played by local town dignitaries. Stages would be mounted on wagons and pulled through the town, each wagon depicting a different scene.

In the New World *Las Posadas* and *Los Pastores*, the direct descendants of the mystery plays, were brought to Mexico in the sixteenth century and later to the Southwest and California by the Spanish. The story of *Las Posadas* ("the inns") is that of Mary and Joseph's search for lodgings in which to spend the night. *Los Pastores* ("the shepherds") recounts how the shepherds responded to the angel's call and sought out the infant Jesus. Performed by

A little child,
a shining star,
A stable rude,
the door ajar.
Yet in that place
so crude, forlorn,
The Hope of all the
world was born.

ANONYMOUS

Neapolitan figures of shepherd with flock

German manger scene, circa 1730, made of paper, brocade, silk, wax, moss, snail shells, twigs and straw

Carved wood Magi from Germany, circa 1520

Were earth a thou-
sand times as fair,
Beset with gold
and jewels rare,
She yet were far
too poor to be
A narrow cradle,
Lord, for Thee.

MARTIN LUTHER

Indian converts under the direction of the Franciscans, these plays first took place in the New World three quarters of a century before Jamestown.

In Europe the traditional Christmas crib had been a fixture in the homes of the peasants and the rich as well as in churches since the time of the Renaissance. Entire families would participate in making the figures out of wood or clay and arranging them. More elaborate crèche scenes were fashioned for the nobility. One such, created for the son of the first Grand Duke of Tuscany in the sixteenth century, included a mechanical crib in which the heavens opened and angels flew about before descending to earth.

But it was not until the eighteenth century in Naples that the crèche reached its most glorious stage of development. King Carlo III made ornate settings for the Nativity scene in his castle, while his queen and her ladies-in-waiting fashioned the costumes. The king even commissioned well-known artists to sculpt his crèche figures. The resulting displays were truly works of art. Other members of the court followed the king's lead and soon entire rooms in Neapolitan palazzos were given over to Nativity scenes with full-time crèche directors hired to set them up. These dreamlike creations depicted the Nativity cycle with hundreds of figures, the making of which required the talents of countless leather workers, jewelers and other craftsmen.

Around the year 1800 a group of peddlers from Naples began selling Nativity and other religious figures in Marseilles, France. The Italians called them *santi belli*, or "beautiful saints." Attracted by the appeal of these brightly colored images, local artisans began crafting similar ones from pottery clay, thus initiating the tradition of *santon* ("little saint") making in the Provence region of France. Regular *santon* fairs were held at Marseilles and Aix, where the craft of santon making persists to this day. As the years passed, markets in Spain and Germany, as well as those in Italy and France, began to fill with the vividly painted clay and plaster figures of the Christ Child in His manger, the Virgin Mary, Joseph, the shepherds, and the Magi.

Aside from the Spanish influence in the Southwest, Christmas celebrations got off to an uncertain start in America. Like their counterparts in England, the Puritans of the New England colonies actually outlawed the celebration of the holiday. It was mainly the immigrants from countries other than England who brought Christmas and the crèche to America.

But if Christmas was late in getting a foothold in the States, Americans are now the world's most fervent celebrators of the holiday, with a variety of customs that is a tribute to their richly mixed heritage. Nativity scenes are much in evidence in the U.S. today. From the old Spanish missions throughout California down through the Southwest all the way to

Texas, Christmas pageants are still performed annually, much as they have been for the last four centuries. In the Midwest at Cleveland's Trinity Episcopal Cathedral an annual pageant takes place that involves a choir of two hundred and over one hundred performers dressed as shepherds, wise men, heralds, and other participants in the original Nativity.

But it is not the size of the crèche that is important, nor the material from which it is made. It is what the crèche symbolizes, the true religious spirit of Christmas, that stands alone among all the traditions of the holiday. And perhaps it is the small inexpensive cardboard stable placed under the family tree that is the most important one of all, peopled by the little plaster figures that have survived for years, some of them a bit the worse for wear, the plaster chipped, the paint faded. And when this crèche is set up, with its animals and shepherds and Mary and Joseph, one figure is conspicuously absent until Christmas morning, when the tiny babe is carefully placed in the empty manger. It is at this moment that we look beyond ourselves and remember once again what Christmas truly signifies.

Spanish crèche from Catalonia

Cornhusk Crèche

All crèches pay loving tribute to that historic event in Bethlehem, but this one, with its primitive look and natural textures, seems especially faithful to the original scene as most of us picture it.

Materials and tools: Dried cornhusks (you may use dried sweet corn or field cornhusks, or purchase husks from craft shops); corn silk or jute twine for hair; cotton balls; fabric dyes (blue, red, green and brown); styrofoam; white glue; thin wire or pipe cleaners; white or off-white crochet thread or thin string; scissors or utility knife; straight pins; pencil; ruler; old bath towel; enamel or stainless steel pot (for dyeing).

General directions: All husks are shaped when damp and thus pliable. For natural, undyed pieces, soak dried husks in warm water 10-15 minutes. For dyed pieces, stir 2 teaspoons of fabric dye into 1 quart gently boiling water until dye is thoroughly dissolved. With liquid simmering, dip each husk in dye bath until desired shade is obtained. Then rinse husks in cold water and set aside for partial drying. Keep dyed husks separate from undyed ones. Cover work surface with an old towel to absorb any excess moisture.

Forming figures: Basic figures are 7 inches to 8 inches high, with the smooth side of the husks facing outward. To form heads, select two large, damp husks, lightly hued and unblemished. Clip off pointed ends so top is about 1½ inches wide. With narrow ends pointing upward, tie husks with string about ½ inch from top and clip husks above the string (see Fig. 1). Place a cotton ball on top of stub. Invert figure and pull husks back down over ball to cover it completely. The string will now be inside the husks. The neck is formed by tying the husk with

Fig. 1: Head

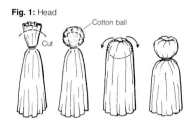

To make the head, clip husks above the string and place a cotton ball on cut stub. Then pull husks back down over ball and tie at neck beneath head.

Fig. 2: Arms

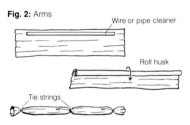

For arms (Fig. 2), roll husk about a wire or pipe cleaner. Tie at center, ends. For sleeves (Fig. 3), tie new husks at ends, fold back, tie at center.

Fig. 3: Sleeves

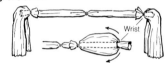

Fig. 4: Adding arms

Fig. 5: Tunic or blouse

To add arms (Fig. 4), insert them through separated husks. Cross tunic in front (Fig. 5), tie at waist.

Fig. 6: Skirt or robe

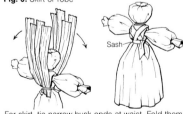

For skirt, tie narrow husk ends at waist. Fold them back down, retie with a sash and trim the bottom.

string beneath the head as in Fig. 1.

The arms (Fig. 2) are made by rolling an 8¼-inch-long husk around a 7½-inch length of wire or pipe cleaner. Tie the roll in the center, and about ½ inch from each end to form the hands.

For the sleeves (Fig. 3), tie two damp husks, 4 inches wide by 5 inches long, to each wrist. Pull the husks back loosely, as with the head, so they completely cover the arms. Flared sleeves, like those on the angel, are a simple variation. Cut husks so that there will be 1 inch extra at the ends of the arms. Roll husks around arms, tie in the middle and fold in excess at ends to provide the flare.

To add the arms (Fig. 4), separate the husks below the neck string. Insert the arms close to the neck and tie around the waist.

For tunic or blouse (Fig. 5), use two lengths of damp husk about 1½ inches wide. Fold them lengthwise, then wrap one over each shoulder and across to the opposite hip. Tie around the waist over previous string. If you wish to make a more prominent tunic, like the one Mary wears in the photograph, attach the skirt first (see below), then add the tunic.

To make the skirt or robe (Fig. 6), use five or six large husks, with the narrow end below the waist and wide end over arms and head. Overlap husks like petals of a flower and tie securely at waist. Gently turn husks down over string at waist, overlapping them slightly. Tie a thin piece of husk around the waist for a sash. Cut the skirt bottom evenly to enable the figure to stand (see photograph) and spread skirt bottom to achieve the desired fullness.

The hair and beard for the figures are made by gluing dried corn silk or separated jute twine to the head.

Fig. 1: Mary's headpiece

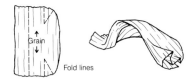

Form on head

Fig. 2: Joseph's headpiece

Cut headpieces to above form, fold. Mold them to fit head, then drape on head and pin during drying.

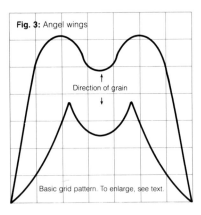

Fig. 3: Angel wings

Direction of grain

Basic grid pattern. To enlarge, see text.

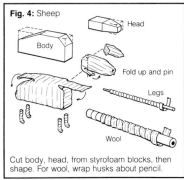

Fig. 4: Sheep

Head

Body

Fold up and pin

Legs

Wool

Cut body, head, from styrofoam blocks, then shape. For wool, wrap husks about pencil.

SPECIFIC FIGURES

Mary: Form the head and arms as specified in general directions. Following the photograph (p. 37), use a dark blue dye for the sleeves. (Hands for all figures are natural, undyed husks.) Use the same blue color for the tunic and skirt, with a green dye for the sash. Then glue on some dried corn silk for the hair.

Fig. 1 (left) shows the shape and formation of Mary's headpiece. Use a natural-colored husk. Drape it on the hair, as shown, and pin it temporarily in place so that it holds shape while drying.

Joseph: Use a brown dye to color the sleeves, tunic and robe. For the shawl, drape a natural-colored husk over the shoulders. The sash is deep purple (a mixture of red and blue). Add the hair.

For Joseph's headpiece (see Fig. 2, left), use a lighter purple dye. Drape it on the hair and pin during drying. For Joseph's staff, wrap a thin strip of natural-colored husk around a 5-inch piece of wire. Bend one end to the shape of a crook and tie or glue it to the hand.

Baby Jesus: This figure is naturally smaller than the other basic figures. Make the head and arms from undyed husks. Do not add sleeves. To simulate a loose robe, drape the skirt from the neck rather than the waist. For a bunting effect, wrap the figure in a husk and tie it loosely, temporarily, until dry. Use a green dye for the blanket. To simulate straw, place some shredded husk or excelsior under the infant.

Angel: Make the figure of natural-colored husks. When it is dry, add a long sash of red-dyed husk across one shoulder, crossing the body to hip, front and back. Tie the sash at waist with a thin, red husk. Use a light-colored corn silk or separated jute twine for hair.

Use Fig. 3 (left) as a reduced model for the angel wings. To enlarge the drawing,

determine the wing height you want. Divide this height into seven vertical rows, and make the enlarged pattern seven rows wide. Then, starting in any square, transfer the drawing square by square. Cut two pairs of wing shapes from this pattern, with the grain running top to bottom. Glue them together and weight down until dry. (Single husk thickness would be too flimsy.) Glue to back of angel.

Sheep: Cut a styrofoam block for the body 1½ inches high x 2¼ inches long x ¾ inch thick and shape with utility knife as shown in Fig. 4. Cover with natural cornhusk, gluing or pinning in place until dry. Cut a second styrofoam block for the head, ½ inch high x 2 inches long x ¾ inch thick, and shape with utility knife. Take two damp husks, gather and tie them near one end. Snip end just past string. Holding stub at the tied end, fold husks back over styrofoam block to form the head. (Head is covered like the head under general directions, except styrofoam block takes the place of cotton ball.) Pin down loose ends at the back of the head until dry. The outer crease at stub end should resemble a mouth.

For the curly wool, wrap ¼-inch-wide strips of damp husk around thin pencils or dowels. Tie with string until dry. Then carefully unwind the strips and cut into 1-inch lengths. Glue these curls to body and top of head. For ears, cut petal-shaped forms from a husk, glue to sides of head. Next, pin the head to the body.

To make the legs for the standing sheep, wind four thin strips of husk around four pieces of wire or pipe cleaner, leaving one end uncovered to stick into body. When the husk windings are dry, insert them into the base of the body.

STABLE ASSEMBLY

Familiarize yourself with the parts list and drawing (Fig. 1, right) of stable. Gather a collection of twigs or fallen branches of suitable thickness, and cut all framing pieces to correct length. Then cut plywood base 9 inches x 14½ inches. Following Fig. 1, mark two lines on base, parallel with each side and ½ inch in from each end. Mark indicated points for each base dowel pin, which will anchor front and back posts and the four vertical rail braces. For these pins drill ³⁄₁₆-inch holes about ¼ inch deep. Drill similar holes at bottom and top ends of each vertical post or rail, and all other places where dowel pins are used. See Fig. 1 for locations of all dowel pins.

Assemble framework of vertical and horizontal beams, posts and pins without glue. Make necessary fitting adjustments by trimming pieces with utility knife. Set aside the angled rail and roof beam braces and the rear roof beam, then glue the rest of the framework together with epoxy glue. While glue dries, hold assembly in place with rubber bands or strips of masking tape.

Next, cut to fit six angled rail braces and two angled roof beam braces. Glue in place, temporarily securing them with masking tape (Fig. 2). Then assemble back pieces. Drill starter holes for nails at tops of back pieces using a ¾-inch x 18 nail with its head cut off for the drill. (This will help prevent the twigs from splitting when they are nailed in place.) Nail the back pieces to rear roof beam (Fig. 3), then glue beam in place to back posts. Similarly pre-drill bottom ends and nail them to base (Fig. 4). Roof pieces are nailed to roof beams in the same manner. Paint the base a flat brown color, then nail the three pieces of trim to the base. Touch up raw-looking ends and cuts with same brown paint used on base.

MANGER ASSEMBLY
Mark leg pieces where they cross each other. (See Fig. 5 for all these steps.) Whittle notched joints at those points, glue legs together. Clamp with clothespin until dry. Mark side pieces where they cross legs. Whittle notched joints, glue to leg pieces, and clamp until dry.

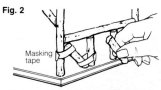
Fig. 2
Masking tape
Secure angled rail braces with tape

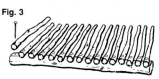
Fig. 3
Nail tops of rear pieces to rear beam

Fig. 4
Base
Nail bottoms of rear pieces to base

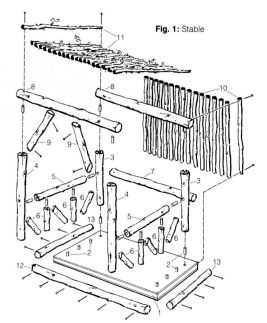
Fig. 1: Stable
Numbers correspond to those in parts list

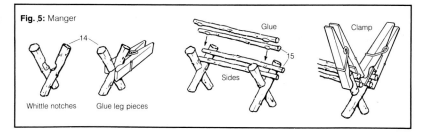
Fig. 5: Manger
Whittle notches   Glue leg pieces   Glue   Sides   Clamp

PARTS LIST

No.	Name	Quantity	Length	Width	Diameter	Material
Stable						
1	Base	1	14½"	9"		⅝" plywood
2	Dowel pins	20	½"			³⁄₁₆" dowel
3	Back posts	2	6½"		⅝"	⅝" twigs
4	Front posts	2	10"		⅝"	⅝" twigs
5	Side rails	2	8"		⅝"	⅝" twigs
6	Rail braces	10	4"		⅝"	⅝" twigs
7	Back rail	1	12⅞"		⅝"	⅝" twigs
8	Roof beams	2	15"		⅝"	⅝" twigs
9	Roof beam braces	2	Cut to fit		⅝"	⅝" twigs
10	Back pieces	15-20	7½"		⅜"	⅜" twigs
11	Roof pieces	15-20	11"		⅜"	⅜" grapevine
12	Base trim, front	1	16"		¾"	¾" twigs
13	Base trim, sides	2	9"		¾"	¾" twigs
Manger						
14	Legs	4	3¼"		³⁄₁₆"	³⁄₁₆" twigs
15	Sides	4	4½"		¼"	¼" twigs

Hardware: Epoxy glue, rubber bands, masking tape; wire nails, ¾" x 18; flat brown paint; 2 clothespins.

The stockings were hung by the chimney with care
In hopes that St. Nicholas soon would be there.

Clement C. Moore: "A Visit from St. Nicholas"

The Christmas Stocking

Oranges. Plums. Jawbreakers. Whistles. Candy canes. Tin soldiers. Doll tea sets. Pincushions. Sachets. Figs. Wind-up cars. Marzipan. Hazelnuts. A toy cornet or a harmonica. Enamel lacquer fans. Chinese puzzles. A stocking hanging from a mantel and bulging with gifts is as quintessentially Christmas as the jack-o'-lantern is the essence of Halloween or a heart-shaped box of candy a symbol of Valentine's Day.

No one knows for certain where the custom of hanging stockings at Christmas Eve began—only that the practice, or some variation of it, persists virtually wherever Christmas is celebrated throughout the world. Conceivably it had its origin in the old legend of the three penniless girls who hung their stockings on the mantel to dry. As the tale goes, St. Nicholas tossed a bag of gold down the chimney where it landed in one of the girls' stockings.

We are reasonably certain that it was in France at the beginning of the twelfth century that nuns began the practice of leaving packages at the homes of poor children at Christmastime, packages filled with good things to eat: fruits and nuts and sweets. These packages may well have been wrapped in stockings. In any event, the custom spread rapidly through Europe among rich and poor alike.

In England children hang stockings by the fireplace. In France and Holland slippers and shoes are left by the hearth to be filled with presents. In China, children hang up stockings made of muslin especially for the occasion and then await *Lam Khoong Khoong* (Nice Old Father) to come

Illustration by Arthur Rackham for "A Visit from St. Nicholas"

and fill them. On Epiphany Eve in Italy the good little witch *Befana* comes down the chimney on a broom and fills the shoes of good Italian boys and girls with toys. Those who have been bad will more likely find their shoes filled with charcoal, rocks and ash.

Wherever Christmas is celebrated, some form of the custom is still in practice. But why stockings? It is strange, is it not, how on one night of the year an object as mundane as a stocking, scarcely noted in the course of our daily lives, suddenly looms extraordinary in our imaginations? Ordinary stockings—wool stockings, argyle stockings, mesh stockings, stockings of bold and vibrant stripes; stockings of every conceivable size and pattern, some as large as a small gunny sack, and some petite enough for Cinderella's tiny foot—all take on an air of something truly mysterious.

To the child, the ritual of hanging the stocking is no light matter. It is an action fraught with the potential not only for great reward but also for catastrophic loss. For, as we all know, the jolly elfin figure who comes down the chimney to fill the stocking can be a figure of fantastic munificence or the conveyor of crushing disappointment.

What small boy or girl waking on Christmas morning, still drowsy but nonetheless eager, has not scurried out to the living room to see what has

42

Christmas Eve—Hanging up the Stockings, an 1879 print

A fringed Christmas card from the 1880s

Victorian Christmas card

been left beneath the tree or hanging from the mantel. He goes with a mixture of joy and dread, for in the months preceding Christmas, hasn't he been repeatedly told that if he doesn't behave, he may well find in his Christmas stocking objects not quite so pleasant as candies and toys?

Tripping warily out into the living room, still gray and chilly in the early dawn, the first things a child sees are merely shadows and shapes. Focusing more closely, he discerns objects in rough outline—boxes, packages of odd shapes all crouched and clustered beneath pine boughs. Then on the mantel he spies the stocking he hung there the night before. But it no longer looks like quite the same stocking. Instead, it gives the appearance of a small sack misshapen by a series of bulges and bumps that might well be caused by objects other than candy and toys.

Moving up on it slowly there is dread anticipation as the child suddenly recalls a long list of recent misdemeanors. Surely the stout old man from the North Pole knows all about them. Isn't it his business to know about such things? Doesn't he have people working for him who keep track of things like that? And if he does, then no doubt the bulges and bumps in the stocking are a reprimand rather than a reward.

Coming closer, approaching cautiously as if it were a ticking bomb, the child sees the stocking within his grasp. At the very top of it, peering out

44

above its rim, is the red-plumed shako of a toy grenadier, the curls of a tiny doll or possibly the gracefully curved handle of a striped peppermint stick.

All is well. The moment of dread passes in a wave of gratitude and delight and is completely forgotten the next moment as the contents of the stocking are tumbled out over the carpet in splendid profusion—dates, nuts, caramels, a noisemaker and a small Chinese puzzle, a drawing pad and a new barrette, a set of jacks and a bag of marbles, a model plane and a tiny furry koala "bear."

Whatever is there, no matter how rich or humble, whether hung on the mantel or at the foot of a four-poster, it is all touched with that air of mystery that comes from believing that it has arrived there through the grace of some supernatural agency. The knowledge of that must be as awesome and satisfying to today's child as it must have been to those small children centuries ago who put shoes filled with oats outside the doors of their rude huts on Christmas Eve for the camels of the Three Wise Men, in the hope that the oats would be replaced with gifts to delight a child.

Thus an ancient practice persists, and even in a world as unsentimental as ours often can be, there is still mystery in a simple and slightly ragged stocking dangling from a mantel.

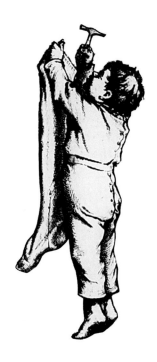

Aran Knit Stockings

These stockings are guaranteed to be an all-around delight. A joy to make, they're a perfect first Aran knit project if you've never tried one before. And what better fun for the children than to have Christmas stockings with their very own names on them! Each stocking takes only a single skein of yarn; the embroidery (done with a simple cross stitch) uses just scraps of red and green yarn.

Materials and tools: 1 skein (3½- to 4-ounce) of knitting-worsted-weight yarn; size 4 knitting needles; 1 double-pointed needle (dpn) for cable; small amounts of red and green yarn and a tapestry needle for embroidery; size G crochet hook for loop.

PATTERN STITCHES

Pat 1 (double moss stitch) over 14 sts: *Rows 1 and 2:* *K 1, p 1, rep from *. *Rows 3 and 4:* *P 1, k 1, rep from *. Rep rows 1 to 4.

Pat 2 (Aran diamond with bobbles) over 14 sts: *Row 1:* K 1; k in front, back, front, back and front of next st (5 sts in 1), k 1, turn; p 5, turn; k 5, turn; p 5, turn; k 5, pass sts 2, 3, 4 and 5 over 1 (bobble made); k 2, place next 2 sts on dpn and hold in back, k 2, k 2 from dpn (cable made); k 2, bobble in next 2 sts, k 1.

Row 2 and all wrong-side rows: P.

Row 3: K 4, place next st on dpn and hold in back, k 2, k 1 from dpn (cross 2 R); place next 2 sts on dpn and hold in front, k 1, k 2 from dpn (cross 2 L), k 4.

Row 5: K 3, cross 2 R, k 2, cross 2 L, k 3.

Row 7: K 2, cross 2 R, k 4, cross 2 L, k 2.

Row 9: K 1, cross 2 R, k 6, cross 2 L, k 1.

Row 11: Cross 2 R, k 8, cross 2 L.

Row 13: Cross 2 L, k 8, cross 2 R.

Row 15: K 1, cross 2 L, k 6, cross 2 R, k 1.

Row 17: K 2, cross 2 L, k 4, cross 2 R, k 2.

Row 19: K 3, cross 2 L, k 2, cross 2 R, k 3.

Row 21: K 4, cross 2 L, cross 2 R, k 4.

Row 22: P. Rep rows 1 to 22.

Stocking front: Beg at top. Cast on 42 sts. *Row 1* (wrong side): *P 1, k 1, rep from *. *Row 2:* K. Rep rows 1 and 2 four times, then rep row 1. Beg pat. *Row 1:* Work 14 sts Pat 1; 14 sts Pat 2; 14 sts Pat 1. Continue patterns as established until 6 rows of fourth diamond have been worked. Beg foot shaping. Inc 1 at beg of every row on right side eight times. (When fourth diamond has been completed, work rows 1 and 2 of Pat 2, then discontinue diamonds and work all sts in Pat 1.) Continue to inc beg of every row on right side. At same time, bind off 2 sts beg of every row on wrong side. When 12 rows have been worked after last diamond, shape toe. Continue binding off 2 on wrong side, but work 4 rows without shaping on right side, inc 1 beg next row, work 7 more rows without shaping on right side, then dec 1 beg next 3 rows on right side. Bind off 2 sts beg next 2 rows, 3 beg next 2 rows, 4 beg next 2 rows. Bind off remaining sts.

Stocking back: Work same as front, but omit bobbles and reverse shaping of foot (that is, for right side read wrong side, and vice versa).

Finishing: Embroider letters in cross st (each st over 2 rows). Sew stocking back to front, wrong sides together, using overcast st. Crochet chain 2½ inches long for loop, attach to corner at top. Refer to the alphabet below to plan the letters you want to use.

Use cross-stitch alphabet above for letters. Be sure each X covers two knit stitches as in the "A", right.

Toyland

The little toy dog is covered with dust,
    But sturdy and staunch he stands;
And the little toy soldier is red with rust,
    And his musket molds in his hands.
Time was when the little toy dog was new,
    And the soldier was passing fair,
And that was the time when our Little Boy Blue
    Kissed them and put them there.

Eugene Field: "Little Boy Blue"

Children and toys have been a magical combination for thousands of years. But if toys belong to childhood, the joy derived from them lasts into old age. It is not difficult for a grandmother or grandfather to remember, while watching young grandchildren at play, the special time in their own lives when the world was magic and the toy dog and the toy soldier came alive.

The memory of a treasured toy of childhood is never more vivid than at Christmastime, when all toyland comes wondrously to life for young and old alike. Stores are chock full of tin soldiers and toy drums, puppets and puzzles, tiny trucks and electric trains, windup toys, pull toys, toys that sing and toys that dance. There are dolls dressed in the latest fashion and soft plush teddy bears. There are kites and merry-go-rounds, rocking horses and circus elephants.

The Michtoms' *Teddy's Bear*

Toyland!
Toyland!
Little girl
and boy land,
While you dwell
within it
You are ever
happy then.

GLEN MACDONOUGH

The custom of exchanging gifts at Christmas probably goes back to the biblical story of the Three Wise Men who brought gifts of gold and frankincense and myrrh to the Christ Child, and of all the many traditions associated with Christmas it is one of the most joyous. For whether the gift be an elegant china doll or a homemade doll of rags, it embodies the generosity of spirit and the love that the Three Kings carried with them to the Child in Bethlehem long ago.

At Christmastime everyone is a child again, merrily participating in the joy of giving and the excitement and anticipation of receiving. In homes everywhere mysterious packages are hidden in the backs of closets, knitting needles click away furiously, and wonderful smells of chocolate and almonds, of gingerbread and cookies come from the kitchen. There is a thrill of expectation in the air. In crowded streets, festive with sparkling decorations, children tug at their parents' coat sleeves, pleading for a stop in front of the toy-store window. Little faces, noses pressed against the glass, peer inside, eyes wide with excitement.

"I WISH . . . ," says one small voice and the eyes fix on a big cuddly teddy bear sitting in a huge rocking chair in the corner of the window. The very first teddy bear had an interesting and even slightly controversial history. One version credits the bear's origin to cartoonist Clifford Berryman who, in 1902, drew a picture for the *Washington Post* that showed President Theodore Roosevelt refusing to shoot a bear during a hunting expedition in Mississippi. A Brooklyn, New York, toy maker named Morris Michtom spotted the cartoon and with the help of his wife set about making a toy replica of the bear. The result was a soft brown animal with black button eyes that Mr. Michtom proudly displayed in his toy-store window with a label reading: *Teddy's Bear*. It sold immediately, and soon the Michtoms were

making as many bears as they possibly could. Eventually their small family enterprise became the Ideal Toy Corporation, one of the largest producers of toys in the world.

A second version claims the first teddy bear was made by the German firm of Steiff, begun in the 1880s by Margarete Steiff. Severely handicapped by polio when she was a child, Margarete Steiff found joy in telling stories to children. Many of her stories were about animals, and soon the children were begging Tante Gretle, as they called her, to let them *see* the animals. So Margarete Steiff, unable to leave her wheelchair, began making stuffed animals. Before long she had created a whole zoo of colorful creatures—elephants, tigers, lions and finally a new fuzzy brown animal called simply "Bear." At the Leipzig Fair in 1903, a buyer from a New York import house fell in love with Bear. He ordered three thousand of them shipped home. There, in a shop window, the White House caterer saw one and decided it would make just the right table decoration for President Theodore Roosevelt's dinner table. He bought several, dressed them in hunting clothes in honor of the President, who was a great outdoorsman, and arranged them as a centerpiece on the table. During dinner one of the guests asked Roosevelt what species of bear decorated the table. Before the President could answer, another guest replied that it was a new species called "Teddy."

Whether the first teddy bear was made by toy-maker Michtom or by the firm of Steiff was unimportant to Teddy himself. Unaware of any controversy surrounding his origin, he gaily made his way into the homes and hearts of children all over the world and became the favorite toy of thousands.

"I WISH . . . ," says another little voice and this time the eyes stare longingly at a shiny electric train going round and round on its tracks. Clickety-clack, clickety-clack, round and round and round it goes, calling

Lionel advertisement from the 1920s

La grande Maison des Poupées.

"The Big Dollhouse," nineteenth century French toy-box cover

the young watcher to far-off adventures. The first electric train was made by nineteen-year-old Joshua Lionel Cowen in New York City during the summer of 1900. Cowen put a small electric motor in a little wooden flatcar and constructed a circle of tracks out of brass strips. He sold the flatcar to a novelty shop and it was an immediate success. Soon there were locomotives, cabooses, passenger cars, cattle cars, milk cars and even refrigerator cars—all close models of real ones. Today there are few people who have not admired the intricate, realistic Lionel toy trains, and one of the most endearing Christmas scenes has long been that of father and child underneath the Christmas tree turning switches to pull the new engine into the station or pushing buttons to unload freight onto the loading dock or deposit toy cattle into the corral.

"I WISH . . .," says still another voice and the wide eyes of this young window-shopper are held by a beautifully furnished dollhouse filled with all the necessary items found in a "real" home. Here in this miniature house the small owner can be in charge, directing the lives of the tiny occupants in a sort of mirror image of reality. But dollhouses are more than toys. They are works of art that reflect the architecture, fashion and customs of their time. As such they can become objects of great value. In 1967, for example, Titania's Palace; a miniature residence built by Sir Nevile Wilkinson over a good part of his lifetime and opened by Queen Mary in 1922, was auctioned by Christie's in London and sold for $75,000. Another miniature mansion, built in 1639, is now on display at the Germanisches National Museum in Nuremburg, Germany. Once owned by the Stromer family, this priceless dollhouse, which stands seven feet, two inches tall, is one of the most

beautiful and elegant ever made. It contains walls of paneled cedar decorated with rich paintings and elaborate needlework hangings, and the kitchen is lined with perfectly crafted pewter plates and copper skillets. The first dollhouses were luxury toys such as Titania's Palace and the 1639 Dollhouse and not really affordable to the parents of most youngsters. But as time passed and dollhouses became more and more popular, homemade buildings constructed of cardboard or wooden crates gave as much joy to children as the most ornate structures.

"I WISH . . ." is heard once more and saucer eyes fasten on a regiment of colorful,

Christmas Morning, nineteenth century print

The 1639 Dollhouse, Germany

53

French Christmas card, late nineteenth century

For girls and boys,
such pretty toys—
I've dolls and drums
and sugarplums
For all little
girls and boys.

ANONYMOUS

Dispatch Rider

very brave soldiers while dreams of victory in battle fill the small head. It was, in fact, the actual victories of Frederick the Great, King of Prussia from 1740 to 1786, that inspired the popularity of the tin soldier, first made in Nuremberg in 1760. And perhaps toy soldiers, more than any other toy, have been responsible for influencing the course of history. Many rulers, including Russia's Tsar Peter III, King Alphonso XIII of Spain and Louis XIV of France, collected model soldiers. It is said that Peter III even court-martialed a rat who had nibbled on one of his toy warriors. In his autobiography, *My Early Life*, Sir Winston Churchill explains how toy soldiers affected his life. One day his father found him playing a game with them and asked him if he would like to go into the Army. Churchill

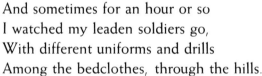
German Grenadier

relates, "I said, 'Yes' at once: and immediately I was taken at my word. . . . The toy soldiers turned the current of my life." Other celebrated collectors of military miniatures include authors H. G. Wells, Anatole France and Robert Louis Stevenson, who wrote affectionately:

> And sometimes for an hour or so
> I watched my leaden soldiers go,
> With different uniforms and drills
> Among the bedclothes, through the hills.

Not all collectors of toy soldiers have been men. The Brontë sisters owned a set of wooden soldiers and spent hours together playing and writing little plays around them. "Mine was the prettiest of the whole," Charlotte Brontë wrote, "and the tallest, and the most perfect in every part. He was the Duke of Wellington."

"I WISH . . ." is heard again, in the softest of whispers from the very smallest window-shopper of all. Bright brown eyes peer in the window and are met by another pair of equally bright blue ones. There, inside, is a beautiful big doll dressed all in white. She is almost as tall as the little girl who stares at her, and her shiny black hair reaches all the way down to her waist.

The history of dolls is a complex one; there have probably been dolls of some sort as long as there have been people. Some, like the Hopi Indian *kachina* and the Egyptian *ushabti*

Hessian Jäger

dolls, are closely linked to religious ceremonies. Others serve in the field of medicine, to teach anatomy, for example, or to aid in the instruction of the handicapped. Some, like puppets and marionettes, are used to entertain, and still others promote the latest fashion or trends in hair design. Once a doll played an important role in a war. Her name was Nina, and she was an agent during the American Civil War. In her hollow head she carried medicine to the Confederate soldiers. The true significance of dolls, however, is as a companion to children, a friend to be loved and cherished,

King's Own Regiment

trusted and cared for more than anything else in all the world. And though the well-loved doll, tattered and torn from years of affection, may one day be lost, it is never forgotten.

The small children continue to stare through the glass window of the toy shop. They stare and they hope and they wish. Christmas will come and the teddy bear and the electric train, the dollhouse, the regiment of toy soldiers and the beautiful blue-eyed doll will disappear from the window. The toy store will be empty and the toys themselves will be stuffed into stockings and hung by the fireplace or crowded under Christmas trees. There the children who peered through the shop window, along with children everywhere, will find their dreams come true.

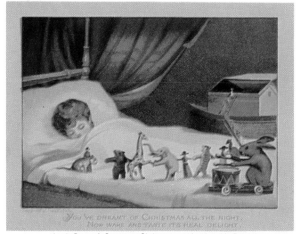

Louis Prang & Company Christmas card, printed in Boston

Cinderella Topsy-Turvy Doll

This Cinderella turns any child into a fairy godmother! Two beautiful dolls in one, she can be transformed with a flick of the wrist. In her calico dress, she's a little housemaid. Flip her over and *voilà*, she's the belle of the ball! Magic though she may be, Cinderella is easy to make, with simple sewing and basic embroidery.

Materials: ½ yard 45-inch pale pink cotton fabric for body and hands

½ yard 45-inch-wide floral print fabric for one dress, ¼ yard contrasting floral print for sleeves

⅝ yard 45-inch-wide plain satin fabric for second dress. (Satin tends to fray, so edges should be overcast.)

½ yard 45-inch-wide lace fabric for overskirt and bodice

¼ yard 45-inch-wide white cotton fabric for petticoat, apron and tie

1½ yards of ¼-inch-wide velvet ribbon for ball gown and hair

1 yard of ⅜- or ¼-inch-wide satin ribbon for braids

2¼ yards of ⅜-inch-wide lace edging for collar, cuffs of both dolls and overskirt of ball gown

1⅜ yards of 1-inch-wide *pregathered* lace edging for petticoat and apron

1 (4-oz.) ball yellow worsted-type yarn for hair

12 inches of ½-inch-wide white woven tape

Small bunch white fabric flowers; stranded embroidery floss for face in white, black, medium blue, brown and dark rose; 4 small buttons for print dress; 1 package tiny pearls for stringing (15 used here from pack of 20); 1½-inch square fabric for apron patch; fiberfill stuffing; sewing threads; tracing paper; dressmakers' carbon paper; tracing wheel.

Making the basic doll: Begin by transferring the pattern pieces for the body, hand and apron, shown next page in Fig. 1, to a sheet of tracing paper. (See the instructions on page 38 regarding the enlargement of a grid pattern.) Mark off the same number of squares, 16 horizontal and 10 vertical on the tracing paper, with each square 1 inch x 1 inch. Then mark on appropriate cloth and cut out hands and apron but not body, so that faces can be embroidered with fabric in embroidery hoop before the body pieces are cut and sewn.

Cinderella's ball gown covers the complete calico twin shown in the lighter lines in the sketch above

Note: You will need two cutouts for the body (front and back) and eight for the hands (one pair, front and back, for each of four hands).

Trace the actual size facial features (Fig. 2) at both ends of *one* body piece, right side, as lightly as possible. Then embroider the features with embroidery floss as follows:

Using 3 strands of black floss, embroider eyebrows in split stitch.

Using 2 strands of black floss, work eyelashes and outline eye in backstitch.

Outline iris with 5 strands medium blue in split stitch. (This won't show when satin stitch is worked over it, but will give a slightly raised effect and insure coverage at outer edge.)

Work eye in satin stitch, using 3 strands white, blue and black (Fig. 2). Work mouth in dark rose. Work nose in 1 strand brown.

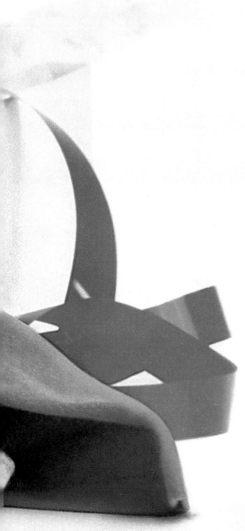

57

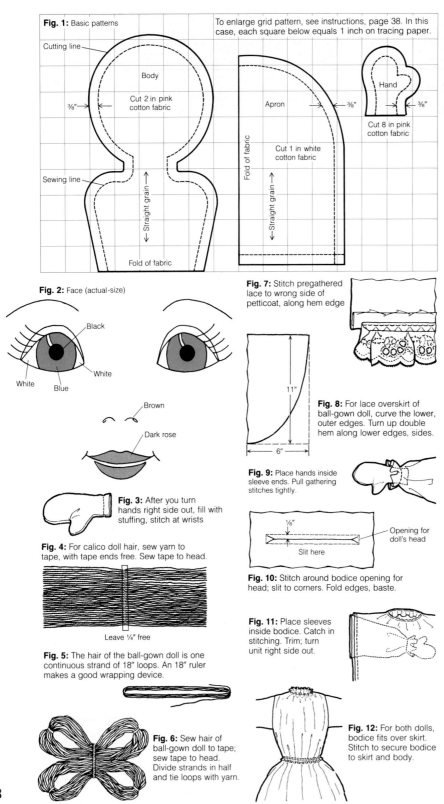

Fig. 1: Basic patterns

Cutting line

Body

Cut 2 in pink cotton fabric

⅜"

Sewing line

Straight grain →

Fold of fabric

To enlarge grid pattern, see instructions, page 38. In this case, each square below equals 1 inch on tracing paper.

Apron

⅜"

Fold of fabric

Cut 1 in white cotton fabric

Straight grain →

Hand

⅜"

Cut 8 in pink cotton fabric

Fig. 2: Face (actual-size)

Black
White
White
Blue
White

Brown

Dark rose

Fig. 3: After you turn hands right side out, fill with stuffing, stitch at wrists

Fig. 4: For calico doll hair, sew yarn to tape, with tape ends free. Sew tape to head.

Leave ¼" free

Fig. 5: The hair of the ball-gown doll is one continuous strand of 18" loops. An 18" ruler makes a good wrapping device.

Fig. 6: Sew hair of ball-gown doll to tape; sew tape to head. Divide strands in half and tie loops with yarn.

Fig. 7: Stitch pregathered lace to wrong side of petticoat, along hem edge

11"

6"

Fig. 8: For lace overskirt of ball-gown doll, curve the lower, outer edges. Turn up double hem along lower edges, sides.

Fig. 9: Place hands inside sleeve ends. Pull gathering stitches tightly.

⅛"

Slit here

Opening for doll's head

Fig. 10: Stitch around bodice opening for head; slit to corners. Fold edges, baste.

Fig. 11: Place sleeves inside bodice. Catch in stitching. Trim; turn unit right side out.

Fig. 12: For both dolls, bodice fits over skirt. Stitch to secure bodice to skirt and body.

When embroidery is complete, cut out body pieces. Place embroidered piece face down on lightly padded surface and press stitching with iron. Then place embroidered piece on plain body piece, right sides together. Stitch around body ⅜-inch from borders, leaving an opening in one side for turning. Clip and notch seam allowance all around. Turn body right side out. Stuff body firmly; turn in edges of opening and sew it closed with slip stitch.

Place hands in pairs, right sides together. Stitch around each pair ⅜-inch from border, leaving wrist edges open. Trim seam allowance all around curves. Turn each hand right side out and stuff firmly. Stitch across each hand at wrist (Fig. 3).

Hair for calico doll: Cut tape length in half (keep one half for second doll). Cut half of the yellow yarn into 18-inch lengths. Lay yarn across tape, with tape in the center, leaving ¼-inch of tape free at each end (Fig. 4). Stitch yarn to tape, using machine zigzag stitch or overcasting by hand. Have yarn thick enough to form solid covering over head.

Place hair on head of calico doll, with stitch line forming center part. Tuck raw tape ends under. Sew hair to head along part with backstitch.

Gather a bunch of hair at each side. Tie yarn around each bunch securely; sew to side of head. Braid hair, again tie securely. Add ribbon bows as shown in photo, page 56.

Hair for ball-gown doll: Hair is one continuous strand of 18-inch loops (Fig. 5). Attach loops of measured yarn to tape as for other doll (Fig. 6). Make sure of ample coverage. Sew tape to head, as above. Divide strands on each side into halves, making two bunches on each side. Tie off loop ends with pieces of yarn (Fig. 6) to facilitate handling.

Working one side at a time, intertwine yarn bunches, secure at back of head. Using 8 inches of velvet per side, interweave ribbon with yarn. Sew bunches to sides of head. Add flower clusters to the hair after the doll has been dressed, as in the photograph at right.

Petticoat: Cut a piece of plain white cotton, 32 inches x 12½ inches. Turn under a small hem along one long edge and hand stitch in place. Attach *pregathered* lace to *wrong* side of petticoat over hem edge, using zigzag stitch or hand overcast (Fig. 7). Fold petticoat in half crosswise, with wrong sides facing and edges matching. Stitch the side edges together with a French seam.

Run two lines of gathering stitches around the top edge of the petticoat. Fit the petticoat around the waist of the doll, with wrong side over face of ball-gown Cinderella and seam at center back. Pull up gathers to fit waist and fasten off.

Apron: Turn under a tiny double hem along sides and lower edges, hand stitch in place. Attach remaining piece of 1-inch *pregathered* lace along hem as on petticoat.

Gather waist edge of apron with two rows of gathering stitches. To make tie, cut a piece of white cotton fabric 1⅞ inches x 36 inches. Fold in half crosswise and mark center. Fold in half lengthwise and, leaving a 5-inch center opening, stitch long edges together, taking a ⅜-inch seam. Turn tie right side out and press. Gather apron top to fit opening; insert, then pin and baste. Topstitch entire length of tie along lower edge, catching top edge of apron in stitching. Apply patch, using embroidery floss and diagonal basting stitch.

Skirt for calico doll: Cut a piece of floral print fabric 32 inches x 11¾ inches. Turn under a tiny double hem along one edge of skirt and stitch. Fold skirt in half crosswise, with wrong sides together and edges matching. Stitch edges together with a French seam.

Run two lines of gathering stitches around top edge of skirt. Place skirt on doll right side up, over petticoat, seam at center back (thus covering head of other doll). Draw up gathers

to fit waist and fasten off threads; secure skirt and petticoat to body.

Skirt for ball-gown doll: Make in same way but use satin fabric. Attach skirt to body. For lace overskirt, cut rectangular piece of lace fabric 32 inches x 11 inches. Curve lower outer edges, following Fig. 8. Turn up tiny double hem along curved sides and bottom edge and stitch by hand. On right side, using machine straight stitch, attach ⅜-inch-wide lace edging as close to edge as possible. Gather upper edge, attach to doll over satin underskirt as for skirt of calico doll.

Sleeves: For calico doll, cut out two 6-inch squares of floral print fabric to contrast with skirt colors. Fold in half, right sides together, and stitch side seams. Turn sleeves right side out.

Turn under ⅜ inch at one end of each sleeve and baste. Cut two 6-inch lengths of ⅜-inch lace edging. Place lace on right side of each sleeve, pin and baste lace edging around hem edge. Stitch close to edge with running stitch. Run a row of gathering stitches just inside this stitch line. Place a hand inside lace-edged end of each sleeve. Pull gathering stitches tight around wrists and secure (see Fig. 9). Sleeves for ball-gown doll are made the same way using satin fabric.

Bodice for calico doll: Cut a piece of first floral fabric 10 inches x 8 inches. Fold bodice piece in half lengthwise, wrong sides together, edges matching. Cut a center opening long enough for doll's head to slip through (about 5 inches). Stitch around opening, ⅛ inch from slash. Slit to corners as in Fig. 10. Fold edges through to wrong side; baste.

Stitch ⅜-inch-wide lace edging to neck edge on right side, as close to edge as possible, using running stitch. Run row of gathering stitches just inside this stitch line. Attach buttons down center front on right side.

Fold bodice with right sides together. Place sleeves inside bodice, with tops of sleeves to top of bodice at sides, and stitch side seams, catching sleeves in stitching (Fig. 11). Trim and

turn bodice-sleeve unit right side out. Turn bodice hem under ⅜ inch at lower edge and sew hem with running stitch, leaving an end loose for gathering.

Put bodice on calico doll; draw up gathering stitches to fit doll's waist, covering raw upper edge of skirt. Fasten off gathering thread securely; stitch to secure bodice to skirt and body (Fig. 12). Draw up gathering thread around neck to fit and fasten off thread securely.

Bodice for ball-gown doll: Make in same way as for calico doll, but use satin fabric together with an overlayer of lace. Baste the lace and satin together before beginning the neckline opening and treat as one layer: i.e., cut an 8-inch x 10-inch rectangle of each and baste around edges, with wrong side of lace attached to right side of satin. Then proceed as instructed above for the calico doll.

Hand stitch one piece of velvet ribbon around the waist of the ball gown and tie in a bow, center front. The bow in photo above consists of three pieces of velvet ribbon: one around the waist; a second looped across center of waist; a third, long strip looped over waist loop and secured beneath it. Insert flowers under bow and attach to skirt as well. Tie apron around waist of calico doll.

59

Toy Wagon

Judging by their popularity as Christmas gifts, toy wagons would seem to be as enduring as wagons themselves. And what better way for a child to cart around all the other gifts?

Cut boards to correct sizes (see Parts List). Then use a 2-inch diameter spice jar to draw rounded corners on floor and side boards. Cut corners and notches (Figs. 1 and 3) with jigsaw; file and sand edges. Using Fig. 1, locate and drill ⅜-inch axle holes in sides, and ⅛-inch pilot screw holes in side and bottom pieces. Insert axle through sides, temporarily fit wheels, dry fit other pieces for right length. Push screws through pilot holes to mark screw holes in end pieces. Remove floor and end pieces, leaving wheels on axles. With 1/16-inch drill, make screw holes ½-inch deep in sides.

To assemble handle, see Fig. 3. Drill holes where shown. Insert T nuts in notches, screws in handle. Saw off screw heads with hacksaw. Apply white glue along inner edges of floorboards. As you press boards together for gluing, also secure handle in notch by inserting screws into T nuts.

After floorboards dry, assemble side and end pieces; apply glue to appropriate edges. Screw pieces together, using finishing washers.

For grip assembly, see Fig. 3. Center 6½-inch length of ¾-inch half-round dowel. Glue and screw it to handle, using two screws and washers. Cut inner pieces to correct fit, glue them to main grip. Use masking tape to secure them while they dry.

Remove wheels, give wagon a final sanding, then apply coat of polyurethane. After it dries, rub it with steel wool. Apply second coat same way.

For permanent wheel attachment, put washers between wagon and wheel and wheel and nut. Secure wheels by placing axle nuts on ends of axles and tapping lightly with hammer.

Fig. 1: Sides and floor
Screws: center ⅞" from ends, 1 1/16" from sides; axle holes: center 3⅛" from ends, ⅝" from bottom

Pilot screw holes
Side board
5½"
⅜" Axle holes

18"
Pilot screw holes
11"
1½"
1½"
Floor (bottom view)
Axles

Center floor screw holes 2" from sides, 1⅞" from ends. Use ⅛" bit for all pilot holes.

Fig. 2: Wagon, exploded view

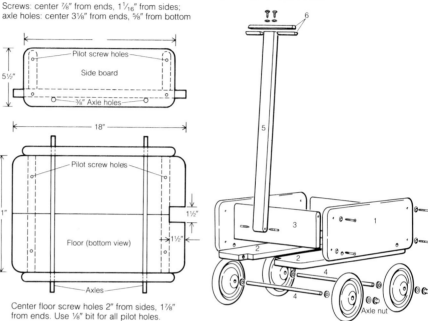

Axle nut

Fig. 3: Handle and grip assembly

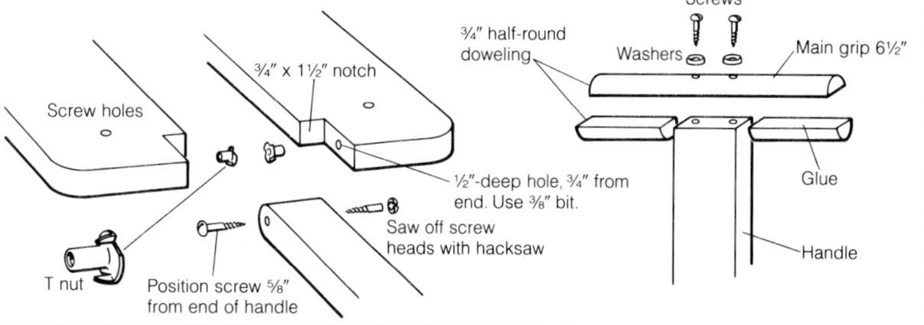

Screw holes
¾" x 1½" notch
¾" half-round doweling
Screws
Washers
Main grip 6½"
Glue
½"-deep hole, ¾" from end. Use ⅜" bit.
Saw off screw heads with hacksaw
Handle
T nut
Position screw ⅝" from end of handle

PARTS LIST

No.	Name	Quantity	Nominal Size	Length	Width	Material
1	Sides	2	1 × 6	16"	5½"	clear pine
2	Floor	2	1 × 6	18"	5½"	clear pine
3	Ends	2	1 × 4	11"	3½"	clear pine
4	Axles	2		15"		⅜" steel rod
5	Handle	1	1 × 2	20"	1½"	clear pine
6	Handle grip	1	¾"	13"		half-round dowel

Tools and hardware: hacksaw, jigsaw; drill with bit sizes ⅜" (for axle holes and T nuts), ⅛" (for screw pilot holes), 1/16" (for screw holes in end pieces and handle); wood files, sandpaper, white glue, combination square ruler or steel tape measure; polyurethane varnish, No. 4/0 steel wool. Fourteen 1¼" No. 6 oval head wood screws; 14 No. 8 finishing washers; 2 3/16" × ½" T nuts, 2 1" No. 6 wood screws; four 4¾" wheels with ⅜" axle holes, 4 ⅜" axle nuts, 8 3/16" washers. ⅜" rods are available in most hardware stores; cut them with hacksaw. Wheels are available in most home service centers.

Christmas Cards

Today's delivery of Christmas cards has arrived. You riffle through them curiously, postponing opening them for a while. You note the shapes and sizes of the envelopes; in the largest envelope, you guess, is a card that will be gilded or embossed or both. And right behind it is the smallest of the batch, complete with tiny writing that must have tried the eyes and patience of a harried postal clerk.

You scan the postmarks and return addresses. There again, as for so many years, is one from that small town a thousand miles distant, from that friend with whom the annual exchange of cards maintains the thread of friendship for both. At the corners of the cards and on their backs, your eyes are caught by the Christmas stamps and seals announcing their own Christmas messages in miniature. There's even an envelope *without* a stamp. Either it slipped through unnoticed in the overwhelming volume that the postal service has been processing, or perhaps some nameless mail sorter, seized by the spirit of the season, allowed it to continue on its way as a small gift both to you and to the forgetful sender.

You reach the last card, restack them all into a neat pile and pause briefly, reflecting. With the holiday approaching, with so much to do in festive preparations and with so many friends and family members in your thoughts, you couldn't possibly have written a note to each to wish the joys of the season, nor they to you, as much as you both enjoy hearing from each other. Among your Christmas blessings, you decide, you'll count the existence of the Christmas card.

Norman Rockwell painting, done for Hallmark cards

As Christmas of 1843 approached, one man could not console himself with such a thought. Again that Christmas, as the director of a London museum and an active man-about-town, Sir Henry Cole had a host of greetings to convey. And it meant writing every one of them by hand. Certainly, he and other seasonal well-wishers could buy sheets of paper decorated with Christmas themes, with space left for a personally written message. There were also cards, usable for any holiday or anniversary, to which the name of the particular occasion could be added. As a child in the early nineteenth century, Cole and the other children had presented handmade "Christmas pieces" to their parents and relations in the form of colored bits of paper showing Bible scenes or decorated with pictures of nature at the top and bottom. The center of each Christmas piece offered examples of youthful penmanship, with messages of "Love to Dearest Mummy at the Christmas Season" or "Holiday Wishes to Aunt Agatha and Uncle Fred."

But Sir Henry was too old for Christmas pieces now and too busy to write personally to all the many people he felt he should. How could he possibly express to them his enthusiasm for the season, his belief that Christmas was a time for young and old together, a time for touching and for toasting? What's more, as an active social reformer and champion of the less fortunate, how could he make all his friends aware of the need to extend a helping hand to the poor at Christmastime?

The answer was simple. He would enlist an artist to portray a scene that depicted his feelings of the season along with a brief message and have this printed and made into cards. On these cards, Cole merely had to write the name of the recipient and at the bottom sign his own.

Thus the first Christmas card was born. The artist Cole commissioned was a friend, John Calcott Horsley, and the card that Horsley finally created is a triptych. On the two outer panels there are scenes that show the feeding and clothing of the destitute. In contrast the larger center panel displays a festive family group embracing one another and offering a cup of cheer to the reader of the card. Below the merrymakers is a simple message—"A Merry Christmas and A Happy New Year To You."

Cole had a thousand such cards printed. Those he didn't use himself he asked a shop to sell on his behalf at one shilling apiece. As Cole rightly guessed, other people found themselves in the same seasonal predicament: too many friends and too little time to write a note to each. Printed Christmas cards were a real success.

The popularity of the cards was aided by two factors. Three years earlier the Postage Act of 1840 allowed a piece of mail to be sent anywhere in the United Kingdom for one penny. The second factor was the development of the steam printing press, which brought considerable improvement in printing and engraving methods in the nineteenth century. In 1862, Charles Goodall & Son, a printing firm that specialized in playing cards, introduced the first broad selection of Christmas cards to the British public. Publishers also turned their presses and the talents of their staffs to the creation of more cards. Among the card designers was a young woman who also illustrated children's books and whose drawings of children have remained classics for over a century: Kate Greenaway.

Yet in the 1860s and 1870s, the favorite Christmas cards of the Victorians depicted children more as small adults, with all the coyness and guile of their elders. Other cards showed fairies dancing on a pond and summer scenes of sunlit meadows which gave no hint of winter, let alone of Christmas. Some were adorned with silk and satin, some came in the shapes of fans and crescents, some squeeled or squeaked and some had to be turned upside-down in order to reveal their true message. Today they appear decidedly un-Christmas-like. But that hardly seems to matter, for in their time they were very popular.

In England, that is, not in the United States. In 1882 the superintendent of the Washington, D.C., post office noted that until a few years earlier "a Christmas card was a rare thing." Previously, Americans who wanted to buy Christmas cards had to make do with a limited number of expensive European imports or with business cards embellished with a holiday motif. The earliest of the native cards that sought to do more was a printed advertisement sent out by "Pease's Great Variety [sic] Store in the Temple of Fancy"

Victorian card

65

Kate Greenaway card

Rare
German mechanical card
of the 1870s

Christmas plum pudding, a Victorian card

A summer scene for Christmas, popular in the nineteenth century

Fringed card by Louis Prang & Company, Boston

Kate Greenaway card

One of many Victorian cards featuring dogs

located in Albany, New York. On this card Santa Claus is shown with a young family who are enjoying their presents while in the background a servant sets a Christmas table. Whether or to what degree the card helped Mr. Pease's business has been lost to history.

It was left to a German immigrant named Louis Prang to make a popular success of the Christmas card in the United States. Arriving in New York as a young man, Prang became an expert lithographer and moved on to Boston where he established a printing business of his own. In the mid-1860s, he began reproducing oil paintings using a technique he had invented which employed as many as forty-five color plates to achieve one picture. He called it his "chromolithograph" technique. Some esthetes denounced Prang's reproductions as frauds, but they caught the public fancy. Then in 1873, in an effort to promote his "chromos" at an exhibition in Vienna, Prang presented decorated business cards. The next step followed naturally: to print a holiday greeting on the cards and sell them as Christmas cards. The first of these, manufactured the next year, were sent to England where a journalist, seeing the British postal service staggering under the weight of Prang's and other cards, denounced them all as "a great social evil." A year later, in 1875, Prang introduced his cards into the United States.

As with Henry Cole before him, Louis Prang had the advantages of an improved postal system and better printing techniques. But he was fortunate in other ways as well. He sensed that as free-spirited and rough-hewn as Americans were, they also longed for sensitivity and beauty in their lives, especially at Christmastime. There was a need to fill and he would fill it. He was right. The highly colored and beautifully designed cards that he produced became immediately popular. Whether the scenes were of animals engaged in seasonal activities customarily reserved for humans, such as ice

A French food merchant's card

skating, or of a child dreaming by a fireside, or of Santa listening to children with a telephone receiver at each ear, the cards made their way into thousands of American homes, so that by 1881 his presses were turning out almost five million Christmas cards and Prang was offering sizable cash prizes to artists who would design more.

If Prang's cards had any disadvantage it was their somewhat expensive price. By the last years of the nineteenth century, a flood of imitators, most of them German,

Homemade card of cutouts, ribbon

67

had overrun the market with inferior but less costly cards. After several unsuccessful years of trying to compete, Prang gave up in discouragement and ceased production. It was not until the outbreak of World War I that German-made Christmas cards were removed from American shelves.

With the influx of European cards limited throughout the war years, American card makers began to fill those shelves. While many of their cards retained familiar Christmas scenes and figures, there were others that caught the temper of the times. The twenties roared for some and their cards reflected their exuberance. Cards of the Depression mirrored the resilience of the nation in the face of economic hardships. Those that appeared during World War II enlisted Santa Claus in the war effort, portraying him on his Christmas Eve rounds with a large American flag flying from his sleigh or in the cap and goggles of a bomber pilot delivering his presents through the bomb bay doors. (Little did Santa know that on space-age cards he would ride atop a rocket ship.) The postwar years introduced a new element to all cards, including those at Christmas. They were the so-called studio cards, which sought with varying degrees of humor and taste to brighten the season.

The postage stamps and seals that adorn the envelopes of Christmas cards have their own unique traditions. When Canada inaugurated the Imperial Penny Postal System in 1898, the government honored the event with the issuance of a special stamp decorated with a Christmas motif. Other countries initiated the tradition of an annual Christmas stamp, the United States adopting it in 1962. With a choice of secular and religious scenes, the latter often from Renaissance art, they have become immensely popular, selling in the billions every year.

Christmas seals, on the other hand, were the inspiration of one man, a Danish postmaster named Einar Holbøll. In 1903 he encouraged the printing and sale of a purely decorative Christmas stamp, the proceeds from which would be donated to a worthy cause. Issued in 1904 and bearing a portrait of Queen Louise of Denmark, more than four million of the stamps were sold. Three years later, through the efforts of the Danish-American writer and reformer Jacob Riis, Christmas seals became known to the American public. Their use was initiated by an enterprising Red Cross worker in Wilmington, Delaware, to benefit her local chapter. Soon other charities were reaping the rewards engendered by their sale. It was in 1920 that the National Tuberculosis Association (now called the American Lung Association) became the sole sponsor and the association's symbol, the double-barred Cross of Lorraine, replaced the Red Cross cross on each seal. Today the Christmas seal is used in almost eighty countries worldwide.

The number of Christmas cards sold has increased dramatically over the years. Nowadays they seem to come from everyone, from everywhere—for every reason. In addition to the cards from friends and relatives, there are the cards from would-be friends and why-not-be business associates, as well as lengthy mimeographed chronicles on How Our Family Spent Its Year, plus cards from the mail carrier and fuel company, the paper boy, the local bank, your insurance agent, the trash man *and* his crew. There are cards with kittens wishing you a "purrfect" holiday and cards on which the first face to appear is that of Washington or Lincoln or, if the recipient is lucky, Andrew Jackson. There are cards that can be hung on a tree and cards that can be nibbled, cards to be wound up and played, round cards and oblong ones and cards that can be refolded into a double tetrahedron with a Christmas message on every face.

We tell ourselves Christmas isn't what it used to be, and we're partly right. In many ways, Christmas—and Christmas cards—have changed and will continue to do so. Some cards will always compete with others in glitter or cleverness. Yet there will still be those that preserve the simple scenes and messages that we remember—carolers, their lanterns held high, singing in the snow; children looking wondrously at a glowing Christmas tree; the star that still shines down on Bethlehem.

What is true of Christmas is true also of its cards. The ways in which we honor Christmas and celebrate it may alter—its spirit will not. It is the spirit of sharing and giving, of well-wishing and warmth, of happiness and the hope that all that Christmas means may be preserved throughout the year.

May thy Christmas happy be,
And naught but joy appear,
Is now the wish I send to thee,
And all I love most dear.

VERSE ON A VICTORIAN CARD

Season's Greetings USA 20c

United States postage stamp, 1982

Handcrafted Cards

Tired of store-bought cards that never quite manage to say what you want them to? Here are three methods of making cards that should provide the family with some easy and interesting possibilities.

OFFICE COPIER CARDS

Many of us take for granted the technological wonders of the office copying machine, yet professional artists have explored it as a creative medium. It is ideally suited for adorning your cards with duplicated family photographs.

Tools and Materials: Tracing paper, rubber cement, white glue, scissors, masking tape, pencil, ruler, felt-tip pens or crayons in assorted colors, family photographs. #5½ envelopes (4⅜ inches x 5¾ inches) for stocking design; #7 envelopes (5¼ inches x 7¼ inches) for house design.

Directions: For house design, use legal-size 8½-inch x 14-inch sheet of white paper; for stocking design, standard size (8½ inches x 11 inches). Most copiers are limited to these two sizes. Fold the sheets into quarters as shown in Figs. 1 and 6 and then spread them open.

The first step in preparing a master for copying is to select and cut out the photographs you want to use, making sure they will all fit comfortably.

Next, draw on tracing paper the design in which you wish to place your photographs. Use the house or stocking illustrated on these pages or make up an original design of your own. As a guide, place tracing paper over lower right quarter of white sheet. You can try out various combinations of photographs and drawings on the tracing paper until you work out the design you like best.

Remove the tracing paper and rub soft pencil over the back of it, then turn it over and tape it in position on the white paper master you will use for copying. Transfer the design to the paper by tracing over the master with a pencil (see Fig. 2). You can also use carbon paper to transfer the design from the tracing paper to the master.

Using a black felt pen or crayon, retrace the pencil lines to make them darker for better copying. Attach your photographs with rubber cement at this point, then pencil in your Christmas greetings as shown in Fig. 3. (It might be a good idea to practice the lettering you want to use on tracing paper first to make sure that it fits the space available.) Retrace the words with felt-tip pen or crayon, as above, to enhance them for copying. If you want to design the back of the card, see Fig. 4.

Professional copying services offer paper of different grades and colors which you may want to try for greater variety. Shop around for the service that will provide the quality you want at the lowest price for the quantity you need.

After the sheets have been finished, the designs can be filled in with colored pens or crayons as the girl is doing in the photograph. Fold the finished sheets as shown in Fig. 5.

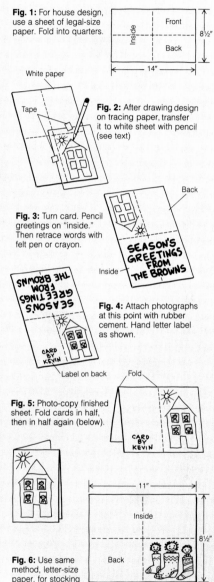

Fig. 1: For house design, use a sheet of legal-size paper. Fold into quarters.

Fig. 2: After drawing design on tracing paper, transfer it to white sheet with pencil (see text)

Fig. 3: Turn card. Pencil greetings on "inside." Then retrace words with felt pen or crayon.

Fig. 4: Attach photographs at this point with rubber cement. Hand letter label as shown.

Fig. 5: Photo-copy finished sheet. Fold cards in half, then in half again (below).

Fig. 6: Use same method, letter-size paper, for stocking

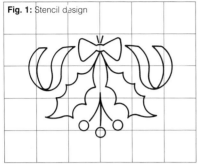

Fig. 1: Stencil design

Basic grid pattern. To enlarge, see page 38.

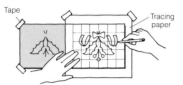

Fig. 2: After rubbing back of tracing paper with soft pencil, trace red ink areas of design on right half of stencil, green ink areas on left half

Fig. 3: Place stencil paper on cutting board and cut out design with knife or single-edge razor

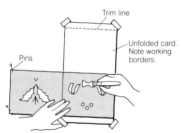

Fig. 4: Tape card to board. Center right stencil, secure at left with pins. Apply red ink with brush.

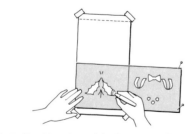

Fig. 5: Allow ink to dry partially. Remove stencil. Let ink dry completely. Apply green ink, left half.

Fig. 6: After the ink has dried fold the card and trim away working borders

72

The two techniques described here can be used for a variety of other designs that may appeal to you.

HOLLY BERRY STENCILS

Many of us learned to make stencils in elementary school, and will remember how much fun it was when the stencil was removed and our bright designs were revealed.

Tools and Materials: Stencil paper, water-base printing ink, tempera or poster paint (red, green, yellow and white), stencil brushes or small sponges, envelopes, heavy white or colored paper for cards; masking tape or push-pins, utility knife or single-edge razor blade, ruler, pencil, tracing paper, cutting board. A paper cutter will make this project easier.

The inks and brushes are available at art and craft supply shops. Because envelope sizes vary, you should adjust the stencil size to fit the dimensions of whatever envelopes are readily available.

Making Stencils: Plan the size of the folded card to fit comfortably into the envelope you have selected (leave about ¼-inch leeway on all sides). Fold the sheet of paper in half and lightly rule in the card size with a pencil. You will use the excess outside the lines as working borders for taping the card in place while you ink the stencil (see Figs. 4-6). When done, you will cut away the working borders, and with them any tape marks.

Next, rule out the actual card size on a piece of tracing paper and leave about an inch of working border all the way around. Then, following instructions on page 38, transfer the design shown in Fig. 1 to the tracing paper after ruling out the squares on the tracing paper within the borders of the card size.

Cut stencil paper to the height of the card but twice its width. Although there are two distinct stencils, they will both be on this single sheet of stencil paper, with the red ink stencil on the right and the green ink stencil on the left (Fig. 3).

Tape the stencil paper to the working surface. Rub a soft pencil over the back of the tracing paper. Tape the tracing paper over the right half of the stencil paper, making sure the design is centered. Trace only those areas that will be the red stencil (see Fig. 2). Then move the tracing paper to the left half of the stencil paper, center it and trace the green portions of the design.

Place the stencil paper on a cutting board and cut out the stencil areas with sharp utility knife (see Fig. 3).

Printing: Squeeze a small amount of red ink onto a plate. Add white and yellow until you get the shade of red you desire. Part of the fun in making stencils lies in developing your own colors, and you may want to experiment beforehand with various shades of red and green.

Before inking your first card, practice with scrap paper to see how much ink to use. If the brush is too heavily loaded, the ink will seep under the stencil and produce a messy image.

Tape the unfolded card paper onto the working surface. Center the right (red) stencil over the card paper, aligning top of stencil with fold, right edge with right edge of card. Secure stencil at the left with pins or tape (see Fig. 4). Apply the red ink, working from the edges toward the center. Allow the ink to dry partially so it won't smudge when the stencil is removed. Then remove the stencil and let the card dry completely before proceeding with the green ink. Apply the green ink as you did the red, centering the stencil on the card and taping or pinning it on the right side (see Fig. 5).

When done, fold the card and trim off the working border (Fig. 6).

CUT PAPER CARDS

These cards are bound to appeal to children still fascinated by the magical power of a pair of scissors. Or does that include us all?

Tools and Materials: White card stock as needed (60-lb. cover weight is a good choice; lighter stock will work). Lightweight cardboard (such as shirt board) for template. Cutting board; cotton (balls or rolls); red construction paper or felt; "monarch" envelopes for dove, 3⅞ inches x 7½ inches; #7 envelopes for Santa, 5¼ inches x 7¼ inches (suggested sizes only—with all card projects it is best to select your envelopes first from readily available sizes, then make the cards to fit the envelopes); scissors, pencil, ruler, single-edge razor blade or utility knife; white glue; nail set, awl or other pointed tool; fine point black felt-tip marker. A paper cutter will also make this project easier.

Directions for Dove: Cut desired number of card stock sheets to 7¼ inches x 7¼ inches. Fold to 3⅝ inches x 7¼ inches. Transfer dove design (Fig. 1) from grid to cardboard template using same procedures as for stencils, page 72. (To enlarge grid, see page 38.) Cut out with scissors and knife to produce template (Fig. 1). Place template on piece of scrap wood and use nail set, awl or other pointed tool to punch an eyehole (see Fig. 2). Position template on folded card stock; trace outline and mark eyehole with pencil (Fig. 3).

Cut dove with scissors along pencil outline (Fig. 4). To cut interior wing shape, place outside section of unfolded card on scrap cardboard or other cutting surface; cut with knife or razor blade (Fig. 5). Bend wing slightly out. Fill eye in with black marker.

Santa: Cut sheets of card stock to 9 inches x 7 inches, then fold in half to 4½ inches x 7 inches. Cut the same number of pieces of red construction paper or felt to size shown in Fig. 8 and glue to tops of folded white card stock to form Santa's hat. Make template, punching eyeholes and cutting nose position with same procedures as for dove. Trace template onto cards and cut them out (Figs. 9 and 10).

Note that the curve of Santa's nose is cut on *unfolded* card (Fig. 11) the same way as the wing of the dove. Finally, glue on twists of cotton for mustache and hat as shown in Fig. 12.

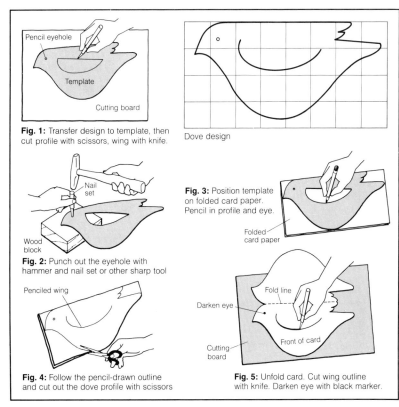

Fig. 1: Transfer design to template, then cut profile with scissors, wing with knife.

Dove design

Fig. 2: Punch out the eyehole with hammer and nail set or other sharp tool

Fig. 3: Position template on folded card paper. Pencil in profile and eye.

Fig. 4: Follow the pencil-drawn outline and cut out the dove profile with scissors

Fig. 5: Unfold card. Cut wing outline with knife. Darken eye with black marker.

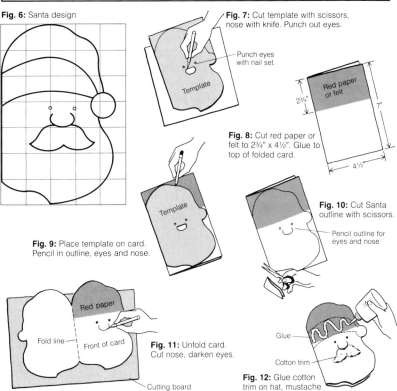

Fig. 6: Santa design

Fig. 7: Cut template with scissors, nose with knife. Punch out eyes.

Fig. 8: Cut red paper or felt to 2¾" x 4½". Glue to top of folded card.

Fig. 9: Place template on card. Pencil in outline, eyes and nose.

Fig. 10: Cut Santa outline with scissors.

Fig. 11: Unfold card. Cut nose, darken eyes.

Fig. 12: Glue cotton trim on hat, mustache

The Plants of Christmas
by Anne Ophelia Dowden

The Greening of Christmas

To: All Wreath Buyers and Makers, Holly and Ivy Festooners, Mistletoe Hangers and Everyone Who Wants to Make the Season Bright with Greenery

From: Your Friendly Florist

I have been watching you as Christmas approaches. I have seen some of you lingering wistfully outside my florist shop, searching for the vivid autumn flowers that filled the windows just a month ago. Others of you, good customers for most of the year, now hurry by, your thoughts on all the things you need to do in preparation for the holidays. Those trees along the street whose bright green leaves delighted you in summer now show little else but dark branches and bare limbs.

But look around again and you'll discover all kinds of other green and growing things appearing every day. You'll use them decorating doors and walls and windows, hanging in gentle arcs from railings and rooflines, nestled around candles, offering an impish invitation from beneath a doorway. What are they? Christmas greenery, of course. Festive wreaths and boughs of evergreens, sprigs of holly with their deep red berries, bits of mistletoe, with which you and your family and your friends and neighbors will soon begin decking your halls.

But before you do, please take a few minutes to read this and reflect. As your florist and supplier of all things botanical from seeds to saplings, I think you would enjoy knowing something of the customs and traditions that are associated with the whole range of Christmas greens. Did you know, for instance, that by bringing into your home even the most modest piece of evergreen to add a touch of seasonal cheer you are carrying on a custom that goes back to prehistoric times?

Perhaps that's why evergreens remain the staple of most Christmas decorations. Whether the evergreen is pine or hemlock, spruce or fir, cedar, juniper or yew, boughs and branches of them are collected by the millions every Christmas in order to be rounded into wreaths, grouped into swags and intertwined in lengthy trains. The fact is that from the beginning of recorded history the evergreen has represented long life and immortality. While most other trees and plants lose their leaves in winter, the evergreen looks ever-living. The Teutonic tribes of Germany believed that godlike spirits inhabited its branches, and the Romans exchanged evergreen boughs as a token of well-wishing. For the rowdy festival of Saturnalia in mid-December, the Romans also eagerly festooned their homes with them. As Christianity evolved, the early persecuted Christians took up the custom too because they didn't want to draw attention to themselves by seeming to ignore it. In doing so, they transformed what was a pagan holiday into the sacred one that has come down to us as Christmas.

It may have been those same first Christians who gave a religious significance to one of the most familiar of all Christmas greens—the holly. With its stiff, thorny leaves and blood-red berries it was suggested as the plant from which Christ's crown of thorns was made. Add to this the English legend that the robin got its red breast when it sought to relieve Christ's sufferings on Calvary by plucking the thorns from His crown. To this day, holly berries remain a favorite food of that and other birds.

Yet even before the birth of Christianity, holly was among the most prized of evergreens. Pagan tribes of Germany and Britain kept it close at hand to ward off evil spirits and bad winter weather, and in the thirteenth

Holly by Anne Ophelia Dowden

But give me holly,
bold and jolly,
Honest, prickly,
shining holly;
Pluck me holly
leaf and berry
For the day when
I make merry.

CHRISTINA ROSSETTI

76

century maidens relied on it as a protector of their virtue. Although the berries of the holly are poisonous for humans to eat, as recently as the nineteenth century its leaves were made into a strong and bitter tea to cure such ills as colic, measles, whooping cough and gout, as well as "winter's ever-bothersome catarrh." And for those of you who may be caroling the English folk song of "The Holly and the Ivy" during Christmas, keep in mind that for centuries holly has been considered a man's plant, ivy a woman's. Perhaps the boldness and the thorniness of holly appears masculine, while ivy with its gentle soft-edged leaves and clinging nature bespeaks femininity. Let me just say that placed together they make a delightful combination.

Speaking of men and women brings me, of course, to mistletoe. In spite of the pleasure it provides those who stand under it, I must admit that mistletoe is, in the horticultural sense, a parasitic weed. Its broad, leathery leaves and pearl-white berries attach themselves high in the branches of certain deciduous trees. But the Druids who inhabited the British Isles centuries ago considered mistletoe a sacred plant. To harvest it, the chief among the Druids had to reach up and remove it with a golden sickle, whereupon it was used to cure illnesses, produce fertility and pacify one's enemies. A kiss beneath it symbolized the end of grievances. A later English custom called upon the man to pluck a berry from the mistletoe every time he kissed a woman, until the mistletoe ran out of berries or he ran out of partners to kiss. And Charles Dickens in his *Pickwick Papers* noted that a newly hung bit of mistletoe "gave rise to a scene of general and most delightful struggling and confusion; in the midst of which [was] Mr. Pickwick . . . now pulled this way, and then that, and first kissed on the chin, and then on the nose, and then on the spectacles: and to hear the peals of laughter which were raised on every side . . ." Today, mistletoe's major contribution to our Christmas festivities continues to be the encouragement of love and laughter.

It's all well and good, you say, to advocate the use of Christmas greens, but in what form? The answer is that you can shape them any way you wish or simply

The shepherd now no more afraid Since custom doth the chance bestow Starts up to kiss the giggling maid Beneath the branch of mistletoe

JOHN CLARE

Ivy by Anne Ophelia Dowden

The Mistletoe Bough by Lizzie Mack, circa 1880

leave them naturally as a spray arrangement or as cuttings in a bowl. Whatever form they take they'll celebrate the spirit of the holiday. Still, of the various decorative displays made of them, wreaths are certainly the most popular.

In the Middle Ages it was customary for a candle to be set in the center of a laurel wreath, lit first on Christmas Eve and then relit every night until January sixth, when the Wise Men are said to have finally found the Christ Child. The wreath that ringed the boar's head at a Tudor Christmas table was made of rosemary and sage. The Advent wreath, which is of Lutheran origin, can be made of any one of several evergreens, with four candles set around it. Beginning on Advent Sunday, four weeks before Christmas, one candle is lighted each week as a symbol of the light given to the world with the birth of Christ.

What sort of evergreen is best for making wreaths is a matter of personal preference and regional abundance. In fact, almost any plant or plant product available in winter can be added to a wreath, from pinecones to berries to dried fruits. (And don't forget the plants and spices that can provide some of the most memorable fragrances of the season. Evergreens have their own distinctive pungency, but it's the rosemary and laurel, bay and sage that give a special essence of their own to whatever green they may be mixed with.)

So far it may appear as if I think of green as the only Christmas color. But red, as you well know, is its customary complement. And no plant I can think of provides it more spectacularly than does the poinsettia. In parts of the United States where evergreens aren't plentiful, poinsettias, with their beautiful long crimson leaves, are nature's most familiar Christmas gift. Actually they had their origin in Mexico and Central America, where the "fire flower" has been the source of many legends. One tells of a poor peasant girl who had no gift for the Christ Child to place at the altar of a great Mexican cathedral on Christmas Eve. And as she wept with sorrow an angel appeared to her and directed her to gather a bouquet of tall weeds that grew nearby and to present them as her gift. The girl obeyed, and as she laid them on the altar the weeds burst into a glorious red bloom.

However, it was an American diplomat and amateur botanist named Joel Poinsett who introduced the plant into the United States. As U. S. minister to Mexico in 1825, he admired seeing them profusely decorating churches, homes and marketplaces during Christmas. Returning to his native South Carolina, he began to grow them and sent cuttings to his fellow botanists around the country. One such grateful friend named the plant after Poinsett, and in time its popularity spread across the country and around the world.

And with this I will conclude my letter to you. As I have been writing, more and more of you have come into my florist shop with questions and orders. It's a busy time for all of us and I will not take more of yours. You have gifts to buy, cards to write and friends to call upon. But now and then do take time to appreciate the lovely plants and trees the season offers us and remember the legends and traditions that have given them a special magic all their own. At a time when we rejoice in the spirit of birth and renewal, the sight of fresh and living things is a reaffirmation that that spirit lives as well. When the world outside our windows shows us only the grays and blacks and whites of winter, then the company and comfort of an evergreen wreath, a bough of holly or a sprig of mistletoe can add joy to our days.

MISTLETOE
by Walter de la Mare

Sitting under the mistletoe
(Pale-green, fairy mistletoe),
One last candle burning low,
All the sleepy dancers gone,
Just one candle burning on,
Shadows lurking everywhere:
Someone came, and kissed me there.

Tired I was; my head would go
Nodding under the mistletoe
(Pale-green, fairy mistletoe);
No footsteps came, no voice, but only,
Just as I sat there, sleepy, lonely,
Stooped in the still and shadowy air
Lips unseen—and kissed me there.

MAKE-IT-YOURSELF PROJECT 8

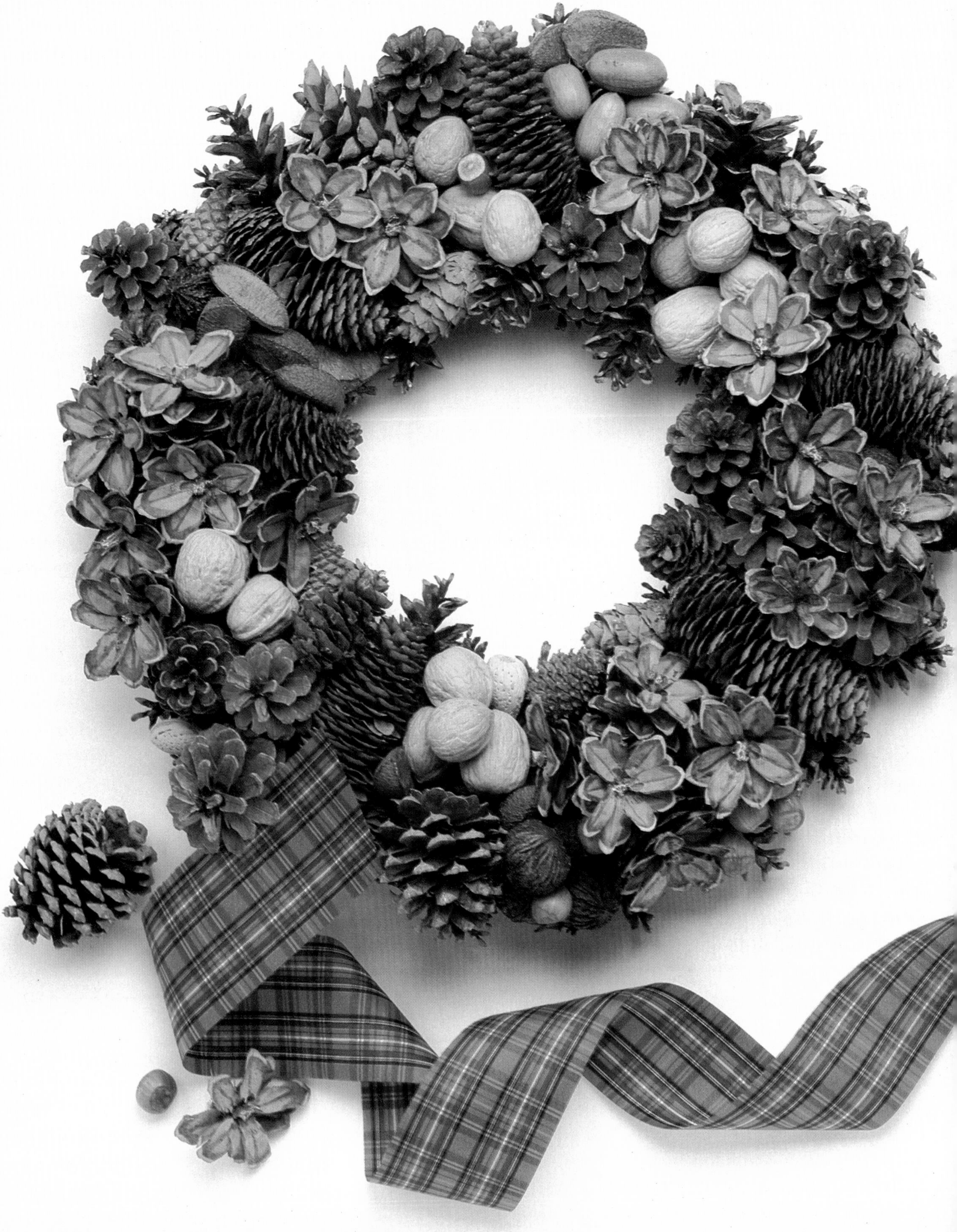

Pinecone Wreath

This is a natural "classic" everyone can enjoy. Not only are the materials readily available, but the pinecones, for many, are free for the taking—or the raking.

Wreaths can be either glued or wired together. Gluing is faster and easier, but glue eventually dries out and the cones may drop off. Wired wreaths take more time, but they will hold together for years.

Materials (for both methods): Pinecones (preferably from white pine trees; they are long and narrow and easier to cut); wire planting frame (normally 10-16 inches in diameter; finished wreath is at least 2 inches larger than frame); pruning shears; assorted cones and nuts; spray can of clear shellac (optional).

For gluing method: If wreath is to hang in an unprotected outdoor area, use a waterproof, linoleum glue. Otherwise, a good quality white glue will suffice. If the wreath is very large, or if several are made, a glue gun is a good investment.

For wiring method: A spool of florist wire, 22-24 gauge; wire cutters; hand or electric drill.

Preparing frame: Soak pinecones in a pail of water until they close (about an hour). Then slip the cones into the planting frame, side by side in alternate directions (see Fig. 1, right).

Hang frame for cones to dry. (This may take two days. If wreath is glued, base must be absolutely dry.)

Assemble the decorative cones and nuts. To make pine "flowers" follow Fig. 2, using cones of white pine for best results. Place the dry base on a working surface and arrange the nuts and cones in a pleasing design. Decide whether you want a random arrangement, or one with a visual focal point, like the star at the top of a Christmas tree. When elements are arranged to your satisfaction, attach them in one of the following ways:

Gluing: Apply glue to bottoms of decorative cones and nuts, one at a time (see Fig. 3). Put back in position. Hold each steady until the glue has slightly firmed.

Wiring: Working with one decorative pinecone at a time, run a wire around it and twist it tight. Push wire through cones comprising wreath base, twist beneath base to secure. Trim wire with clippers. To wire nuts to base, drill holes in shells. Work a wire through newly made holes and twist close to nut. Then proceed as with cones. Small nuts can be wired together and secured to the base as a group.

After the wreath is assembled, you can give it a glossier finish by spraying it thoroughly with clear shellac.

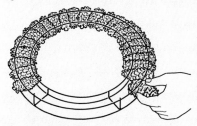

Fig. 1: Preparing the base

Insert the pinecones between the wires of the metal frame so they will face in alternate directions

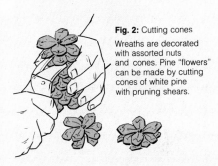

Fig. 2: Cutting cones
Wreaths are decorated with assorted nuts and cones. Pine "flowers" can be made by cutting cones of white pine with pruning shears.

Fig. 3: Decoration
After deciding on arrangement, glue the cones and nuts one at a time. Hold each until glue begins to firm.

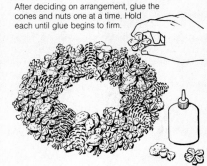

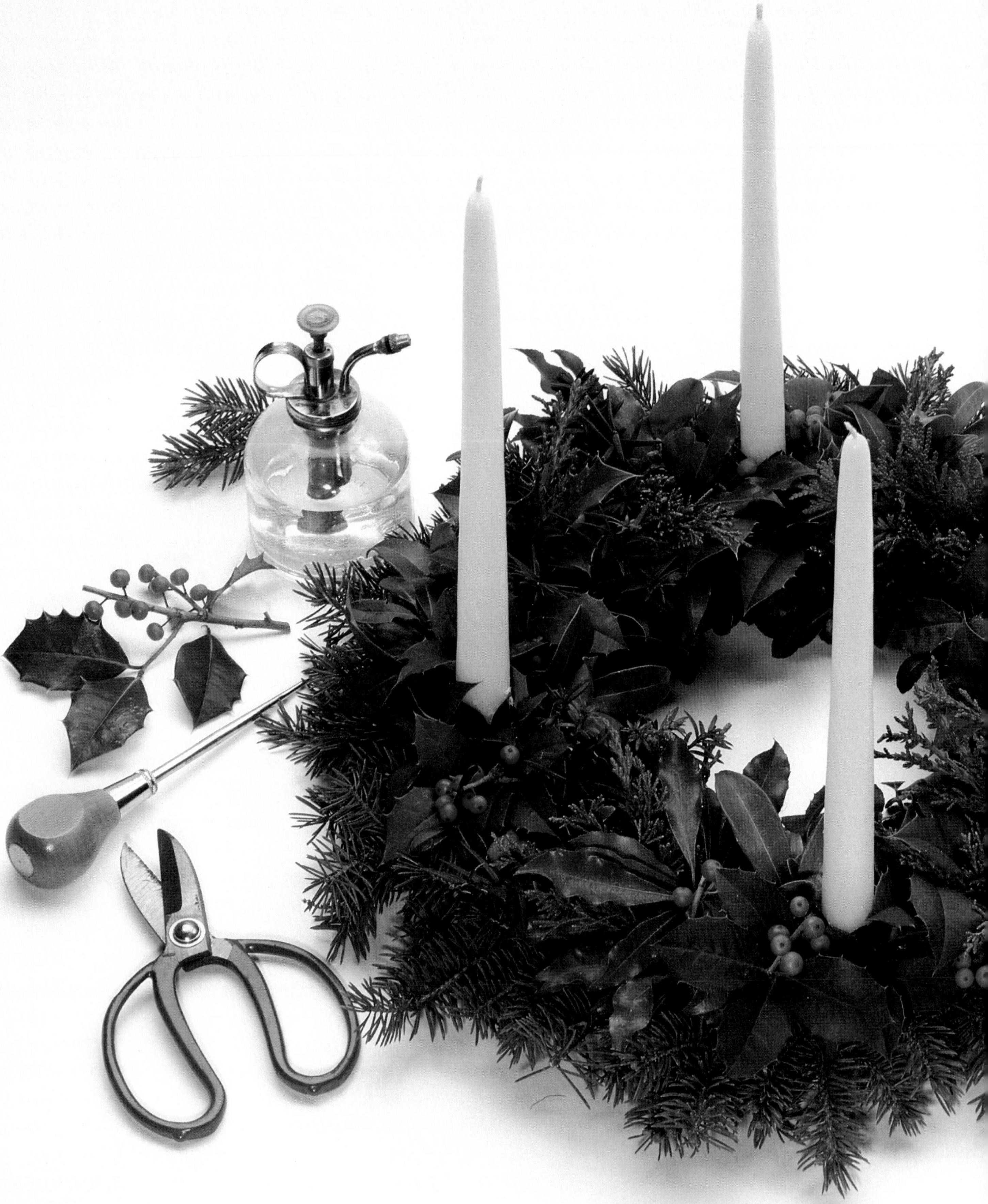

Advent Wreath

Easy to make and long-lasting, this "living wreath" pays tribute to an age-old tradition. The circle shape represents eternity, and each of the four candles is also symbolic. The first Sunday's candle is the Prophesy Candle; the second is the Bethlehem Candle. The third represents the Shepherd's Candle, and the fourth is the Angel's Candle.

Materials: Long shredded, unmilled sphagnum moss; wire planting frame, 10-16 inches in diameter (finished wreath is at least 2 inches larger than planting frame); dark green plastic trash bag; roll of wire; advent candle wreath frame (you can also use candle picks or florist's clay); large nail or awl; assorted greens and berries (see Note below); 4 white candles.

Note: The best greens for the wreath are juniper, yew, spruce, fir, box, rhododendron, holly and ivy. Pine and hemlock do not hold up very well indoors.

Preparing frame: Soak the moss in a pail of water until thoroughly wet. Squeeze out excess water. Then, working on a waterproof or protected surface, pack planting frame with moss.

Cut the plastic bag into one continuous strip about 2 inches wide. Wrap the strip firmly around moss-packed frame, overlapping the edges slightly (see Fig. 1, below). Secure end by wrapping wire around it.

Wire candle frame to planting frame (see Figs. 2, 3). If you don't use candle frame, insert candle picks in planting frame, or make four holes and fill with florist's clay.

Adding greens: Clip greens 4-6 inches long. Strip the stems about 1 inch. Working along the rim of the frame, punch holes through plastic strips with nail or awl and firmly insert clippings (see Fig. 3). Continue around rim, shaping and trimming to keep circle even. Similarly, work inside of wreath, but use shorter clippings to avoid closing the center. If necessary, angle the greens.

You can fill in the top by working the greens first around the candle holders, making sure they are covered, then filling the areas between. Or you can cover the top as you go along. You can also stick to one kind of green and berry, or use a greater variety. If you wish, you can add bows and other decorative touches. Traditionally, bows of purple ribbon are used with the first two candles. Pink ribbons are used with the third and fourth candles.

A wreath will last through the holidays; misting it every other day will help keep it fresh. After the holidays, remove the greens, hang the frame to dry, then store it in an airy place. The following year, soak the wreath and add fresh greens. After a few years, you may need to replenish the moss or replace the plastic strips.

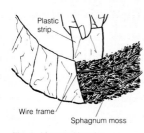

Plastic strip

Wire frame

Sphagnum moss

Fig. 1. After packing the planting frame with wet moss, firmly wrap it with plastic strip, overlapping slightly

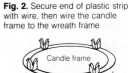

Fig. 2. Secure end of plastic strip with wire, then wire the candle frame to the wreath frame

Candle frame

Wrap wire around plastic strip

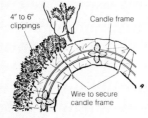

4" to 6" clippings

Candle frame

Wire to secure candle frame

Fig. 3. Working along rim, punch holes through plastic strips, insert clippings. Fill inside of circle in the same way, then decorate the top.

Santa Claus

Tough Questions for Santa Claus in a Tough No-Nonsense World

"He knows if you've been bad or good . . ."

1. How do you know? Did my little brother snitch on me?

2. How can you visit every kid's house all over the world in one night?

3. How can you remember the names and addresses of every little kid and recall what each one asked for? Do you have all this on a computer?

4. How can you get zillions of gifts into that one dinky little sack?

5. How can a chubby guy like you fit through the chimney?

6. Don't you ever get tired of the milk and cookies kids leave out? How would you feel about a grilled cheese and cocoa?

7. What do your reindeer like for a snack?

8. Don't you get cold living at the North Pole?

9. What's Mrs. Claus like? How come you never had kids of your own?

10. How come I saw you at three different department stores? Then again out at the corner of Main and 4th? How can you be in all those places at one time?

11. If there's no snow on Christmas Eve, will the sleigh still be able to land on our roof?

Norman Rockwell, *Saturday Evening Post* cover, December 21, 1935

"Greetings from St. Nicholas," old German card

If you live with small children, you have undoubtedly at one time or another been subjected to an interrogation comprised of some or even all of the above questions for Santa Claus. Rather than try to provide answers for each, it may be more useful to offer a blanket reply. For example: Santa Claus, as we all know, is a remarkable fellow with extraordinary powers. Unencumbered by purely human limitations, he is able to circumvent the globe in a single night, visit the home of every child whether that home has a chimney or not, and leave appropriate gifts for each little girl and boy. He has no difficulty in being in three, four, a dozen or even an infinite number of places at the same moment. He is, quite simply, fantastic, and at a certain time of the year, given the proper spirit within ourselves, the fellow can do the impossible—that is, he can pervade all gloom and shatter all skepticism and doubt.

Sinterklaas to the Dutch, Father Christmas to the English, *Père Noël* to the French. The Germans call him *Weihnachtsmann*, as well as *Christkindl*, or Christ Child, while in Russia they once spoke of the Miracle Maker but now simply refer to him as Grandfather Frost. The Chinese have their *Lam Khoong-Khoong*, meaning Nice Old Father, and the Japanese have *Hoteiosho*, who has eyes in both the back and front of his head and carries a big bag of toys. On January fifth, Epiphany Eve in Italy, Santa Claus is a woman called *Befana*, who comes down the chimney bearing gifts for good little girls and boys.

Who is this universally beloved magical figure with the power to melt hard hearts and suspend shrewd doubts during the Season of Peace? Well, the story of Santa Claus begins with the birth of St. Nicholas, approximately 270 A.D., along the Mediterranean coast of northern Turkey.

According to one account, Nicholas was born to a childless couple after thirty years of marriage and was orphaned at the age of nine. Reared by guardians thereafter, he developed a strong sympathy for the poor and needy and devoted a great deal of his time to providing food, clothing and often money to the underprivileged. Much of his gift giving was accomplished in secret and, invariably, at night.

A story often told of the young St. Nicholas involves the three daughters of an impoverished nobleman who was not able to provide them with dowries. Without dowries they had no hope of suitors. Out of desperation one of the girls volunteered to sell herself into slavery in order to provide marriage portions for her two sisters. Informed of their difficulties, Nicholas came by one night and tossed a small bag of gold down the chimney or through the open window of the eldest girl's bedroom where, according to the legends, it fell into a stocking hanging up to dry. Shortly thereafter the

Around the World with **SANTA= CLAUS**

87

Cover from a children's book published in the United States in the 1890s

Santa Claus selling soap

Before the days of radio and television, merchants often used Christmas cards as a way to advertise their wares. A European example of this practice can be seen on page 67. The American merchants whose cards are featured on these two pages all gave star billing to that famous old man in the red suit.

eldest daughter was married. This same act of generosity was repeated for the other two daughters with equally happy results.

While perhaps still in his teens, Nicholas became the Bishop of Myra, subsequently to be identified in early manuscripts as a saint and miracle worker. Destined to become patron saint of children, Russia, bankers, sailors, pawnbrokers, vagabonds and thieves, when Nicholas died, probably on the sixth day of December around the year 340 A.D., he was well on his way to becoming universally revered as St. Nicholas of Myra.

The practice of bringing gifts in the name of St. Nicholas probably began in France at the start of the twelfth century. The fifth of December, proclaimed the Eve of St. Nicholas, was the time when nuns would leave gifts at the doorstep for the small children of poor families. The custom spread rapidly into other parts of Europe and was soon being celebrated by both rich and poor alike. But it was not until 1626 that St. Nicholas made his way across the Atlantic to North America. He came in the form of a figurehead on the prow of a Dutch ship, *The Good Housewife*, filled with settlers from Holland. Their destination was New Amsterdam at the southern tip of Manhattan Island. It was here that St. Nicholas's foothold in the New World was firmly established. Even after New Amsterdam fell to the British in 1664, the Dutch persisted in the custom of celebrating

A merchant's card showing Santa in a sleigh pulled by just two reindeer

A lean Santa Claus wearing a long coat

A plumper version dressed for rooftop activity

Welcome, friend!
St. Nicholas, welcome!
Welcome to
this merry band!
Happy children
greet thee, welcome!
Thou art glad'ning
all the land!

MARY MAPES DODGE

St. Nicholas Eve. Popular pronunciation over the years managed to contract Saint Nicholas into *Sinterklaas*, which was eventually corrupted to *Sancte Claus*. With *Sancte Claus* now on the scene, could Santa Claus be far behind?

Three people are generally credited with the further transformation of St. Nicholas from the gift-bearing good Bishop of Myra to our own beloved gift-bearing Santa Claus. They are the author and humorist Washington Irving, Clement Clarke Moore, a professor at a theological seminary, and the renowned political cartoonist Thomas Nast.

Under the name of Diedrich Knickerbocker, Washington Irving, author of such favorite tales as "Rip Van Winkle" and "The Legend of Sleepy Hollow," published his beloved *A History of New York from the Beginning of the World to the End of the Dutch Dynasty*. Along with a great deal of gentle humor about the Dutch in New York, Irving also dealt with their enormous affection for St. Nicholas. In his physical description of the beloved saint, the bishop's robes are replaced by more traditional Flemish attire. Instead of the mitred hat of a bishop, there was a wide-brimmed hat, hose and a long Dutch clay pipe. And Irving spoke of the saint flying about in a wagon over the rooftops of New Amsterdam, dropping gifts into the chimneys of little children. The author describes him as visiting on only one night a year and making his entrance via the chimney. This comes close to our own

89

An elflike Santa Claus by Arthur Rackham in an illustration for "A Visit from St. Nicholas"

Old Kris by N. C. Wyeth, *The Country Gentleman*, December 1925

conception of Santa Claus, but it was not until 1822 when Clement Clarke Moore penned his timeless poem, "A Visit from St. Nicholas," that Santa really took on the appearance of the familiar figure loved by millions today.

Using as the model for his Santa Claus Irving's conception of St. Nicholas in *A History of New York*, Moore created the "jolly old elf" with merry dimples and twinkling eyes. He dressed him in fur, gave him a stump of a pipe and provided him with a team of eight reindeer to draw a miniature sled. The

Le Père Noël, drawing by Pablo Picasso

Santa Claus has long been a favorite of artists and illustrators, and each has a somewhat different idea of how the old man should look. On these two pages are Santas by four famous artists. While looking unalike in many ways, they are all unmistakably Santa Claus.

rest is history. In several years the poem had established itself as a classic, appearing in hundreds of newspapers and periodicals.

During the mid-1800s in America many embellishments were added to the constantly evolving image of Santa Claus. This occurred particularly in the area of illustration. Toy workshops, elfin helpers and jingle bells for the reindeer team were but a few of the new innovations.

It was not until the period of the Civil War, however, that the political cartoonist Thomas Nast produced a figure that became affixed forever in the minds of people as Santa Claus. Nast drew his first Santa Claus for the cover of *Harper's Weekly*, the leading newspaper of the day. More a recruiting poster for the Union side during the Civil War than a decorative Christmas feature, Santa was pictured by Nast as a figure dressed in stars and stripes dispersing gifts. Between the years of 1864 and 1886 Nast's drawings of Santa Claus, eagerly awaited by a large public, appeared annu-

A Thomas Nast Santa, *Harper's Bazaar*, January 1, 1881

91

A Christmas Fairy by Lizzie Mack

*All the house
was asleep,
And the fire
burning low,
When, from far
up the chimney,
Came down
a "Ho! ho!"*

MRS. C. S. STONE

ally. In these he generally appears as a portly, bewhiskered, befurred old gent, climbing in and out of chimneys with an enormous sack of toys on his back.

Up until 1886 Nast had always drawn Santa in black ink. Asked by a publisher to produce color drawings of Santa for a book, Nast had the brilliant inspiration of giving him a bright red suit with white ermine trim. Jolly, plump, bewhiskered and all in red, here at last was the Santa Claus we know so well today.

It has taken more than sixteen centuries for the good Bishop of Myra to evolve into jolly old St. Nick. In an age of computers, genetic engineering and interplanetary space travel, it is tempting to speculate on what additional changes the next sixteen centuries might impose on this beloved figure.

But even if Santa does trade in his red flannels for a thermostatically controlled space suit, and the reindeer for a glittering titanium space capsule, the spirit of the good gift-bearing Bishop of Myra with his unfailing concern for the needy and less fortunate will never change. Sixteen hundred years from now, ten thousand years, or even for the next one hundred millennia, of one thing you may be certain—on Christmas Eve all over the world the children will still be asking tough questions, hanging stockings and eagerly awaiting his arrival.

"Yes, Virginia, There Is a Santa Claus"

The following first appeared on the editorial page of the New York Sun on September 21, 1897. Francis Church was the newspaperman who wrote this now-famous response to a little girl's probing question about Santa Claus.

Dear Editor:

I am 8 years old. Some of my little friends say there is no Santa Claus. Papa says "If you see it in *The Sun* it's so." Please tell me the truth, is there a Santa Claus?

Virginia O'Hanlon,
115 West 95th Street

Virginia, your little friends are wrong. They have been affected by the skepticism of a skeptical age. They do not believe except they see. They think that nothing can be which is not comprehensible by their little minds. All minds, Virginia, whether they be men's or children's, are little. In this great universe of ours man is a mere insect, an ant, in his intellect, as compared with the boundless world about him, as measured by the intelligence capable of grasping the whole of truth and knowledge.

Yes, Virginia, there is a Santa Claus. He exists as certainly as love and generosity and devotion exist, and you know that they abound and give to your life its highest beauty and joy. Alas! how dreary would be the world if there were no Santa Claus. It would be as dreary as if there were no Virginias. There would be no childlike faith then, no poetry, no romance to make tolerable this existence. We should have no enjoyment, except in sense and sight. The eternal light with which childhood fills the world would be extinguished.

Not believe in Santa Claus! You might as well not believe in fairies! You might get your papa to hire men to watch in all the chimneys on Christmas Eve to catch Santa Claus, but even if they did not see Santa Claus coming down, what would that prove? Nobody sees Santa Claus, but that is no sign that there is no Santa Claus. The most real things in the world are those that neither children nor men can see. Did you ever see fairies dancing on the lawn? Of course not, but that's no proof that they are not there. Nobody can conceive or imagine all the wonders there are unseen and unseeable in the world.

You may tear apart the baby's rattle and see what makes the noise inside, but there is a veil covering the unseen world which not the strongest man, nor even the united strength of all the strongest men that ever lived, could tear apart. Only faith, fancy, poetry, love, romance, can push aside that curtain and view and picture the supernal beauty and glory beyond. Is it all real? Ah, Virginia, in all this world there is nothing else real and abiding.

No Santa Claus! Thank God he lives, and he lives forever. A thousand years from now, Virginia, nay, ten times ten thousand years from now, he will continue to make glad the heart of childhood.

A New Picture Book by Lizzie Mack, 1889

Santa's Dream Dollhouse

This spectacular dollhouse is an ambitious project overall, but the individual steps are quite simple. The major material, corrugated cardboard, is strong and easily cut. Glue will be your primary tool, and you won't need a workshop. Just about any well-lighted place will do.

The rewards don't end with the finished facade, for much of the real fun will come from decorating and furnishing the rooms to your taste. The result? A unique, enduring dollhouse of exceptional charm—with no mortgage.

Materials: 4 sheets of heavyweight corrugated cardboard (or foamcore), 30 inches x 40 inches x ¼ inch; 7 eight-foot-long pieces of wood lattice, ¼ inch x ⅞ inch; 2 eight-foot-long pieces of wood screen trim, ¼ inch x ⅝ inch; one-quart can of spackle or other vinyl-type patching compound.

If you paint the interior: alcohol base primer-sealer; latex paint, any colors you wish. (Primer helps prevent cardboard from warping.) For wallpapering the interior, use heavy gift wrapping, scraps of household wallpaper or other wall covering.

White glue; 1 roll 1-inch masking tape; 1 roll 2-inch black masking tape; 1 pint dark brown flat latex paint or opaque stain (for wood trim); 1 sheet illustration or poster board, 20 inches x 30 inches x 1/16 inch, for interior moldings and trim; 1 sheet acetate, 20 mil thickness (for windows), 9 inches x 12 inches; 1 roll 1/16-inch chartmakers' tape (optional; available at art and craft shops).

Tools: Handsaw (preferably backsaw); utility knife or single edge razor blade; metal straightedge ruler (36-inch, ideal); a 2- to 3-inch putty knife; medium artists' sable paintbrush (for touchup); 1½- to 2-inch paintbrush or mini-roller (if you paint interior); large cutting board; mitre box.

The open back of the house permits you to arrange your own furniture. Note Christmas tree, second floor.

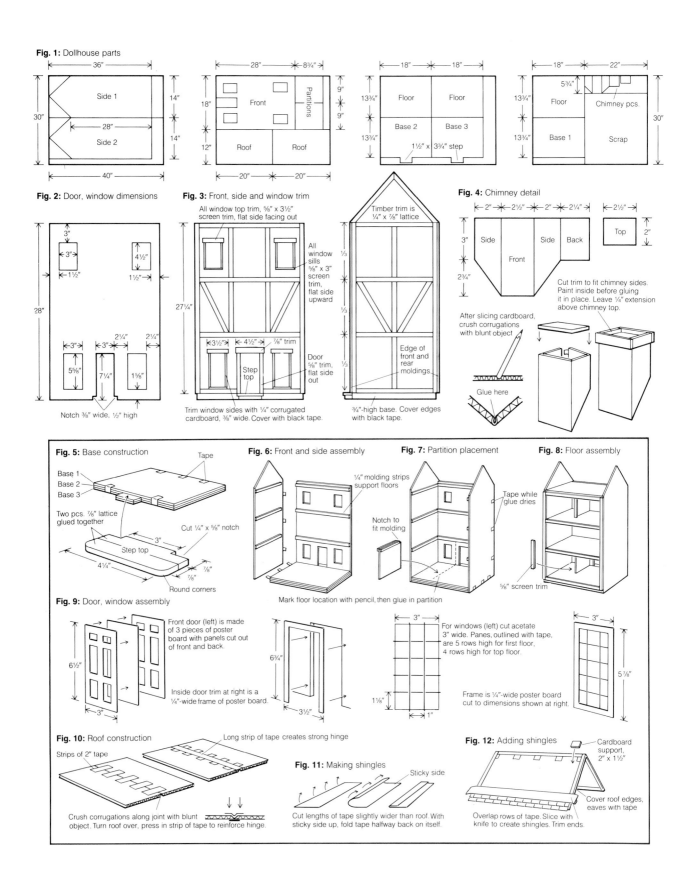

Fig. 1: Dollhouse parts

36″ — Side 1 — 14″ — 28″ — Side 2 — 14″ — 30″ — 40″

28″ — 8¾″ — Front — Partitions — 9″ 9″ — 18″ — Roof — Roof — 12″ — 20″ — 20″

18″ — 18″ — Floor — Floor — 13¾″ — Base 2 — Base 3 — 13¾″ — 1½″ x 3¾″ step

18″ — 22″ — 5¾″ — Floor — Chimney pcs. — 13¾″ — Base 1 — Scrap — 13¾″ — 30″

Fig. 2: Door, window dimensions

3″ — 3″ — 1½″ — 4½″ — 1½″ — 28″ — 3″ — 3″ — 2¼″ — 2¼″ — 5⅝″ — 7¼″ — 1⅝″
Notch ⅜″ wide, ½″ high

Fig. 3: Front, side and window trim

All window top trim, ⅝″ x 3½″ screen trim, flat side facing out
All window sills ⅝″ x 3″ screen trim, flat side upward
27¼″
3½″ — 4½″ — ⅞″ trim
Step top
Door ⅝″ trim, flat side out
Trim window sides with ¼″ corrugated cardboard, ⅜″ wide. Cover with black tape.

Timber trim is ¼″ x ⅞″ lattice
⅓ ⅓ ⅓
Edge of front and rear moldings
¾″-high base. Cover edges with black tape.

Fig. 4: Chimney detail

2″ — 2½″ — 2″ — 2¼″ — 2½″ — Top — 2″
3″ — Side — Front — Side — Back — 2¾″
Cut trim to fit chimney sides. Paint inside before gluing it in place. Leave ¼″ extension above chimney top.
After slicing cardboard, crush corrugations with blunt object
Glue here

Fig. 5: Base construction
Tape
Base 1 — Base 2 — Base 3
Two pcs. ⅞″ lattice glued together
Cut ¼″ x ⅝″ notch
3″ — Step top — 4¼″ — ⅞″ — ⅞″
Round corners

Fig. 6: Front and side assembly
¼″ molding strips support floors
Mark floor location with pencil, then glue in partition

Fig. 7: Partition placement
Notch to fit molding
Tape while glue dries

Fig. 8: Floor assembly
⅝″ screen trim

Fig. 9: Door, window assembly
Front door (left) is made of 3 pieces of poster board with panels cut out of front and back.
6½″ — 3″
Inside door trim at right is a ¼″-wide frame of poster board.
6¾″ — 3½″
3″ — 1⅛″ — 1″
For windows (left) cut acetate 3″ wide. Panes, outlined with tape, are 5 rows high for first floor, 4 rows high for top floor.
Frame is ¼″-wide poster board cut to dimensions shown at right.
3″ — 5⅞″

Fig. 10: Roof construction
Long strip of tape creates strong hinge
Strips of 2″ tape
Crush corrugations along joint with blunt object. Turn roof over, press in strip of tape to reinforce hinge.

Fig. 11: Making shingles
Sticky side
Cut lengths of tape slightly wider than roof. With sticky side up, fold tape halfway back on itself.

Fig. 12: Adding shingles
Cardboard support, 2″ x 1½″
Cover roof edges, eaves with tape
Overlap rows of tape. Slice with knife to create shingles. Trim ends.

The cardboard for the dollhouse need not be perfect, since any blemishes will be covered by spackle. And the spackle itself can be renewed over and over again if it chips or cracks.

Construction: Following drawings on Fig. 1, lay out measurements on cardboard. Label the pieces, cut them out. Glue together the three pieces forming the base (Fig. 5). Secure with masking tape and weight down with books on a flat surface. While they dry, you may cut the front step top at this point and paint it, but add it later after the trim. See Fig. 5 for dimensions.

Pencil mark door and window locations (Fig. 2), cut them out. Similarly mark main chimney piece and chimney top (Fig. 4); cut these two pieces. To fold chimney, pencil mark fold lines on inside. Lightly slice along these lines, then use blunt end of pen or pencil to crush corrugation. Apply thin layer of glue along folds and the two outside edges. Fold chimney, tape joint while drying and set aside for later. Glue on chimney top.

Pencil mark the three floor locations along inside of front and side walls to correspond to horizontal trim positions in Fig. 3. Cut ¼-inch strips of poster board for ceiling molding (see Figs. 6,7). Make sure side moldings are 1/16 inch shorter than side walls to allow space for front molding when sides and front are joined. Because these strips support the floors, glue them along lower lines of floor locations.

Proceed next to assemble the walls. Glue front wall to base (Fig. 6); add side walls and secure with masking tape. Remove excess glue with damp paper towel and scrap poster board.

Mark placement of first-floor partition (Fig. 7). Glue ¼-inch-wide strips of poster board to both sides of partition, flush along top edge. Apply glue along top edge of first-floor ceiling molding and along all but rear edge of partition. Hold partition in place while you position second floor on top of molding and on top of partition. Add third-floor, third-floor partition and attic floor in the same way.

Pencil mark locations for the exterior trim—the lattice beams and door and window trim (Fig. 3). Cover trim locations with strips of 1-inch masking tape, then trim tape with ruler or knife to equal width of latticework. Do not cut through cardboard.

To simulate stucco, cover outer walls with spackling about 3/16 inch thick. Use putty knife. You may overlap tape, but do not cover it completely. Carefully remove tape before "stucco" hardens, exposing cardboard where lattice trim is to be glued.

Following Fig. 3 for lattice location, cut the pieces of trim to fit after the house is assembled. Apply brown paint or stain with small rag (faster than brushing). After the pieces have dried, glue them in position.

Cut, paint and glue windowsills in position next, following dimensions and materials in Fig. 3. Then add window and door side trim, followed by window and door top trim. Window side trim is made with ⅜-inch-wide strips of ¼-inch cardboard covered with black masking tape and painted to hide the corrugations.

After window and door trim have dried, paint or paper the interior. Prime all surfaces to be painted; then apply latex finish coat in the colors of your choice to floors, ceilings and walls (if you do not intend to paper them). To paper, cut pieces to fit, then glue them in position.

Assemble door, windows, and door and window inside trim, following details in Fig. 9. Prime and paint doors and trim, allow to dry, then glue in place. You can either glue the acetate windows in position first and then add the trim, or you can glue trim and acetate together and glue windows in place as a unit.

Next, decorate all exposed edges of rear walls with wood screen trim, fluted side facing out. (See Fig. 8 and photo, p. 95.) Cut the strips to fit, glue them to rear edges, including partitions. After partition trim dries,

paint it to match interior colors. Glue front step in place.

Paint chimney top black. Cut chimney top trim to fit chimney sides (Fig. 4). Paint inside of trim black, outside and top edges brown. Glue trim to chimney. Apply "stucco" spackling to rest of chimney, set aside to dry.

Cover the exposed cardboard of the base with black masking tape.

To make roof, hinge the halves together with black masking tape (Fig. 10). Cover roof edges and eaves with tape (Fig. 12).

For shingles, cut tape strips a bit wider than roof. Fold one edge back on itself (Fig. 11), leaving half of sticky part exposed. Starting at bottom edge of roof, tape on strips, overlapping rows until roof is covered (Fig. 12). With knife, slice exposed, doubled tape edge every inch or so to simulate shingles, then trim ends.

Mark chimney position on front half of roof (rear half lifts up for storage) and cut away a 2-inch x 2½-inch area of roof tape. Cut cardboard support as shown in Fig. 12 and glue it to this spot. Position roof, glue to front half of house only, then glue chimney to support.

Christmas in the Kitchen

Christmas Remembered

by James Beard

Christmas has always held a special delight for me, ever since my childhood in Portland, Oregon. In those days the celebration began almost a year ahead, because my mother believed in making her fruitcake, mincemeat and puddings well in advance so they could be packed in airtight containers and kept mildly intoxicated over a period of time to age and mellow. The large tin boxes of fruitcake, several pounds each, were given some Christmas cheer about once a month by means of a cheesecloth wrung out with brandy or rum. Although the mincemeat was made with plenty of spirits to begin with, it continued to get an additional drink every now and then. It was never entirely used up, and so new batches were added to it. I still keep this habit going and have in my kitchen a large jar of mincemeat that was begun nine years ago and to which more mincemeat and considerably more alcohol have been added, so that by now it is incredibly flavorful, fruity and boozy, and makes great tarts, pies and puddings.

A ritual went along with Mother's Christmas puddings. When one was put to boil, everyone in the household had to stir it and make a wish. This pleasant little conceit carried over from my mother's Welsh and English

days, and she believed firmly it would bring good luck. Well, if good luck meant great results in the kitchen, she was right, because I've never had puddings that were as rich and as palate-tingling as those. When they were heated and brought blazing to the table, they were indeed a joy. Two sauces were served with them—one, a rather syrupy sauce, well laced with cognac; and the other, a traditional hard sauce, made with confectioners' sugar, butter and whatever flavoring one wanted.

My father had a very strange treatment for his mince pie, which was always served quite hot. He would lift the upper crust and place a large square of butter and a chunk of Roquefort cheese under it and let them melt into the mincemeat before he ate it.

The holiday cakes were made at the last. There would be a seed cake and an English currant cake, and often a Scots Bun, or "Black Bun," as it is more properly called, which is extremely spicy and pungent and cooked in a crust. Nowadays, I have decided, people are afraid of spices and intense flavor—something I notice particularly when I sample fruitcakes, spice cake or mincemeat. I don't think that cooks ever follow a good recipe accurately when it calls for a quantity of spices, yet one of the important things in Christmas cooking is the blessing of cloves, cinnamon and nutmeg in combination with fruits.

Christmas cookies never played as much a part in our lives as they did in other households, although we enjoyed a few specialities, such as macaroons; oatmeal cookies made with nuts and raisins; and sugar cookies, rolled paper thin and sprinkled with sugar, almonds and, sometimes, a touch of cinnamon. They were crisp and buttery and a satisfying contrast to the richness of the cakes and tarts.

Our family celebration of Christmas was far different from that of other Portlanders, and its centerpiece was my spectacular godfather, General Summers, who had been in the Spanish-American War in the Philippines. He was a handsome human being, with a flowing white mustache, beautiful white hair, and a figure that showed the wear and tear of self-indulgence in food and drink. His nicely rounded belly often tempted my mother's old Chinese chef, Let, to pat him and say, "Nice General," which I always thought was a wonderful tribute. At any rate the general, who was jovial and amusing, became my image of Santa Claus as far back as I can remember.

On Christmas Eve the folding doors leading from the parlor to the sitting room would be closed, to serve later as theater curtains. We had already put up our tree. It was decorated with a collection of exquisite old German ornaments that were carefully handled and seemed to last for years. From time to time something new was added. I recall particularly a brilliant green bell that tinkled delicately and musically, and that bell was used to signal the moment to open the folding doors and behold the symbol of Christmas. There stood the General, who did not simply dress up as Santa Claus. He *was* Santa Claus.

We all exchanged lovingly wrapped packages—they didn't look like something out of a department store—and drank champagne or, if the weather was crisp, hot toddy. Sometimes there would be punch and fine rye or bourbon. Everyone was soon laughing and tearing open packages.

I'll never forget the year the General played a joke on my mother. She was a large woman and wore something called "outsize" stockings. There was an enormous box under the tree for her this particular Christmas, really enormous. Mystified, she opened it to find that it contained a pair of "outsize" stockings, stuffed to the hilt with popcorn and beautifully tied, forming a tasty pair of outsize legs. That was one of the choicest moments of all my Christmases, because it hit home, and my mother's laughter and the General's and everyone else's was irresistible.

In the middle of the festivities, my mother's chef, Let, would sneak upstairs to a balcony on the second floor and unwrap one of those giant packages of firecrackers that used to be part of Chinese festivals, and they would hang all the way down to the ground. Then he would slip outside to light the fuse, and we would have an explosive serenade breaking the silence of the night.

Next there was supper, which Mother varied from year to year so that it was unpredictable but always interesting. It could center around something as simple as turkey and ham—the turkey having been cooked in the afternoon so that it was neither hot nor cold; and the ham, a fine country specimen, nicely glazed. These were accompanied by a good potato salad, cole slaw or perhaps a vegetable salad, along with relishes and pickles made during the summer season. And more than likely, there would be hot Parker House rolls. For dessert there was fruitcake, both light and dark, cut fairly thin, and there were always Christmas candies. We had two friends who made exquisite candy and were more than generous with it. We also had a close friend who managed one of Portland's best sweetshops, and the boxes of candy from there were huge and delicious. In my earlier years, I wouldn't eat chocolates but used to satisfy myself by picking off all the candied violets that adorned them.

When the evening was over, I had to carry every one of my gifts upstairs and arrange them around my bed before I could go to sleep, so that I could look at them again as soon as I awoke in the morning.

Before going to church early Christmas Day, we would have a rather astonishing breakfast. My mother felt that the supreme dish at this point should be a very thick porterhouse steak, grilled perfectly, and served with either hash brown or home fried potatoes, toast or toasted stollen, or perhaps coffee cake or brioche. I can also remember such things as codfish cakes for Christmas breakfast, and if my father had a hand in it, it might be fried or sautéed chicken with bacon and hot biscuits.

After our rather elaborate buffet meal on Christmas Eve and a substantial breakfast the next morning, we never felt the need to sit down to the great Christmas dinner. My father would entertain his cronies from ten or eleven o'clock in the morning until the middle of the afternoon with rounds of Tom and Jerrys. I would go visit my friends. Meanwhile, my mother would be telephoning people she was fond of, or she went out to lunch or dinner. Thus we all went our separate ways when most families were just beginning to get together.

I didn't establish a pattern of my own for Christmas until I came to New York much later in life. During one period I used to have a Christmas breakfast and surround myself with close friends—those who could break away from family matters for part of the day. There would often be twenty or twenty-five guests. A buffet was served between noon and one or one-thirty, allowing plenty of time for those going on to Christmas dinner. My menus were usually international. I can recall serving *zampone*, for one thing—a cut of pork that includes the pig's foot and most of the shank, which is boned, stuffed with a savory sausage mixture, and then cured or smoked. It is cooked for two or three hours and when presented makes a very festive looking and unusual holiday dish.

I also used to do a wonderful Portuguese codfish dish that is based on puréed potatoes, cream, cooked dried codfish, garlic and good fruity olive oil, all mixed together into a very light texture and then topped with buttered bread crumbs and baked. At times I would have large platters of smoked fish and scrambled eggs, thinly sliced onions, tomatoes and plenty of hot bagels. On other occasions I did tiny individual omelets, or I offered a collection of sausages—Italian, Chinese, Portuguese, French, Spanish, spicy, sweet, hot—all prepared in various ways and accompanied by a cream roll or a baked egg dish. There were good breads, butters and preserves. And I still made fruitcakes (a year ahead), Christmas puddings, pound cakes and seed cakes. For drinks there was champagne, orange juice, tomato juice, vodka. Guests could make their own combinations, such as the highly popular champagne and orange juice, which I first learned to like during the war.

My circle of friends seems to have changed completely, and I now observe Christmas in a way I never did before—having a few people in for evening dinner. I have the things I like best, simple things. I am apt to splurge and start with caviar, iced vodka and champagne. The fine black beluga, so luscious, is frighteningly expensive, but there is good black "fresh" caviar that is less costly; and in the last two or three years I have used golden caviar, the roe of whitefish, which is delicate in color but deliciously mild in flavor.

The pièce de résistance is generally a fine, rare roast of beef, sirloin or prime rib, which I suppose reverts to my English-Welsh background, and equally traditional is the accompanying Yorkshire pudding that bubbles up and crisps in the beef fat. Another custom that I more or less established for myself is a purée of parsnips, made with a touch of Madeira and lots of butter. After that comes good cheese. I still love Roquefort and the cheeses of Switzerland, and I have become a follower of goat cheese. Finally there are mince tarts or a pudding of mincemeat, apples and streusel. There is fruitcake, too, and once in a while a good Christmas pudding, for old times' sake. Sometimes in lieu of a genuine pudding I steam fruitcake, which answers the same purpose, although nothing is as good as my mother's pudding, which was black, sticky, fruity and heady.

Apart from the pleasures of holiday eating, I find a special joy at Christmas in picking gifts for people I love. I choose things that I myself like; that's always my gauge. And I try to surprise. Lately I have been sending things for the kitchen. I have tracked down the sources for good, aged ham throughout the country, in Missouri, Kentucky, Virginia, the Carolinas, Oregon. I also send pounds and pounds of nuts. There are beautiful pecans to be bought, especially welcome to people who enjoy baking; filberts, from my home state of Oregon, unmatched anywhere; and seductive pistachios from California.

My love of Christmas has never diminished, and I am grateful to have seen so many Christmases. But if I were asked which ones stick in the memory most vividly, I would have to say those earliest days—the joy of the blazing pudding, the General's appearance as Santa, my mother's wonderful Christmas breakfast, and Let's firecrackers echoing through the silent night.

―――――

The four Christmas dinners that follow and their recipes were created by Mr. Beard especially for A Family Christmas. *See pages 106 through 125.*

Roast Beef and Yorkshire Pudding

James Beard Christmas Menu 1

DRINKS
AROUND THE FIRE

Spiced walnuts
Buttery almonds

DINNER

Oysters & clams
with mignonette sauce

Prime ribs of beef

Yorkshire pudding

Puréed parsnips
with Madeira

Horseradish cream

Assortment of cheeses

Mincemeat & apple tart
with hard sauce

Sand tarts

Coffee

SPICED WALNUTS

Place shelled walnut halves on a baking pan. Dot with butter and sprinkle with sugar and a little grated nutmeg. Bake at 350°F. for 10 to 15 minutes.

BUTTERY ALMONDS

Combine almonds with a pinch of salt, dot with butter, and toast under the broiler. Be careful not to let them burn.

OYSTERS AND CLAMS WITH MIGNONETTE SAUCE

Serve freshly opened oysters and cherrystone clams on the half shell in a bed of ice with mignonette sauce—a combination of freshly ground black pepper, malt vinegar, and a little finely chopped shallot, to taste. Garnish with lemon wedges.

PRIME RIBS OF BEEF

Place a 3- to 4-rib roast on a rack in a shallow pan. Preheat the oven to 350°F. Roast, allowing 15 to 17 minutes per pound for rare (meat thermometer, 120° to 125°F.) or 17 to 20 minutes per pound for medium rare (meat thermometer, 135°F.). Allow the roast to stand at least 10 minutes before carving.

YORKSHIRE PUDDING

2 eggs
1 cup milk
1 cup sifted all-purpose flour
½ teaspoon salt
½ teaspoon freshly ground black pepper
¼ cup beef drippings, heated

Beat the eggs with a whisk or electric hand beater until quite light, then gradually beat in the milk and flour. Or you can put those ingredients in an electric blender or electric mixer and blend or beat just until the batter is smooth. Season with the salt and pepper.

Preheat the oven to 450°F. Put an 11-by-14-by-2½-inch baking pan in the oven and let it get very hot. Remove pan and pour in the hot drippings and then the batter. Put pan on the center shelf of the oven and bake for 10 minutes, then reduce the heat to 375°F. and continue to bake until the pudding has risen and is puffed and brown, but do not open the oven door during the first 20 minutes of baking. Cut in squares and serve immediately with roast beef.

PURÉED PARSNIPS WITH MADEIRA

5 to 6 pounds parsnips
½ cup (1 stick) butter, melted
½ cup Madeira
¼ cup heavy cream
¼ teaspoon grated nutmeg
Salt
Finely chopped walnuts
⅓ stick unmelted butter

Wash and trim the parsnips and put them in a 6- to 8-quart pan with salted water to cover. Simmer until they can be pierced, drain, and let them cool until they can be handled. Peel them and cut into pieces 3 to 4 inches long. Put the pieces through a food mill, blender or processor, and combine the purée with the melted butter, Madeira, heavy cream, nutmeg, and salt to taste. Beat the purée well, adding more butter or cream if it seems too dry. Spoon into a 6-cup baking dish, sprinkle with the chopped walnuts, and top with pieces of butter. Heat the purée in a 375°F. oven for about 20 minutes, or until heated through.

HORSERADISH CREAM

½ cup cream cheese
½ cup sour cream
½ cup coarsely grated fresh horse-

radish or ⅓ cup drained bottled horseradish

Beat the cream cheese and sour cream to a paste and mix in the horseradish.
Makes approximately 1 cup. Serve with the beef.

MINCEMEAT AND APPLE TART

1 recipe tart pastry (see below)
6 tart apples, peeled, cored and cut into sixths
4 tablespoons (½ stick) butter
1 teaspoon vanilla extract
2½ cups mincemeat

Line a deep 9-inch tart pan with the pastry and place it in the refrigerator while preparing the filling.

Simmer the apples in the butter and vanilla in a heavy skillet, covered, over medium heat. Do not let the apples get mushy. Cool them slightly. Place one-half of the mincemeat in the prepared tart pan. Cover with the apples. Spread the rest of the mincemeat on top and bake at 375°F. for 30 to 35 minutes or until the crust is baked and well browned. Cool the tart and serve with hard sauce.

Pastry:
2¼ cups all-purpose flour
¾ teaspoon salt
⅔ cup shortening
4 to 6 tablespoons cold water

Mix the flour and salt in a large bowl. Cut in the shortening with a pastry blender or two knives until the mixture looks mealy. Sprinkle the water, one tablespoon at a time, evenly over the flour mixture. Lightly stir with a fork and continue to add only enough water to make a soft dough that will hold together in a ball. Chill for at least 30 minutes before rolling.

Hard Sauce:
¾ cup (1½ sticks) butter, softened
1½ cups confectioners' sugar
Dash of salt
Brandy or rum

Cream the butter and gradually beat in the sugar and salt until creamy and quite light. Add the brandy or rum to taste, and continue beating till thoroughly blended. Chill before serving.

SAND TARTS

8 tablespoons (1 stick) unsalted butter, softened
1 cup sugar
¼ teaspoon salt
1 egg
2 cups sifted cake flour
½ teaspoon vanilla extract

Topping:
2 egg whites
2 tablespoons sugar
½ teaspoon ground cinnamon

Beat the butter in a bowl until creamy and fluffy, then beat in the sugar, salt and egg, and continue to beat until very light, fluffy and pale. Beat in the sifted flour and the vanilla until thoroughly combined. When the dough is well blended, form it into a ball, wrap in waxed paper, and chill in the refrigerator for at least 3 hours.

Roll out the dough between sheets of waxed paper until very thin, less than ¼ inch, and cut into 3- or 3½-inch rounds with a plain or fluted cookie cutter.

After cutting out the cookies, preheat the oven to 375°F. Butter 3 cookie sheets. Arrange the cookies on the sheets, lifting them from the waxed paper with a flexible, thin-bladed metal spatula.

Beat the egg whites lightly with a fork, and, using a pastry brush, brush the tops of the cookies with the beaten egg white. Sprinkle the tops with the sugar and cinnamon, to taste. Do not overdo either the sugar or the cinnamon.

Bake the cookies until they turn a deep yellow around the edges, about 10 to 12 minutes. Remove from the oven and cool slightly, then remove from the pans with a metal spatula and put on wire racks to cool. Makes about 2½ dozen. These cookies are better used within a week, but they will stay crisp for 3 or 4 weeks if stored in an airtight tin in a cool place.

Cornish Game Hens with Sausage Stuffing

James Beard Christmas Menu 2

DRINKS IN
THE DRAWING ROOM

Caviar, toast & lemon

DINNER

Smoked salmon and sturgeon
with thin rye bread sandwiches

Cornish game hens
with crumb & sausage stuffing

Beet and carrot purée

Soufflé of Hubbard squash

Watermelon rind pickles

Assortment of cheeses

Frozen pudding

Scots black bun

Vadis bars

Coffee

Candies

CAVIAR, TOAST AND LEMON

Buy the best grade of caviar you can.
(About 2 ounces per person is considered an ample serving.) Serve it in a
glass bowl placed in another bowl full
of chopped ice, or if you prefer, use a
silver bowl. Place lemon wedges and
toast alongside.

SMOKED SALMON AND
STURGEON WITH
THIN RYE BREAD SANDWICHES

If you have someone who can carve
smoked salmon and sturgeon cor-
rectly—in thin, longish slices, almost
translucent—then have him perform
in the dining room; otherwise, have

the fish sliced perfectly beforehand.
Serve with capers, oil, and lemon,
and thinly sliced onion. Include rye
bread, sliced thin and buttered, and
be sure to pass the pepper grinder.

CORNISH GAME HENS
WITH CRUMB
AND SAUSAGE STUFFING

6 to 8 Rock Cornish hens (one for
each person)

Bread and Sausage Stuffing:
1 small yellow onion
1 cup (2 sticks) unsalted butter
½ cup green onions, thinly sliced
1 tablespoon chopped fresh tarragon
    or 1 teaspoon dried tarragon
2 teaspoons salt
1 teaspoon freshly ground black
    pepper
1 pound sausage meat
6 cups fresh bread crumbs
⅓ cup finely chopped parsley

Remove the gizzard, heart and liver
from the cavity of each hen. Place the
giblets and the whole onion in a small
saucepan with water to cover. Simmer
for 30 minutes.

Meanwhile, prepare the stuffing.
Melt butter in a large skillet or pan.
Sauté the green onions over medium
heat until just limp. Add the tarragon,
salt, pepper and sausage meat. Cook
over medium heat for 4 to 5 minutes
to partially cook the sausage meat.
Add the bread crumbs and parsley and
toss to blend well. When they are
cooked, remove the gizzards, hearts
and livers from the saucepan and chop
fine. Add to the stuffing mixture.

Fill cavities of hens with the stuffing, truss, and arrange the birds on
their sides on a roasting rack in a
shallow pan. Roast in a preheated
400°F. oven for 15 minutes, then turn
on the other side, baste well with the
pan juices, and roast a further 15 minutes. Then turn hens on their backs
and roast breast up for 10 to 15

minutes, until just tender but not over-
cooked. Test for doneness by wiggling
the legs (should move easily) and by
puncturing the joint between body and
thigh with a paring knife (juices should
be faintly tinged with pink).

NOTE: If you have additional
stuffing, place it in a small casserole,
dot it with butter, and cook it in the
oven, covered, during the last 15
minutes of roasting.

BEET AND CARROT PURÉE

6 medium-size beets
6 medium-size carrots
6 tablespoons (¾ stick) unsalted butter
1 teaspoon salt
¼ teaspoon grated nutmeg

Wash the beets without puncturing
the skin. Leave on the roots, and trim
off all but about 1½ inches of the
tops. Wrap each beet securely in aluminum foil, leaving about an inch of
the stalk protruding from the foil.
Bake on the middle rack of a preheated
450°F. oven, allowing 1½ hours.

Scrape the carrots and place them
in a pan in enough boiling water to
cover, and cook until just tender,
about 20 minutes. Drain.

Remove the foil from the beets, peel them, and remove the stems and root ends.

Combine the beets and carrots in the beaker of a food processor or food mill and purée with the butter, salt and nutmeg.

You may prepare this in advance and reheat it in the top of a double boiler or in a microwave oven.

SOUFFLÉ OF HUBBARD SQUASH

2 cups puréed steamed Hubbard squash (see below)
1 teaspoon salt
½ teaspoon freshly ground black pepper
½ teaspoon grated nutmeg
6 tablespoons (¾ stick) butter
6 egg yolks
8 egg whites

To prepare the squash, place pieces in a steamer over boiling water. Cover, and steam until tender—20 to 25 minutes. Remove the squash from the steamer and scrape the flesh from the shell with a fork or spoon. Purée in a blender or food processor.

Combine the squash with the seasonings and butter and beat lightly. Mix in the egg yolks, one at a time, beating well after each addition. Beat the egg whites until stiff but not dry. Fold one-quarter of the whites into the purée, incorporating thoroughly. Lightly fold in the remaining whites. Pour mixture into a well-buttered 2½-quart soufflé dish, stand dish in a roasting pan half filled with hot water, and place on top of the stove over medium heat for 5 minutes. (This will help stabilize the soufflé and quicken the rising process.) Preheat the oven to 375°F. Remove the dish from the water and bake in the oven for 30 to 35 minutes.

WATERMELON RIND PICKLES

4 quarts prepared watermelon rind cubes (see below)
½ cup salt
1 teaspoon powdered alum
Cold water
3 cups white wine vinegar or white distilled vinegar
2 sticks cinnamon or 3 or 4 drops oil of cinnamon
1 rounded teaspoon whole cloves (about 16 cloves) or 1 or 2 drops oil of cloves
3 cups sugar

To prepare the rind, cut away all the outside green, leave a bare rim of red inside, and cut into ½-inch (or up to ¾-inch) cubes. Measure, and place in a large glass, plastic, or crockery mixing bowl. Mix the salt and alum together very well. Add about 1 quart cold water and stir well to dissolve the salt. Pour over the rind, then add enough more water to cover it. The cubes will float, so it is best to weight them down with a plate. Let stand at least 8 hours or up to 24 hours. Drain well and rinse for several minutes under cold running water. Drain well again. Bring the vinegar to boil in an 8-quart kettle. If using whole spices, tie them in cheesecloth or other thin cloth bag and simmer in the vinegar 10 minutes. The amount of oil of spice used will depend upon its strength, which often varies, and upon your taste. Therefore it is best to use very little at first.

Add 1 cup sugar to the vinegar, stir well, and add the watermelon rind. Bring just to simmer. Remove from the heat and let stand off the range until cool. Add another cup of sugar and again bring just to the boil. Again remove from the heat and let cool. Now taste for sweetness. This amount of sugar will give a sour-sweet flavor. If more sugar is desired, after the melon has cooled, add the last cup of sugar and again bring to the boil. Remove the spice bag and simmer the rind just

113

until it looks translucent. Stir occasionally to make sure all the watermelon cubes are cooking. Seal in hot sterilized jars. Makes 4 pints.

FROZEN PUDDING

1 pint light cream
4 egg yolks
½ cup sugar
1 can (8¾ ounces) puréed chestnuts
¼ cup Malaga or sherry
½ cup currants
¼ cup seedless raisins
½ cup sugar
½ cup water
¾ cup heavy cream
Marrons glacés for garnish
Whipped cream for garnish

Heat the light cream in a saucepan until a film shines on top. Beat the egg yolks in a mixing bowl until light and thick, then gradually beat in ½ cup sugar. Add the heated cream gradually and pour back into the saucepan. Cook over a very low heat, stirring constantly, until custard thickens slightly and coats a spoon. Remove from heat, and stir in the chestnut

purée and Malaga or sherry. Cool and half freeze, preferably in an ice cream freezer, since the fruits are added later and should be all through the pudding when it is presented.

Cook the currants, raisins, sugar and water together over a moderate heat until the fruit plumps up and the syrup thickens. Cool slightly. Beat the heavy cream until it holds a soft shape. Stir the fruit and whipped cream into the frozen custard. Pack mixture into a melon or charlotte mold and freeze until firm in a freezer or refrigerator freezer compartment. Unmold on a handsome, chilled platter, and garnish with marrons glacés and whipped cream.

NOTE: If you do not have an ice cream freezer, you may fold the cooked fruit and the whipped cream into the cooled custard. Pour the mixture into a melon or charlotte mold and freeze until firm.

SCOTS BLACK BUN

Pastry:
3⅓ cups all-purpose flour, sifted
¼ teaspoon salt

2 sticks butter, cut into small pieces
2 egg yolks beaten with 8 tablespoons cold water and 2 tablespoons oil

Batter:
2 cups all-purpose flour
1 teaspoon baking soda
1 teaspoon cream of tartar
2 teaspoons cinnamon
2 teaspoons ginger
2 teaspoons grated nutmeg
½ teaspoon ground cloves
1 teaspoon allspice
½ teaspoon black pepper
¼ teaspoon salt
4 cups raisins, chopped
4 cups currants
1 cup slivered almonds
½ cup diced mixed candied peel
1 cup sugar
4 eggs, beaten
½ cup cognac
1½ cups buttermilk, or 1 cup milk
1 egg yolk beaten with 1 tablespoon cold water

Pastry Combine the flour and salt in a bowl. Cut in the butter until you have a texture of coarse cornmeal. Add the beaten egg mixture and combine with a fork to form a ball of pastry. Dust lightly with flour and wrap in waxed paper. Refrigerate for 1 hour.

Roll out two-thirds of the pastry to fit a 2½-quart mold or baking dish, leaving a ¼-inch overhang. Roll out remaining pastry to form the top.

Batter Sift together the flour, baking soda, cream of tartar, cinnamon, ginger, nutmeg, cloves, allspice, pepper and salt. Combine the fruits, nuts and candied peel in a large mixing bowl with the sugar. Sift the flour mixture over this and toss until thoroughly mixed. Add the eggs, cognac and buttermilk or milk, and mix to form a very thick paste. Turn into the pastry-lined pan. Moisten edges of the bottom pastry. Cover filling with top crust and crimp edges closed with a fork. Prick the top pastry with a fork, and run a skewer through the top of the pastry to the bottom in about 4 places. Bake in a 350°F. oven for ½ hour, then reduce heat to 300°F. and continue to bake for an additional 3 hours. After 2½ hours, brush with the egg yolk mixture. If you wish you may anoint your Scots Black Bun with a little cognac or brandy after removing it from the oven.

NOTE: Let it mellow for 3 to 4 days before serving.

VADIS BARS

4 cups sifted all-purpose flour
6 tablespoons sugar
1½ cups (3 sticks) unsalted butter, softened
1 teaspoon salt
4 teaspoons grated lemon zest (the colored outer surface of the rind)
6 hard-boiled egg yolks, mashed
4 raw egg yolks

Butter Crunch Topping:
2 cups sugar
2 teaspoons lemon juice
½ cup heavy cream
1 cup (2 sticks) unsalted butter
3 cups blanched and sliced toasted almonds or filberts
2 teaspoons vanilla extract

Place the flour in a bowl, make a well in the center, and add all the remaining ingredients to the well except the topping ingredients. With the fingertips, make a paste of the center ingredients, then gradually incorporate the flour to form a smooth, firm ball of dough. Work quickly so the butter does not become oily. When the sides of the bowl are left clean, wrap the dough in waxed paper and chill until it is firm enough to roll.

Roll out the dough between sheets of waxed paper into a rectangle about 11 by 16 inches, and press into a lightly greased 11-by-16-inch jelly-roll pan. Prick well with a fork, and chill.

Meanwhile, make the butter crunch topping. Combine the sugar and lemon juice in a heavy saucepan or skillet. Stir over low heat until the sugar is completely melted and golden brown, then add the cream and butter, and let the mixture boil. (At first the sugar will harden, but it will soon melt and blend with the liquid.) Stir until smooth. Stir in the nuts and set the mixture aside to cool. Just before using, stir in the vanilla.

Remove the dough from the refrigerator and bake it in a 350°F. oven for about 45 minutes, or until almost completely baked. Remove from the oven and spread with the topping. Return to the oven, placing the pan on a high rack, and bake 8 to 15 minutes longer, or until the top is bubbling. Remove from the oven and cool slightly before cutting into very small bars with a greased knife. Makes about 140 bars.

Saddle of Venison with Game Sauce

James Beard Christmas Menu 3

FOIE GRAS AND TOAST

Imported foie gras is an elegant choice, but if that seems too expensive, shop around for good domestic pâté made with chicken liver. Serve chilled and turned out on a platter. Surround with thin slices of toast.

OXTAIL CONSOMMÉ

3 oxtails, cut in sections
1 veal knuckle, cracked
4 quarts water
3 carrots, cut in strips
3 leeks, well cleaned
1 onion stuck with 2 cloves
1 bay leaf
1 teaspoon rosemary
1 tablespoon salt
8 to 10 peppercorns
Beaten egg whites (optional)
Madeira
Lemon slices for garnish (optional)

Arrange the oxtails on the rack of a broiling pan about 4 inches from the heat. Broil, turning the pieces frequently, until they are well browned on all sides and crisp at the edges.

Remove oxtail pieces to an 8-quart pot and add the veal knuckle and water. Bring to a boil and boil rapidly for 5 minutes, removing the scum from the surface. Add the carrots, leeks, onion, bay leaf, rosemary, salt and peppercorns. Reduce the heat, cover, and simmer for 4 to 5 hours. Remove the bones. Strain the stock through a cheesecloth-lined colander and cool overnight. Remove the fat. Heat, taste for seasoning, and if you wish, clarify with beaten egg whites before serving. Serve in soup cups, adding 1 tablespoon Madeira to each cup. Makes 2 to 3 quarts. Garnish with lemon slices if desired.

CHEESE STICKS

2 cups sifted all-purpose flour
½ teaspoon salt
¼ teaspoon baking powder
⅔ cup shortening
⅓ cup finely grated sharp cheddar cheese
1 egg yolk lightly beaten with 4 tablespoons cold water
Cayenne

Sift the dry ingredients together. Add the shortening and chop with a pastry blender until mixture looks like coarse meal. Add the cheese, then the egg yolk mixture. Mix with a knife until dough cleans bowl of flour. If necessary, add a few drops more water, as little as possible. On a lightly floured surface, roll the dough a scant ¼ inch thick. Cut in very narrow finger-length strips. Dust with cayenne.

Bake in a 400°F. oven for 10 to 12 minutes. Do not overbake. Serve cold, but fresh baked.

MARINATED SADDLE OF VENISON WITH GAME SAUCE

Saddle of venison, 4 to 5 pounds
Olive or vegetable oil

Marinade:
½ cup olive or vegetable oil
2 carrots cut in rounds
1 large onion, thinly sliced
1 rib celery cut in chunks
2 garlic cloves, crushed
2 or 3 sprigs of parsley
1 teaspoon rosemary
½ teaspoon savory
1 bay leaf
1 teaspoon freshly ground black pepper
1 bottle (1/5 gallon) red wine

Rub the venison well with oil. Place it in the marinade, cover, and let it remain several days in a cool place, turning once or so a day.

Remove the meat and wipe it dry. Place it on a rack in a rather shallow roasting pan. Roast at 450°F. for 30 minutes. Reduce the heat to 400°F. and continue roasting until the internal temperature, as indicated by a meat thermometer, reaches 125°F. (approximately 12 to 25 minutes per pound). Salt about 15 minutes before removing from the oven. Transfer to a hot platter.

Game Sauce:
1 cup reduced marinade (see below)
1 cup strong beef broth
Beurre manié (2 tablespoons very soft butter blended thoroughly with 2 tablespoons flour)
1 to 2 tablespoons chopped parsley
Salt and freshly ground black pepper

While the roast is cooking, strain the marinade and reduce it to 2 cups over high heat. Reserve half of it for future use as a marinade or sauce.

Combine the remaining cup of marinade with the beef broth, and stir in the beurre manié. Continue stirring until thickened. Reduce the heat and let sauce simmer 20 to 25 minutes, stirring occasionally and taking care it does not burn. Add the chopped parsley, salt and freshly ground pepper to taste, and serve with the roasted venison.

FRIED CORNMEAL SQUARES

4 cups boiling water
1 teaspoon salt
1 cup yellow cornmeal

Bring the water and salt to a boil either in the top of a double boiler or in a heavy saucepan. Stirring constantly, pour the cornmeal gradually into the water. When all is added, let it come to a boil and boil 5 minutes. Continue to stir. Then place it over simmering water to cook 1 hour, or if cooking in a saucepan, cook over medium flame 45 to 50 minutes, stirring often. Pour into a mold or bread pan and let it chill thoroughly. Remove, cut into slices, and sauté in butter or fat until crisp and brown. Makes 12 to 18 squares, according to size of pan.

TOMATO TIMBALES

1 cup heavy cream
4 eggs
Salt, pepper, to taste
½ teaspoon basil
1½ cups finely chopped tomato pulp (from peeled, seeded and squeezed fresh tomatoes), well drained
Butter
Parchment cooking paper

Whisk the cream, eggs and seasonings together in a bowl and add the finely chopped tomato pulp. Mix well. Butter generously six 2½-inch custard cups or 9 small timbale molds, or one 3-cup charlotte mold or soufflé

dish. Line the bottoms with parchment cooking paper and butter that also. Pour in mixture. Cover the molds with parchment paper with a small vent hole cut in the center. Place the timbales in a large baking pan and pour in just enough water to come halfway up the sides of the molds. Place in a 375°F. oven and bake for 20 to 25 minutes for small molds, or for 45 to 50 minutes for charlotte mold or soufflé dish. Remove top parchment. Run a knife around the edges, unmold, then lift off and discard the rest of the parchment and serve.

FLAMING CHRISTMAS PUDDING WITH ARMAGNAC SAUCE

½ pound beef suet, finely chopped
1½ cups all-purpose flour
¾ cup seedless raisins
1 cup sultana raisins
½ cup currants
½ pound mixed candied peel
3 cups fresh bread crumbs
Zest and juice of 1 orange
Zest and juice of 1 lemon
6 to 7 tart apples, peeled, cored and chopped
½ cup ground filberts
1 cup firmly packed brown sugar
½ teaspon ground cloves
2 teaspoons cinnamon
1 teaspoon ginger
1 teaspoon mace
1 teaspoon salt
1½ cups cognac, rum or brandy
6 eggs, lightly beaten
½ to ¾ cup Armagnac

Sprinkle the suet with ½ cup flour. Dust the raisins, currants and mixed candied peel lightly with flour. Combine the raisins, currants, mixed peel, bread crumbs, zest (the colored outer surface of the rind) and juice of the orange and lemon, and the suet in a large bowl with the remaining flour. Add the apples, ground filberts, brown sugar, cloves, cinnamon, ginger, mace and salt. Add ½ cup

cognac, rum or brandy and place the mixture in a cold spot or in the refrigerator for 5 days. Add ¼ cup more spirits each day and stir mixture well each time. On the last day stir it well again. Stir in the lightly beaten eggs thoroughly. Pour the well-mixed pudding into a buttered mold and cover it with a floured, buttered, damp cloth or seal it with aluminum foil. Cook it in a boiling water bath for 6 hours. Remove mold from water and let stand 5 minutes before removing cloth or foil cover. Unmold the pudding on a warm platter. Heat ½ to ¾ cup Armagnac, but do not let it come to the boil. Ignite and pour carefully but quickly over the pudding so it will run down the sides. Serve with the Armagnac sauce.

Time Saver Beef suet, mixed candied peel, fresh bread crumbs, zest of orange and lemon, apples and filberts may all be chopped or ground in a food processor. Follow manufacturer's directions.

Armagnac Sauce:
1 cup heavy cream
3 egg yolks
2 tablespoons sugar
Pinch of salt
⅓ cup Armagnac

Combine the cream, egg yolks, sugar, salt and Armagnac in the upper part of a double boiler, blending well. Stir the sauce over hot water until it thickens slightly.

Roast Turkey
and Glazed
Country Ham

James Beard Christmas Menu 4

BUFFET

Deviled crab and shrimp

Finger salad
with mustard vinaigrette

Tiny cream biscuits

Glazed country ham

Roast turkey

Mustard mayonnaise

Gratin of brussels sprouts

Dirty rice (using turkey giblets)

Wilted celery salad

Christmas fruit bowl with kirsch

Fruitcake

Cornmeal butter wafers

Assortment of cheeses

Coffee

DEVILED CRAB AND SHRIMP

1 pound crabmeat
½ pound small shrimp, cooked and
  shelled
2 cups coarsely rolled cracker crumbs
¾ cup finely diced celery
¾ cup chopped onion
¾ cup (1½ sticks) butter, melted
¼ cup milk, or more if needed
1 teaspoon dry mustard
½ teaspoon salt
Few grains cayenne pepper
2 tablespoons chopped parsley
2 tablespoons chopped green pepper

Combine the crabmeat and shrimp
with the crumbs, celery and onion, and
moisten generously with the butter
and milk. Season with the mustard,
salt, cayenne, parsley, and green pep-

per. Mix thoroughly, pile into scallop
shells or a casserole, and bake in a
350°F. oven for about ½ hour.

FINGER SALAD WITH MUSTARD VINAIGRETTE

Arrange various salad greens attrac-
tively on a platter and serve with a
mustard vinaigrette for dipping.

I don't use large lettuce leaves, but
rather small Bibb lettuce, leaf lettuce
and Boston lettuce leaves, and endive.
You may also use cucumber fingers
and cherry tomatoes. I find that
people enjoy dipping into a good
vinaigrette and don't mind using their
fingers.

Mustard Vinaigrette:
1 teaspoon coarse (kosher) salt
½ teaspoon freshly ground black pepper
½ teaspoon Dijon mustard
2 tablespoons wine vinegar
8 tablespoons fruity olive oil

Mix the salt, pepper, mustard, vinegar, and oil with a wooden spoon or a
fork, then taste and add more oil,
vinegar or mustard if you feel the
dressing needs it.

TINY CREAM BISCUITS

2 cups all-purpose flour
1 teaspoon salt
1 tablespoon double-acting baking
  powder
2 teaspoons sugar
¾ to 1 cup heavy cream
Melted butter

Sift the dry ingredients together and
fold in the heavy cream until it makes
a soft dough that can be easily handled. Turn out on a floured board,
knead for about 1 minute, and then
pat to a thickness of about ½ to ¾
inch. Cut into 1-inch squares with a
knife, dip in melted butter, and arrange on a buttered baking sheet or in
a square baking pan. Bake in a preheated 425°F. oven for 15 to 18 minutes and serve very hot. Makes 2 to 3
dozen biscuits.

GLAZED COUNTRY HAM

Real smoked country ham is available
in many parts of the country and the
different kinds can require different
treatments. It is best to follow the
directions on the wrapping. However, most hams need final baking,
even the ready-to-eat ones. Hams
range in size from 10 to 20 pounds,
but if a whole ham is too large you can
buy a half.

After baking, cool the ham thoroughly. Bring 1½ pints apricot jam to
a boil and let it cook 3 minutes. Add
¼ cup brandy or bourbon, if you like,
and put the jam through a strainer.
Rub the ham fat with a little dry mustard. Spoon or brush the glaze over
the ham to cover it completely. Let it
set before serving. Grape, apple, or
quince jelly may be used instead of
apricot preserves.

blade of the processor when making mayonnaise. Put 1 whole egg and 1 egg yolk, the salt, mustard, and lemon juice in the beaker and process until blended, about 2 or 3 seconds. Then, with the machine still running, gradually pour in the oil until thick and smooth; then stop processing.

Makes 1¾ cups. Serve with the turkey, which is served tepid.

GRATIN OF BRUSSELS SPROUTS

3 pints brussels sprouts

Cheese Sauce:
2 tablespoons (¼ stick) butter
2 tablespoons all-purpose flour
Salt and freshly ground black pepper
1½ cups milk or cream
¾ cup sharp cheddar cheese, grated—plus additional for topping
Dash of Tabasco

Cut off the stem ends and remove the outer leaves and any leaves which seem to be yellowed or ravaged with wormholes. Discard the stems. Soak the sprouts in water 15 to 20 minutes before cooking.

Put a small amount of water (about a quarter inch) in a heavy saucepan and bring to a boil. Add the prepared sprouts, cover tightly, and steam 5 to

ROAST TURKEY

1 turkey, 10 to 14 pounds (preferably fresh)
1 stick (½ cup) or more butter, softened
Strips of fresh or salt pork, or bacon rind

Remove the neck from the bird if not already done and discard or use for broth. Remove the liver, gizzard and heart and reserve for the dirty rice.

Truss the turkey with twine. Massage the turkey well with softened butter, and then salt and pepper it. Line a rack with strips of fresh or salt pork or with the rind of bacon, which you can sometimes buy from your butcher when he cuts down a whole slab. Set the rack in a fairly shallow roasting pan, and place the turkey breast side down on the rack. Roast 1 hour at 350°F. Remove the pan from the oven, turn the turkey on one side, and rub with softened butter. Return the turkey to the oven and roast another hour. Remove the pan, turn the turkey on its other side, and rub with butter. Roast for another 30 minutes, turn the turkey on its back, and rub the breast with butter. Return to oven

and continue roasting till the turkey tests done.

Note that the cooking time may vary depending on the bird. If you use a meat thermometer, be sure to insert the thermometer in the thigh but not touching the bone.

Remove the turkey from the oven and place it on a hot platter. Allow it to cool gently at room temperature. Remove all the twine before serving.

MUSTARD MAYONNAISE

2 egg yolks
1 teaspoon coarse (kosher) salt
2 tablespoons Dijon mustard
1½ cups olive oil, or half olive and half peanut oil
1 tablespoon lemon juice

Beat the egg yolks, salt, and mustard in a bowl with an electric mixer or wire whisk until the yolks become thick and sticky. Gradually beat in the oil, drop by drop, until the mayonnaise starts to thicken and stiffen, then beat in the remaining oil more rapidly, making sure it is incorporated before adding more. When all the oil is beaten in, beat in the lemon juice. *Food Processor Method* Use the metal

123

10 minutes, or until they are just crisply tender. Drain the sprouts well and return to the saucepan to dry out. Pour the sprouts into a well-buttered baking dish.

Cheese Sauce Melt the butter in a saucepan, combine with the flour, salt and pepper, and cook over low heat a few minutes to cook the starchy taste out of the flour. Stir in the milk or cream and continue stirring until the mixture thickens. Stir in the grated cheddar cheese and Tabasco. Let the cheese melt in the hot sauce. Do not stir too much after melting or the cheese may become stringy and rather disagreeable in texture.

Pour the cheese sauce over the brussels sprouts. Sprinkle lavishly with additional grated cheddar cheese and heat in a 350°F. oven just long enough to melt the cheese.

DIRTY RICE

½ pound turkey or chicken gizzards, trimmed of excess fat and finely chopped
½ pound turkey or chicken livers, finely chopped
2 medium-size onions, peeled and finely chopped
½ cup finely chopped celery
2 tablespoons olive oil
1½ teaspoons salt

½ teaspoon freshly ground black pepper
1½ cups uncooked long-grain white rice
3 cups water
½ cup finely chopped fresh parsley

Combine the gizzards, livers, onions and celery together. Heat the olive oil in a 4- to 5-quart casserole over moderate heat. Add the chopped giblets mixture, stir in the salt and black pepper, and reduce the heat to low. Stirring occasionally, cook uncovered until the bits of giblets are richly browned, about 30 minutes.

Meanwhile, place the rice in a heavy 2-quart pot, stir in the water, and bring to a boil over high heat. Reduce the heat to low, cover tightly, and simmer for 20 to 25 minutes, or until the rice has absorbed all the liquid in the pan and the grains are tender. Remove the pan from the heat and let the rice rest, still tightly covered, for 10 minutes or so. Fluff the rice with a fork and add it to the casserole. With a fork, toss the rice and the chicken mixture together gently but thoroughly.

Taste for seasoning and toss with the parsley.

WILTED CELERY SALAD

1 large stalk (bunch) or 2 small stalks celery
1½ cups vinaigrette sauce (made with 1 to 1½ tablespoons Dijon mustard)
Romaine
Chopped chives or green onions

Clean the celery and save the outer ribs and large leaves for flavoring soups and stews. Cut the inner ribs, heart and small leaves into fairly small pieces. Pour the vinaigrette sauce over them and let stand for several hours to mellow and wilt. Turn the celery often to be sure it is evenly bathed. Serve on romaine with a garnish of chopped green onions or chives.

CHRISTMAS FRUIT BOWL WITH KIRSCH

Arrange in a decorative salad bowl a combination of sliced pears, orange and grapefruit sections, sliced apples and bananas, and grapes. Toss with kirsch to taste.

WHITE FRUITCAKE

1½ cups seedless raisins
1½ cups white raisins
1½ cups currants
1 tablespoon grated orange zest
1 teaspoon grated lemon zest
3 cups chopped mixed candied fruits
1 cup candied cherries, whole or cut in half
1 cup moist-dried apricots, cut in small strips (optional)
2 cups halved or very coarsely chopped walnuts, pecans, almonds, Brazil nuts or filberts
1 cup flour

Batter:
2 cups (4 sticks) butter, softened
2 cups sugar
8 to 10 large eggs, separated
2 tablespoons rum, brandy, or orange juice
1 teaspoon vanilla extract
3½ cups sifted all-purpose flour
¾ teaspoon salt
Parchment paper

Glaze:
White corn syrup

Rinse the raisins and currants with hot tap water and spread on a paper towel to dry. They will plump slightly. Or instead of plumping them, put all the fruits in a glass bowl, add ½ cup sherry, brandy, or light rum, and let stand overnight, stirring a number of times until the fruit has absorbed the liquor. Add the nuts to all the fruits and rinds and sprinkle with the cup of flour.

Batter Using the largest mixer bowl you have, cream the butter until very fluffy (easiest done with an electric mixer). Cream in all the sugar, or reserve ½ cup for the egg whites. The butter and sugar mixture should be like sweetened whipped cream in texture. If using a mixer, drop the egg yolks in one at a time with mixer on

medium to high speed. Stir or beat in the flavorings. Sift the flour with the salt. Stir into the creamed mixture until well blended.

In another bowl beat the egg whites until foamy, and if you like add 1 teaspoon lemon juice or cream of tartar to stabilize the egg whites. If you have reserved ½ cup of sugar, add it gradually during beating of whites. Beat until stiff but not dry—the mixture should hold soft peaks. Fold into the cake batter with a rubber spatula. Fold rather than stir the fruits and nuts into the batter.

The baking pans should be filled not more than two-thirds full and should be well greased and lightly floured. If using tube pans, crown molds, or loaf pans that are old and blackened, better line the pans, both bottom and sides, with one or two layers of greased parchment paper.

Bake the cakes in a preheated 275°F. oven for 1 to 3 hours, depending upon the size of the pans used. An ordinary 9-by-5-by-3-inch loaf pan will take about 1½ hours or slightly more, depending upon how full it is. If the cake springs back when pressed lightly in the center, it is done. It will also have begun to shrink from the sides of the pan.

When the cakes are done, glaze the tops by brushing on white corn syrup, preferably while they are still hot.

This is also a good time to stick on any fruit and nut decorations you might like on the top. Cool in the pans. Remove, brush with brandy, bourbon, rum, or other liquor. Wrap well in aluminum foil—or easier, put into freezer bags—and seal. Brush with more liquor from time to time, if you like. Makes three to four 9-by-5-by-3-inch loaves.

CORNMEAL BUTTER WAFERS

½ pound (2 sticks) unsalted butter, softened
1 cup sugar
2 egg yolks
1 teaspoon grated lemon zest
1½ cups all-purpose flour
1 cup yellow cornmeal

Combine the butter and sugar and beat until light and well blended. Add the yolks and mix well, then stir in the lemon zest (the colored outer surface of the rind), flour and cornmeal, blending thoroughly. Chill the dough until firm. It may then be rolled into a long cylinder and cut into ¼-inch rounds, or rolled out and cut into different shapes. Arrange the cookies on ungreased baking sheets and bake in a 350°F. oven for 10 to 12 minutes. Makes about 24 cookies.

125

Cookies Grandmas used to make . . . and still do

Favorites that say "Merry Christmas!" and how to make them

The very first enticing aromas from the kitchen at Christmas often contain tantalizing hints of cinnamon, nutmeg, chocolate and butter—a sure signal that cookies are in the works! Here are eighteen all-time favorites, as attested to by their popularity in cookbooks and among generations of homemakers. Some, like chocolate chips, are as American as apple pie. Others spring from the rich traditions of Europe. But all are irresistible—especially when still warm from the oven and popped into an eagerly waiting little mouth.

GINGERBREAD MEN

½ cup (1 stick) butter or margarine
½ cup sugar
½ cup molasses
1½ teaspoons white vinegar
3 cups sifted all-purpose flour
½ teaspoon baking soda
½ teaspoon ground cinnamon
½ teaspoon ground ginger
¼ teaspoon salt
1 egg, beaten

Combine butter or margarine, sugar, molasses and vinegar in a saucepan. Bring to a boil and let cool. Resift flour together with baking soda, cinnamon, ginger and salt. Stir beaten egg into molasses mixture, then blend sifted ingredients into molasses mixture. Mix well, then chill dough, covered, in refrigerator.

Preheat oven to 375°F. Grease several cookie sheets. Break off one-third of the dough, form into a ball, and roll out on a lightly floured surface to approximately ⅛-inch thickness. Cut into gingerbread boy or other favorite shapes with cookie cutters dipped in flour.

Place on greased cookie sheets and decorate with raisins, cinnamon candies or silver balls (or decorate with icing after baking as below). Bake 8 to 10 minutes. Remove from oven and cool on wire racks. For icing decorations after baking, use icing recipe given for Sugar Cutouts. Makes approximately 10 large and 14 medium-size "men."

DATE NUT PINWHEELS

Filling:
1 10-ounce package pitted dates, chopped
1 cup water
¼ cup sugar
2 teaspoons lemon juice
1 cup finely chopped walnuts

Dough:
3½ cups unsifted all-purpose flour
½ teaspoon baking powder
½ teaspoon salt
¼ teaspoon baking soda
1 cup (2 sticks) butter or margarine, softened
2 cups firmly packed light brown sugar
2 eggs

Filling In a medium saucepan combine dates, water, sugar and lemon juice. Bring to boil; reduce heat and simmer, stirring occasionally, 10 to 12 minutes until thickened. Fold in chopped walnuts and let cool to room temperature.

Dough Combine flour, baking powder, salt and baking soda and set aside. In mixer bowl cream butter or margarine, brown sugar and eggs with electric mixer until fluffy. Gradually add flour mixture to creamed mixture. Beat until just blended. Divide dough into thirds. Wrap in waxed paper and refrigerate until easy to handle.

Roll each third between lightly floured sheets of waxed paper into a

rectangle approximately 12 by 18 inches. Remove top sheet of waxed paper and spread each rectangle of dough with the date-nut filling (approximately ⅔ cup of filling per rectangle).

Starting with the long side of the dough, roll up each rectangle jelly-roll fashion. Wrap them in waxed paper and refrigerate overnight.

Preheat oven to 350°F. Grease 2 large cookie sheets. Cut each roll into ¼-inch slices and place 1 inch apart on cookie sheets. Bake 10 to 12 minutes and cool on wire racks. Makes approximately 8 dozen.

PFEFFERNÜSSE

3 eggs
1 cup granulated sugar
3 cups all-purpose flour
¼ teaspoon baking powder
¼ teaspoon salt
⅛ teaspoon white pepper
1 teaspoon ground cinnamon
⅛ teaspoon ground cloves
½ cup chopped candied lemon peel
¼ cup ground blanched almonds
½ cup confectioners' sugar
2 apple slices

Beat eggs and granulated sugar in a large mixer bowl with electric mixer at medium speed. Add flour, baking powder, salt, white pepper, cinnamon and cloves and continue to beat until well mixed, scraping bowl occasionally. Beat in the lemon peel and almonds until well combined. Wrap in waxed paper and chill dough for 1 hour.

Preheat oven to 350°F. Grease 2 large cookie sheets. Roll dough out onto lightly floured surface to approximately ¼-inch thickness. Cut out circles with 1-inch round cookie cutter. Place on cookie sheets. Bake for 15 minutes or until lightly browned. Cool on wire racks. Reroll scraps, bake and cool. Place confectioners' sugar in a bag, add the cookies and shake until well coated.

Because these cookies are very hard, place them in a tightly covered container with the apple slices, cover, and allow to ripen for 2 to 3 weeks (they'll soften). Makes about 9 dozen.

POPPY SEED BUTTER COOKIES

½ cup (1 stick) butter, softened
½ cup sugar
1 egg, well beaten
1 teaspoon almond extract
2 cups sifted all-purpose flour
½ teaspoon baking powder
⅛ teaspoon salt
¼ cup poppy seeds

Preheat oven to 400°F. Combine butter, sugar, beaten egg and almond extract in large mixer bowl. Cream with electric mixer until well blended.

Resift flour with baking powder and salt. At a low mixer setting, slowly and gradually add resifted flour mixture and poppy seeds to other ingredients. Use spatula often to help blend the ingredients completely. The dough will seem very heavy.

Chill dough. Fill cookie press with dough and press out shapes on an ungreased cookie sheet. Bake 10 to 12

minutes. Watch carefully—the completed cookie should be a pale tan, not browned. Makes 2 to 3 dozen small cookies.

FLORENTINES

2 cups quick-cooking oats (not instant)
6 tablespoons all-purpose flour
2 eggs
1 cup sugar
1 teaspoon vanilla extract
1 teaspoon lemon juice
1 cup (2 sticks) butter or margarine, melted
4 squares (1 ounce each) semi-sweet chocolate

Preheat oven to 350°F. Line cookie sheets with foil. Combine oats and flour and set aside.

Beat eggs slightly, add sugar, vanilla and lemon juice and mix together. Add melted butter or margarine and stir. Add oats and flour combination all at once and stir until thoroughly combined.

Drop batter onto foil-lined sheets in ½-teaspoon dabs, no more than 8 to a sheet. Bake 8 minutes, but watch carefully—the edges should be golden, but not brown. Remove from oven and allow to cool on sheets. Do not try to peel cookies off foil until cold or they may stick and break.

While cookies are cooling, melt the chocolate over hot water. When

129

cookies have thoroughly cooled, peel from foil and lay flat side up.

Spread chocolate on flat side of one cookie with pastry brush. (Keep chocolate hot while spreading.) Stick second cookie flat side down on chocolate filling. If chocolate is slow to harden, put on cookie sheet and place in freezer for a few minutes, then store in refrigerator in a well-sealed container. Makes approximately 4 dozen.

CHOCOLATE MERINGUE DROPS

1 cup (6 ounces) semi-sweet chocolate bits
2 egg whites
⅛ teaspoon salt
½ cup sugar
½ teaspoon vanilla extract
½ teaspoon white vinegar
¾ cup finely chopped nuts

Preheat oven to 350°F.

Melt chocolate bits over hot water.

Beat egg whites with salt until foamy. Add sugar gradually and beat until stiff peaks form. Add vanilla and vinegar. Fold in melted chocolate and nuts.

Drop by teaspoonfuls onto a greased cookie sheet and bake for 10 minutes. Makes approximately 3 dozen.

TUILES À L'ORANGE

½ cup sugar
⅛ teaspoon vanilla extract
2 egg whites
⅓ cup sifted all-purpose flour
¼ cup (½ stick) butter, melted
½ cup slivered blanched almonds
Grated peel of ½ orange

Grease and flour 3 cookie sheets; set aside. Combine sugar, vanilla and egg whites in a bowl; beat with whisk for 1 minute or until foamy. Add remaining ingredients, mixing well.

Preheat oven to 400°F. Drop batter from teaspoon about 3 inches apart onto prepared sheets, leaving enough space to allow for spreading. Bake 5 to 6 minutes or until edges are browned. While still hot, remove from cookie sheets and cool on wire racks or on rolling pin long enough to maintain curved "roof tile" shape when cold. Makes about 2 dozen.

SUGAR CUTOUTS

1 cup (2 sticks) butter *or* ½ cup (1 stick) butter plus ½ cup (1 stick) margarine, softened
1 cup sugar
2 eggs, well beaten
2 teaspoons vanilla extract
3½ cups sifted all-purpose flour
2 teaspoons baking powder

Preheat oven to 375°F. Combine butter, sugar, beaten eggs and vanilla in large mixer bowl. Cream with electric mixer until fluffy. Resift flour with baking powder and blend with other ingredients at low speed, slowly and gradually, until well mixed.

Chill dough thoroughly in refrigerator. Then tear off one-quarter to one-third of the dough, form into a ball, and roll out on lightly floured waxed paper until approximately ¼-inch thick. Cut out shapes with floured cookie cutters.

Decorate cookies before baking with green or red sugar crystals, nonpareils, silver balls or cinnamon candies—or after baking with icing described below. Place on greased cookie sheet, and bake for 10 to 15 minutes, or until golden. Remove and cool on wire rack. Repeat with rest of dough. Makes about 4 dozen, depending on size of cutters.

Icing:
3 egg whites
½ teaspoon cream of tartar
1 16-ounce box confectioners' sugar
Red or green food coloring (optional)

Beat together egg whites, cream of tartar and confectioners' sugar, mixing in food coloring if desired. Spread icing on cookie with a knife or decorate cookie using a pastry bag.

MOLASSES COOKIES

¾ cup (1½ sticks) butter or margarine
1 cup sugar
¼ cup molasses
1 egg
2 cups sifted all-purpose flour

2 teaspoons baking soda
½ teaspoon ground cloves
½ teaspoon ground ginger
½ teaspoon salt
1 teaspoon ground cinnamon
Extra granulated sugar for coating

Melt butter or margarine over low heat; remove and let cool. After cooling add sugar, molasses and egg. Hand beat well.

Combine flour, baking soda, cloves, ginger, salt and cinnamon and resift together. Add to molasses mixture and mix well by hand. Place in refrigerator for 1 hour.

Preheat oven to 375°F. Grease cookie sheets. Remove dough from refrigerator and stir. Form into 1-inch balls, roll balls in granulated sugar, place on greased cookie sheets, press thumb into center of balls, and bake for 8 to 10 minutes. Remove and place on wire racks to cool. Makes approximately 4 dozen.

BOURBON BALLS

1 cup crushed vanilla wafers
1 cup confectioners' sugar
1 cup finely chopped pecans
2 tablespoons unsweetened cocoa
2 tablespoons light corn syrup
¼ cup bourbon
½ cup granulated sugar

Mix together all ingredients except granulated sugar. Roll mixture into 1-inch balls. Roll balls in the granulated sugar. Place in a covered container and refrigerate for a few days before serving for maximum flavor. Continue to store in refrigerator or freezer until used up. Makes approximately 2 dozen.

SWEDISH SPRITZES

1½ cups (3 sticks) butter *or* 1 cup (2 sticks) butter plus ½ cup (1 stick) margarine, softened
1 cup sugar
1 egg, well beaten
2 teaspoons vanilla extract
4 cups sifted all-purpose flour
1 teaspoon baking powder

Preheat oven to 400°F. Combine butter, sugar, beaten egg and vanilla in large mixer bowl. Cream with electric mixer until fluffy. Resift flour with baking powder. At a low mixer setting, slowly and gradually add resifted flour mixture to other ingredients. Use spatula often to help blend the ingredients completely.

Chill dough. Fill cookie press with dough and press out shapes on an ungreased cookie sheet.

Decorate before baking with green or red sugar crystals, nonpareils, silver balls or cinnamon candies. Bake 8 to 10 minutes. Remove from sheet and cool on wire rack. Makes approximately 6 dozen small spritzes.

CHOCOLATE CHIPS

2¼ cups sifted all-purpose flour
1 teaspoon baking soda
1 teaspoon salt
½ cup (1 stick) margarine, softened
½ cup (1 stick) butter, softened
¾ cup granulated sugar
¾ cup firmly packed brown sugar (light or dark)
1 teaspoon vanilla extract
2 eggs
2 cups (12 ounces) semi-sweet chocolate bits
1 cup chopped walnuts or pecans

Preheat oven to 375°F. Lightly grease 2 cookie sheets.

Resift flour with baking soda and salt. Set aside.

In a large mixer bowl combine margarine and butter, granulated sugar and brown sugar and vanilla extract; beat with an electric mixer until creamy. Beat in eggs until well blended. Gradually add flour mixture, mixing well after each addition, scraping bowl occasionally with a rubber spatula. Stir in chocolate bits and chopped nuts.

Drop by rounded teaspoonfuls onto greased cookie sheets. Bake 8 to 10 minutes, cool on wire racks, and store in a covered container. Makes approximately 9 dozen.

ENGLISH TOFFEE SQUARES

1 cup (2 sticks) butter
1 cup sugar
2 cups sifted all-purpose flour
1 egg yolk
1 teaspoon vanilla extract
1 egg white, lightly beaten
2 cups finely chopped walnuts or pecans

Preheat oven to 350°F.

Melt butter in a large saucepan; add sugar, flour, egg yolk and vanilla. Mix well. Spread evenly in a 9-by-12-inch baking pan. Spread lightly beaten egg whites over top of mixture and sprinkle evenly with chopped nuts.

Bake 20 minutes or until lightly browned. Remove from oven and let sit in pan for 3 to 4 minutes. Cut into squares while still in pan and allow to cool thoroughly before removing. Makes about 2 dozen.

FILBERTINES

½ cup (1 stick) butter or margarine, softened
½ cup sugar
1 egg
1⅓ cups unsifted all-purpose flour
½ teaspoon baking soda
⅛ teaspoon ground cardamom
½ cup finely chopped filberts or hazelnuts

In a large mixer bowl with electric mixer at medium speed, cream butter or margarine and sugar until light and fluffy, scraping bowl occasionally. Add egg and beat until well blended. Beat in flour, baking soda and cardamom. Chill for 1 hour.

Preheat oven to 350°F. Grease 2 large cookie sheets; set aside. Shape dough into 1-inch balls and roll them in chopped nuts. Place on baking sheets, 2 inches apart. Bake for 15 minutes or until lightly browned and firm to the touch. Cool on wire racks. Makes about 2 dozen.

"STAINED GLASS" COOKIES

½ cup sugar
⅓ cup (⅔ of a stick) margarine, softened
1 egg
½ teaspoon vanilla extract
¼ teaspoon salt
2 cups sifted all-purpose flour
1 teaspoon baking powder
2 tablespoons milk
4–5 rolls assorted fruit-flavored hard candies
¼ cup light corn syrup

In a large mixer bowl cream sugar and margarine with electric mixer until light and fluffy. Beat in egg, vanilla and salt.

Resift flour with baking powder.

Slowly add flour mixture to creamed mixture, alternating with milk. Mix thoroughly, using spatula to help blend the ingredients completely.

Wrap dough in waxed paper and chill overnight or until dough handles easily.

Preheat oven to 350°F. Line cookie sheets with foil and grease generously.

Roll out small amounts of dough on floured surface with rolling pin to ⅛-inch thickness. Cut out desired shapes with cutters dipped in flour. While still on floured board cut holes in shapes in desired sizes and patterns. Remove excess dough from cutouts with toothpick. With metal spatula place cutouts on foil-lined sheets.

Cut hard candies with a knife and fill holes in cookies with hard candy pieces (a ½-inch hole takes half a round candy). Decorate with silver balls if desired. Bake for 9 minutes, then cool on foil-lined cookie sheets before removing.

When thoroughly cooled, remove from foil and brush each cookie with corn syrup that has been boiled for 2 minutes. Reboil corn syrup before glazing each batch. Allow to harden for at least 24 hours. Makes 2 dozen.

PEANUT BLOSSOMS

1¾ cups all-purpose flour
1 teaspoon baking soda
½ teaspoon salt
½ cup granulated sugar
½ cup firmly packed light brown sugar
½ cup shortening
½ cup creamy peanut butter
1 egg
2 tablespoons milk
1 teaspoon vanilla extract
48 milk chocolate kisses, unwrapped

In a large mixer bowl, stir the all-purpose flour, baking soda and salt together. Add all of the remaining ingredients except chocolate kisses and mix at the medium speed of an electric mixer until well combined, scraping the bowl occasionally. Chill the dough for 30 minutes.

Preheat oven to 375°F. Roll small amounts of dough into 1-inch balls. Place on an ungreased cookie sheet and bake for 12 minutes or until they turn a light brown color.

Remove from oven and immediately press a chocolate kiss into the center of each (the cookie will crack around the edge). Repeat with remaining dough. Makes 4 dozen.

THUMBPRINTS

1 cup (2 sticks) unsalted butter, softened
½ cup sugar
2 egg yolks
1 teaspoon vanilla extract
2 cups all-purpose flour
½ teaspoon salt
¼ cup apricot, raspberry or strawberry jam

In large bowl of electric mixer with mixer at medium speed, cream butter and sugar until light and fluffy. Beat in egg yolks and vanilla. Gradually add flour and salt until well blended. Refrigerate dough for 1 hour.

Preheat oven to 350°F. Work with only one quarter of the dough at a time; keep the remainder refrigerated. Roll into 1-inch balls. Place on ungreased cookie sheets about 2 inches apart. Using your thumb or the end of a wooden spoon, make a depression in the center of each ball. Bake 10 minutes. Remove cookies from oven. Make the depression again. Fill each depression with ¼ teaspoon jam and return to oven to bake for 5 more minutes. Cool on wire rack. Repeat with remaining dough. Makes about 4 dozen.

NUT THINS

1 cup (2 sticks) butter or margarine, softened
1 cup sugar
2 eggs, well beaten
1½ cups sifted all-purpose flour
½ teaspoon salt
1 teaspoon vanilla extract
1 cup chopped walnuts or pecans
5 dozen nutmeat halves

Preheat oven to 375°F. Grease 2 large cookie sheets.

Cream softened butter or margarine and sugar together in large mixer bowl; add well-beaten eggs. Resift flour with salt and add gradually to creamed mixture while beating with electric mixer at low speed. Add the vanilla extract. Remove beaters and stir in chopped nuts.

Drop by teaspoonfuls onto greased cookie sheets, spacing well apart as these cookies spread while baking. Place a nutmeat half in the center of each cookie.

Bake for approximately 10 minutes, or until edges are lightly browned. Cool for a minute or two on cookie sheets before removing and placing on wire racks for final cooling. Makes approximately 5 dozen.

133

Gingerbread House

The world's most famous gingerbread house is probably one described in a Grimm brothers' fairy tale. Remember how Hansel and Gretel, frightened and famished in the forest, first set eyes on the witch's abode?

"When they were quite near they saw that the cottage was made of gingerbread and covered with cakes, while the windows were made of transparent sugar."

Surely a sight to make any child lick his or her lips! From what drawing board, or rolling board, did this confection originally spring? We have no exact way of knowing. Jacob and Wilhelm Grimm based their fairy tales, including *Hansel and Gretel*, on stories handed down by word of mouth, and the genesis of these tales is shrouded in the mists of time.

But ginger cookies have been around for quite awhile, as well as what might be called the "pictorial school of cooking." The cooks of Germany and Central Europe have long been known for their skill at making cookies in different shapes. To this day French chefs turn their floury fingers to doll-cakes named *naulets* and cakes shaped like yule logs—the celebrated *bûche de Noël*.

As for gingerbread houses, they have ties to real houses as well. They lent their name to a Victorian architectural style. And the thatched roofs of European huts and chalets have long smacked of gingerbread ancestry. Which inspired which?

In any case, the gingerbread house today stands firmly on its own aromatic foundation, as enticing and magical a holiday sight as the cottage first glimpsed by Hansel and Gretel.

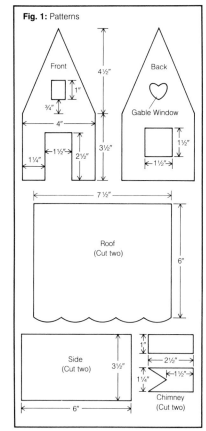

Fig. 1: Patterns

Front
4½"
1"
¾"
4"
3½"
2½"
1½"
1¼"

Back
Gable Window
1½"
1½"

Roof
(Cut two)
7½"
6"

Side
(Cut two)
3½"
6"

Chimney
(Cut two)
1"
2½"
1¼"
1½"

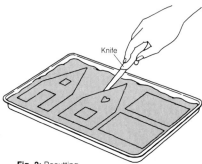

Knife

Fig. 2: Recutting
Remove cookie sheet with baked dough from oven. Using same patterns, quickly recut all lines.

Fig. 3: Base
Overlap doilies to fit: secure to base with icing. Cover with icing, letting lace edge show.

These simple instructions will make the elegant and tasty gingerbread house depicted in the photograph on the preceding pages:

Utensils, materials: 1 10-inch × 12-inch medium-weight piece of cardboard for base; lightweight cardboard (such as shirt board) for pattern pieces, as necessary; 2 lace placemats large enough to cover base; cookie sheets, pastry tube or icing decorator, spatula, rolling pin, sharp knife, assorted candies (see list on opposite page).

House pattern: Cut pattern pieces out of lightweight cardboard following the dimensions given in Fig. 1. In the process, cut out the front door, front window and rear gable window.

Gingerbread recipe:
¾ cup shortening
¾ cup molasses
¾ cup sugar
3¾ cups flour
1 teaspoon baking soda
1 teaspoon nutmeg
1 teaspoon salt
3 teaspoons ground ginger

Melt the shortening in a large saucepan. Stir in the molasses and sugar, using a wooden spoon. Remove from heat.

Sift together the flour, baking soda, nutmeg, salt and ginger. Stir into the molasses mixture, using hands to work in completely. The dough will be stiff and crumbly, so use it as soon as possible. If necessary, the dough may be wrapped and refrigerated, but this will make it harder to work with.

Baking the pieces: Preheat the oven to 350° F. Slightly grease the cookie sheets. Roll out one-half of the dough on one cookie sheet to ⅛-inch thickness. Cover the remaining dough. Lay out the pattern pieces on the dough for the front, back and sides. Arrange the pieces (including the door and window shutters) as close together as possible. Cut through the dough around all patterns, including the door and window apertures. To make the shutters, halve the dough

cut from the front window. Do not remove excess dough. Bake 10-15 minutes until deep brown but not burned.

Don't overbake. On the other hand, underbaked dough will be too soft and the house may collapse. Remove cookie sheet from oven. Using the pattern pieces again, recut all lines (see Fig. 2). Work quickly; the dough hardens as it cools.

With the remaining half of the dough, repeat above steps for the roof and chimney pieces.

Frosting "glue": This frosting hardens well and is used to cement the house together, to attach the chimney, door, shutters and candies, and to simulate icicles. In a large bowl with electric mixer at high speed, beat until frothy:
2 egg whites
⅛ teaspoon cream of tartar
2 teaspoons water

Gradually add 3 cups of sifted confectioner's sugar and continue to beat until the mixture is of spreading consistency. You may need more sugar. The icing should be firm enough to hold a soft peak.

Cover with a damp towel to prevent drying out. The icing may be stored in the refrigerator in an airtight container for later use.

Assembling the house: Secure the doilies to the base with icing, overlapping them to fit (see Fig. 3). Cover the doilies with icing, swirling it to look like snow; leave the lace edges exposed.

Pipe frosting around the bottom and inside edges of the back wall and set it in place (Fig. 4).

Pipe frosting around the edges of one side and place it in position against the back (Fig. 5). Repeat this procedure with the other side. Then pipe frosting around the bottom and inside edges of the front and add it to the house.

Pipe frosting along the top edges of the front and back and carefully position the roof pieces (Fig. 6). Hold them in place while the icing sets.

Pipe icing along the roof peak for greater stability.

When the roof is securely set, you are ready to add the details. "Glue" the chimney pieces together with icing and set it on the roof peak where desired (Fig. 7). Use icing to attach the shutters. Decorate the door with *heart candies* and frost it in place in front of the doorway (Fig. 8). The door may be angled open or remain closed.

Pipe frosting along the sides of the chimney and the peak of the roof. Set *gumdrops* along the peak.

Pipe frosting under the eaves of the roof and add round *mints* (Fig. 9).

Attach candies to the front and back of the house. Use icing to add *mint leaves* for the bushes and *gumdrops* for the shrubs. Use *nonpareils* for the roof tiles. Add small *heart candies* to the chimney and shutters. Attach *candy canes* at each corner as shown in the photograph on the preceding pages.

As a final touch, use the remaining icing to add decorative icicles to all edges of the house. Cover any remaining openings around the chimney, and top the shutters, chimney and front door with "snow."

You may also add a path in front consisting of additional gingerbread hearts similar to the one cut out of the gable window or heart candies.

Candies used in sample house:

½ pound gumdrops
¼ pound round mints
½ pound mint leaves
¼ pound nonpareils
15 small heart candies
4 small candy canes

Additional decorating ideas:

1. Using cookie cutters, make small gingerbread boys and girls to stand in front of the house.

2. Add a purchased candy snowman and/or a Santa Claus.

3. You can make pretty gable windows and pathstones with a small, heart-shaped aspic cutter.

4. Cut a wreath for the front door from a mint-leaf candy.

Fig. 4: Adding back
Position back wall at an angle as above. Pipe frosting along bottom edges, set in place.

Fig. 5: Sides
To secure sides to base, pipe frosting along bottom edge and inner joints between back, sides.

Fig. 6: Roof
Pipe frosting along top edges of front, back, then add roof. Hold roof in place while it sets.

Fig. 7: Chimney
After roof has set, assemble chimney pieces with frosting; place in position on roof.

Fig. 8: Door, shutters
Use frosting to attach shutters. Decorate the door with candy hearts and frost it in place.

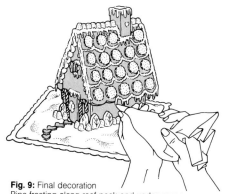

Fig. 9: Final decoration
Pipe frosting along roof peak and under eaves. To add other decorative touches, see text.

A Christmas Storybook

A MISERABLE,
MERRY CHRISTMAS

by Lincoln Steffens

My father's business seems to have been one of slow but steady growth.
He and his local partner, Llewelen Tozer, had no vices. They were devoted
to their families and to "the store," which grew with the town, which, in
turn, grew and changed with the State from a gambling, mining, and
ranching community to one of farming, fruit-raising, and building. Immi-
gration poured in, not gold-seekers now, but farmers, businessmen and
home-builders, who settled, planted, reaped, and traded in the natural
riches of the State, which prospered greatly, "making" the people who will
tell you that they "made the State."

As the store made money and I was getting through the primary school,
my father bought a lot uptown, at Sixteenth and K Streets, and built us a
"big" house. It was off the line of the city's growth, but it was near a new
grammar school for me and my sisters, who were coming along fast after me.
This interested the family, not me. They were always talking about school;
they had not had much of it themselves, and they thought they had missed
something. My father used to write speeches, my mother verses, and their
theory seems to have been that they had talents which a school would have
brought to flower. They agreed, therefore, that their children's gifts should
have all the schooling there was. My view, then, was that I had had a good
deal of it already, and I was not interested at all. It interfered with my own
business, with my own education.

And indeed I remember very little of the primary school. I learned to
read, write, spell, and count, and reading was all right. I had a practical use

for books, which I searched for ideas and parts to play with, characters to be, lives to live. The primary school was probably a good one, but I cannot remember learning anything except to read aloud "perfectly" from a teacher whom I adored and who was fond of me. She used to embrace me before the whole class and she favored me openly to the scandal of the other pupils, who called me "teacher's pet." Their scorn did not trouble me; I saw and I said that they envied me. I paid for her favor, however. When she married I had queer, unhappy feelings of resentment; I didn't want to meet her husband, and when I had to I wouldn't speak to him. He laughed, and she kissed me—happily for her, to me offensively. I never would see her again. Through with her, I fell in love immediately with Miss Kay, another grown young woman who wore glasses and had a fine, clear skin. I did not know her, I only saw her in the street, but once I followed her, found out where she lived, and used to pass her house, hoping to see her, and yet choking with embarrassment if I did. This fascination lasted for years; it was still a sort of super-romance to me when later I was "going with" another girl nearer my own age.

What interested me in our new neighborhood was not the school, nor the room I was to have in the house all to myself, but the stable which was built back of the house. My father let me direct the making of a stall, a little smaller than the other stalls, for my pony, and I prayed and hoped and my sister Lou believed that that meant that I would get the pony, perhaps for Christmas. I pointed out to her that there were three other stalls and no horses at all. This I said in order that she should answer it. She could not. My father, sounded, said that someday we might have horses and a cow; meanwhile a stable added to the value of a house. "Someday" is a pain to a boy who lives in and knows only "now." My good little sisters, to comfort me, remarked that Christmas was coming, but Christmas was always coming and grown-ups were always talking about it, asking you what you wanted and then giving you what they wanted you to have. Though everybody knew what I wanted, I told them all again. My mother knew that I told God, too, every night. I wanted a pony, and to make sure that they understood, I declared that I wanted nothing else.

"Nothing but a pony?" my father asked.

"Nothing," I said.

"Not even a pair of high boots?"

That was hard. I did want boots, but I stuck to the pony. "No, not even boots."

"Nor candy? There ought to be something to fill your stocking with, and Santa Claus can't put a pony into a stocking."

That was true, and he couldn't lead a pony down the chimney either. But no. "All I want is a pony," I said. "If I can't have a pony, give me nothing, nothing."

Now I had been looking myself for the pony I wanted, going to sales stables, inquiring of horsemen, and I had seen several that would do. My father let me "try" them. I tried so many ponies that I was learning fast to sit a horse. I chose several, but my father always found some fault with them. I was in despair. When Christmas was at hand I had given up all hope of a pony, and on Christmas Eve I hung up my stocking along with my sisters', of whom, by the way, I now had three. I haven't mentioned them or their coming because, you understand, they were girls, and girls, young girls, counted for nothing in my manly life. They did not mind me either; they were so happy that Christmas Eve that I caught some of their merriment. I speculated on what I'd get; I hung up the biggest stocking I had, and we all went reluctantly to bed to wait till morning. Not to sleep; not right away. We were told that we must not only sleep promptly, we must not wake up till seven-thirty the next morning—or if we did, we must not go to the fireplace for our Christmas. Impossible.

We did sleep that night, but we woke up at six A.M. We lay in our beds and debated through the open doors whether to obey till, say, half-past six. Then we bolted. I don't know who started it, but there was a rush. We all disobeyed; we raced to disobey and get first to the fireplace in the front room downstairs. And there they were, the gifts, all sorts of wonderful things, mixed-up piles of presents; only, as I disentangled the mess, I saw that my stocking was empty; it hung limp; not a thing in it; and under and around it—nothing. My sisters had knelt down, each by her pile of gifts; they were squealing with delight, till they looked up and saw me standing there in my nightgown with nothing. They left their piles to come to me and look with me at my empty place. Nothing. They felt my stocking: nothing.

I don't remember whether I cried at that moment, but my sisters did. They ran with me back to my bed, and there we all cried till I became indignant. That helped some. I got up, dressed, and driving my sisters away, I went alone out into the yard, down to the stable, and there, all by myself, I wept. My mother came out to me by and by; she found me in my pony stall, sobbing on the floor, and she tried to comfort me. But I heard my father outside; he had come part way with her, and she was having some sort of angry quarrel with him. She tried to comfort me;

143

besought me to come to breakfast. I could not; I wanted no comfort and no breakfast. She left me and went on into the house with sharp words for my father.

I don't know what kind of a breakfast the family had. My sisters said it was "awful." They were ashamed to enjoy their own toys. They came to me, and I was rude. I ran away from them. I went around to the front of the house, sat down on the steps, and, the crying over, I ached. I was wronged, I was hurt—I can feel now what I felt then, and I am sure that if one could see the wounds upon our hearts, there would be found still upon mine a scar from that terrible Christmas morning. And my father, the practical joker, he must have been hurt, too, a little. I saw him looking out of the window. He was watching me or something for an hour or two, drawing back the curtain ever so little lest I catch him, but I saw his face, and I think I can see now the anxiety upon it, the worried impatience.

After—I don't know how long—surely an hour or two—I was brought to the climax of my agony by the sight of a man riding a pony down the street, a pony and a brand-new saddle; the most beautiful saddle I ever saw, and it was a boy's saddle; the man's feet were not in the stirrups; his legs were too long. The outfit was perfect; it was the realization of all my dreams, the answer to all my prayers. A fine new bridle, with a light curb bit. And the pony! As he drew near, I saw that the pony was really a small horse, what we called an Indian pony, a bay, with black mane and tail, and one white foot and a white star on his forehead. For such a horse as that I would have given, I could have forgiven, anything.

But the man, a disheveled fellow with a blackened eye and a fresh-cut face, came along, reading the numbers on the houses, and, as my hopes— my impossible hopes—rose, he looked at our door and passed by, he and the pony, and the saddle and the bridle. Too much. I fell upon the steps, and having wept before, I broke now into such a flood of tears that I was a floating wreck when I heard a voice.

"Say, kid," it said, "do you know a boy named Lennie Steffens?"

I looked up. It was the man on the pony, back again, at our horse block.

"Yes," I spluttered through my tears. "That's me."

"Well," he said, "then this is your horse. I've been looking all over for you and your house. Why don't you put your number where it can be seen?"

"Get down," I said, running out to him.

He went on saying something about "ought to have got here at seven o'clock; told me to bring the nag here and tie him to your post and leave him for you. But, hell, I got into a drunk—and a fight—and a hospital, and—"

"Get down," I said.

He got down, and he boosted me up to the saddle. He offered to fit the stirrups to me, but I didn't want him to. I wanted to ride.

"What's the matter with you?" he said angrily. "What you crying for? Don't you like the horse? He's a dandy, this horse. I know him of old. He's fine at cattle; he'll drive 'em alone."

I hardly heard, I could scarcely wait, but he persisted. He adjusted the stirrups, and then, finally, off I rode, slowly, at a walk, so happy, so thrilled, that I did not know what I was doing. I did not look back at the house or the man, I rode off up the street, taking note of everything—of the reins, of the pony's long mane, of the carved leather saddle. I had never seen anything so beautiful. And mine! I was going to ride up past Miss Kay's house. But I noticed on the horn of the saddle some stains like raindrops, so I turned and trotted home, not to the house but to the stable. There was the family, father, mother, sisters, all working for me, all happy. They had been putting in place the tools of my new business: blankets, currycomb, brush, pitchfork—everything, and there was hay in the loft.

"What did you come back so soon for?" somebody asked. "Why didn't you go on riding?"

I pointed to the stains. "I wasn't going to get my new saddle rained on," I said. And my father laughed. "It isn't raining," he said. "Those are not rain-drops."

"They are tears," my mother gasped, and she gave my father a look which sent him off to the house. Worse still, my mother offered to wipe away the tears still running out of my eyes. I gave her such a look as she had given him, and she went off after my father, drying her own tears. My sisters remained and we all unsaddled the pony, put on his halter, led him to his stall, tied and fed him. It began really to rain; so all the rest of that memorable day we curried and combed that pony. The girls plaited his mane, forelock, and tail, while I pitchforked hay to him and curried and brushed, curried and brushed. For a change we brought him out to drink; we led him up and down, blanketed like a racehorse; we took turns at that. But the best, the most inexhaustible fun, was to clean him. When we went reluctantly to our midday Christmas dinner, we all smelt of horse, and my sisters had to wash their faces and hands. I was asked to, but I wouldn't, till my mother bade me look in the mirror. Then I washed up—quick. My face was caked with the muddy lines of tears that had coursed over my cheeks to my mouth. Having washed away that shame, I ate my dinner, and as I ate I grew hungrier and hungrier. It was my first meal that day, and as I filled up on the turkey and the stuffing, the cranberries and the pies, the fruit and the nuts—as I swelled, I could laugh. My mother said I still choked and sobbed now and then, but I laughed, too; I saw and enjoyed my sisters' presents till—I had to go out and attend to my pony, who was there, really and truly there, the promise, the beginning, of a happy double life. And—I went and looked to make sure—there was the saddle, too, and the bridle.

But that Christmas, which my father had planned so carefully, was it the best or the worst I ever knew? He often asked me that; I never could answer as a boy. I think now that it was both. It covered the whole distance from brokenhearted misery to bursting happiness—too fast. A grown-up could hardly have stood it.

GO TELL IT ON THE MOUNTAIN
American Black Spiritual

Go tell it on the mountain,
Over the hills and everywhere;
Go tell it on the mountain,
That Jesus Christ is born.

When I was a sinner,
I prayed both night and day;
I asked the Lord to help me,
And He showed me the way.

When I was a seeker,
I sought both night and day;
I asked the Lord to help me,
And He taught me how to pray.

Down in a lowly manger
The humble Christ was born;
And God sent out salvation
That blessed Christmas morn.

Go tell it on the mountain,
Over the hills and everywhere;
Go tell it on the mountain,
That Jesus Christ is born.

THE LEGEND OF THE CHRISTMAS ROSE

by Selma Lagerlöf

Robber Mother, who lived in Robbers' Cave up in Göinge forest, went down to the village one day on a begging tour. Robber Father, who was an outlawed man, did not dare to leave the forest. So his wife took to the road with her five youngsters, each wearing a ragged leathern suit and birch-bark shoes and with a sack on his back as long as himself. Robber Mother and her brood were worse than a pack of wolves, but when she stepped inside the door of a cabin, no one dared refuse to give her whatever she demanded; for she was not above coming back the following night and setting fire to the house if she had not been well received.

As Robber Mother went from house to house and begged, she came one day to Övid, which at that time was a cloister. She rang the bell of the cloister gate and asked for food. The watchman let down a small wicket in the gate and handed her six round bread cakes for herself and each of the five children.

While the mother was standing quietly at the gate, her youngsters were running about. Now one of them came and pulled at her skirt, as a signal that he had discovered something which she ought to come and see, and Robber Mother followed him promptly.

The entire cloister was surrounded by a high and strong wall, but the youngster had managed to find a little back gate which stood ajar. When Robber Mother got there, she pushed the gate open and walked inside without asking leave, as it was her custom to do. Övid Cloister was managed at that time by Abbot Hans, who knew all about herbs. Just within the

148

cloister wall he had planted a little herb garden, and it was into this that the old woman had forced her way.

It was high summertide, and Abbot Hans's garden was so full of flowers that Robber Mother's eyes were fairly dazzled by the blues, reds and yellows. But presently an indulgent smile spread over her features, and she started to walk up a narrow path that lay between many flower beds.

In the garden a lay brother walked about, pulling up weeds. It was he who had left the door in the wall open, that he might throw the weeds on the rubbish heap outside. When he saw Robber Mother coming in, with all five youngsters in tow, he ran toward her and ordered them away. But the beggar woman walked right on as before and took no notice whatever of him.

He thought she had not understood and wanted to take her by the arm and turn her toward the gate. But when she saw his purpose, she straightened herself to her full height. "I am Robber Mother from Göinge forest; so touch me if you dare!" It was obvious that she was certain she would be left in peace.

And yet the lay brother dared to oppose her. "You must know, Robber Mother, that this is a monks' cloister, and no woman in the land is allowed within these walls."

But Robber Mother walked straight ahead among the little flower beds, looking at the honeysuckles, which were full of deep orange-colored flower clusters. The lay brother knew of no other remedy than to run into the cloister and call for help. He returned with two stalwart monks, and Robber Mother saw that now it meant business! With feet firmly planted on the path she let out a perfect volley of shrieks, and, throwing herself upon the monks, clawed and bit at them, as did the youngsters. The men soon learned that all they could do was to go back into the cloister for reinforcements.

As they ran through the passageway which led to the cloister, they met Abbot Hans, who came rushing out to learn what this noise was about. They told him that Robber Mother from Göinge forest had come into the cloister and confessed they were unable to drive her out without assistance.

Abbot Hans upbraided them for using force and forbade their calling for help. He sent both monks back to their work, and although he was an old and fragile man, took with him only the lay brother. When he came out in the garden, Robber Mother was still wandering among the flower beds. He was certain that she had never before seen an herb garden; yet she sauntered leisurely between all the small patches, each with its own species of rare flower, and looked at them as if they were old acquaintances.

Abbot Hans loved his herb garden as much as it was possible for him to love anything earthly and perishable, and he couldn't help liking that the old woman had fought with three monks for the privilege of viewing the garden in peace. He came up to her and asked in a mild tone if the garden pleased her.

Robber Mother turned defiantly toward Abbot Hans, but when she noticed his white hair and bent form, she answered peaceably, "First, when I saw this, I thought I had never seen a prettier garden; but now I see that it can't be compared with one I know of."

When Abbot Hans heard her say that, a faint flush spread over his withered cheek. The lay brother, who was standing close by, immediately began to censure the old woman. "This is Abbot Hans," said he, "who with much care and diligence has gathered the flowers from far and near for his herb garden. We all know that there is not a more beautiful garden to be found, and it is not befitting that you, who live in the wild forest all the year around, should find fault with his work."

"If you could see the garden of which I am thinking you would uproot all the flowers planted here and cast them away like weeds," Robber Mother said.

But the Abbot's assistant was hardly less proud of the flowers than the Abbot himself, and he laughed derisively. "It must be a pretty garden that you have made for yourself amongst the pines in Göinge forest! I'd be willing to wager my soul's salvation that you have never before been within the walls of an herb garden."

Robber Mother grew crimson with rage and she cried out: "It may be true that until today I had not; but you monks, who are holy men, certainly must know that on every Christmas Eve the great Göinge forest is transformed into a beautiful garden, to commemorate the hour of our Lord's birth. We who live in the forest have seen this happen every year. And in that garden I have seen flowers so lovely that I dared not lift my hand to pluck them."

The lay brother wanted to continue the argument, but Abbot Hans gave him a sign to be silent. Ever since his childhood, Abbot Hans had heard it said that on every Christmas Eve the forest was dressed in holiday glory. He had often longed to see it, but he had never had the good fortune. Eagerly he begged Robber Mother that he might come up to the Robbers' Cave on Christmas Eve. If she would send one of her children to show him the way, he could ride up there alone, and he would never betray them—on the contrary, he would reward them, insofar as it lay in his power.

Robber Mother said no at first, for she was thinking of Robber Father and of the peril which might befall him should she permit Abbot Hans to ride up to their cave. At the same time the desire to prove to the monk that the garden which she knew was more beautiful than his got the better of her, and she gave in.

"But more than one follower you cannot take with you," said she, "and you are not to waylay us or trap us, as sure as you are a holy man."

This Abbot Hans promised, and Robber Mother went her way. Abbot Hans commanded the lay brother not to reveal to a soul that which had been agreed upon. He feared that the monks, should they learn of his purpose, would not allow a man of his years to go up to the Robbers' Cave.

Nor did he himself intend to reveal his project to a human being.

Then it happened that Archbishop Absalon from Lund came to Övid and remained through the night. When Abbot Hans was showing him the herb garden, he got to thinking of Robber Mother's visit, and told the Bishop about Robber Father, who these many years had lived as an outlaw in the forest, and asked him for a letter of ransom that the man might lead an honest life among respectable folk.

But the Archbishop replied that he did not care to let the robber loose among honest folk in the villages. It would be best for all that he remain in the forest.

Then Abbot Hans grew zealous and told the Bishop about Göinge forest, which, every year at Yuletide, clothed itself in summer bloom around the Robbers' Cave. "If these bandits are not so bad that God's glories can be made manifest to them, surely we cannot be too wicked to experience the same blessing."

"This much I will promise you, Abbot Hans," the Archbishop said, smiling, "that any day you send me a blossom from the garden in Göinge forest, I will give you letters of ransom for all the outlaws you may choose to plead for."

Abbot Hans thanked Bishop Absalon for his good promise and said that he would surely send him the flower.

The following Christmas Eve Abbot Hans did not sit at home in Övid Cloister, but was on his way to Göinge forest. One of Robber Mother's wild youngsters ran ahead of him, and close behind him was the lay brother.

Abbot Hans had been longing to make this journey, but it was a different matter for the lay brother accompanying him. Abbot Hans was very dear to him, and he would not willingly have allowed another to attend him and watch over him. But he didn't believe that he should see any Christmas Eve garden. He thought the whole thing a snare which Robber Mother had, with great cunning, laid for Abbot Hans, that he might fall into her husband's clutches.

While Abbot Hans was riding toward the forest, he saw that everywhere they were preparing to celebrate Christmas. In every peasant settlement great hunks of meat and bread were being carried from the larders into the cabins, and from the barns came the men with big sheaves of straw to be strewn over the floors. As he rode by the little country churches, he observed that each parson, with his sexton, was busily engaged in decorating his church.

When Abbot Hans saw all these Christmas preparations, his haste increased, thinking of the festivities that awaited him, which were greater than any others. But the lay brother grew more and more anxious, and implored Abbot Hans to turn back and not to throw himself deliberately into the robber's hands.

Abbot Hans went straight ahead, paying no heed. They left the plain behind and came up into desolate and wild forest regions. The farther they rode, the colder it grew, and after a while they came upon snow-covered ground. It turned out to be a long and hazardous ride through the forest.

They climbed steep paths, crawled over swamp and marsh, and pushed through windfall and bramble. Just as daylight was waning, the robber boy guided them across a forest meadow, skirted by tall, naked trees and green firs. Back of the meadow loomed a mountain wall, and in this wall they saw a door of thick boards.

Now Abbot Hans dismounted. The child opened the heavy door for him, and he looked into a mountain grotto, with bare stone walls. Robber Mother was seated before a log fire that burned in the middle of the floor. Alongside the walls were beds of pine and moss, and on one of these beds lay Robber Father asleep.

"Come in, you out there!" shouted Robber Mother without rising. Abbot Hans walked boldly into the cave, and the lay brother followed. Here were wretchedness and poverty! and nothing was done to celebrate Christmas. Robber Mother had neither brewed nor baked; neither had she washed nor scoured. The youngsters were lying on the floor around a kettle, eating; but no better food was provided for them than a watery gruel.

Robber Mother spoke in a tone as haughty and dictatorial as any well-to-do peasant woman. "Sit down by the fire and warm yourself, Abbot Hans," said she; "and if you have food with you, eat, for the food we in the forest prepare you wouldn't care to taste. And if you are tired after the long journey, you can lie down on one of these beds to sleep. I shall awaken you in time to see that which you have come up here to see."

Abbot Hans obeyed Robber Mother and brought forth his food sack; but he was so fatigued after the journey he was hardly able to eat, and as soon as he could stretch himself on the bed, he fell asleep.

Gradually fatigue got the better of the lay brother, too, and he dropped into a doze. When he woke up, he saw that Abbot Hans had left his bed and was sitting by the fire talking with Robber Mother. The outlawed robber sat also by the fire, pretending not to be listening. He was a tall, rawboned man with a dull, sluggish appearance.

Abbot Hans was telling Robber Mother all about the Christmas preparations he had seen on the journey, reminding her of Christmas feasts and games which she must have known in her youth, when she lived at peace with mankind. "I'm sorry for your children, who can never run on the village street in holiday dress or tumble in the Christmas straw," said he.

At first Robber Mother answered in short, gruff sentences, but by degrees she listened more intently. Suddenly Robber Father turned toward Abbot Hans and shook his fist. "You miserable monk! did you come here to coax from me my wife and children? Don't you know that I am an outlaw and may not leave the forest?"

"Sit down by the fire and warm yourself, Abbot Hans," said she.

153

Abbot Hans looked him fearlessly in the eyes. "It is my purpose to get a letter of ransom for you from Archbishop Absalon," said he. He had hardly finished speaking when the robber and his wife burst out laughing. They knew well enough the kind of mercy a forest robber could expect from Bishop Absalon!

"If I get a letter of ransom from Absalon," said Robber Father, "then I'll promise you that never again will I steal so much as a goose."

Suddenly Robber Mother rose. "We are forgetting to look at the forest," she said. "Now I can hear, even in this cave, how the Christmas bells are ringing."

The words were barely uttered when they all sprang up and rushed out. But in the forest it was still dark night and bleak winter. The only thing they marked was a distant clang borne on a light south wind. "How can this bell ringing ever awaken the dead forest?" thought Abbot Hans. For now, as he stood out in the winter darkness, he thought it impossible that a summer garden could spring up here.

When the bells had been ringing a few moments, a sudden illumination penetrated the forest; it pushed its way forward between the stark trees, like a shimmering mist. Then Abbot Hans saw that the snow had vanished from the ground and the earth began to take on a green covering. The ferns shot up their fronds, rolled like a bishop's staff. The heather that grew on the stony hills quickly dressed itself in new bloom, the moss-tufts thickened and raised themselves, and the spring blossoms shot upward their swelling buds.

Abbot Hans's heart beat fast as he marked the first signs of the forest's awakening. "Old man that I am, shall I behold such a miracle?" thought he, and the tears wanted to spring to his eyes. Then it grew so hazy that he feared the darkness would once more cover the earth; but almost immediately there came a new wave of light. The leaves of the trees burst into bloom, crossbeaks hopped from branch to branch, the woodpeckers hammered on the limbs, and a flock of paradise starlings lighted in fir tops to rest, the brilliant red tips of their feathers glittering like so many jewels.

Again, all was dark for an instant, but soon there came a new light wave. A fresh, warm south wind blew and scattered over the forest meadow little seeds that took root and sprang up the instant they touched the earth. Cranes and wild geese shrieked in the air, and the baby squirrels began playing on the branches of the trees. The juniper berries changed color every second, and forest flowers covered the ground till it was all red, blue and yellow.

Abbot Hans bent down to the earth and broke off a wild strawberry blossom, and, as he straightened up, the berry ripened in his hand.

. . .a flock of paradise starlings lighted in fir tops to rest, the brilliant red tips of their feathers glittering like so many jewels.

154

The mother fox came out of her lair with a litter of black-legged young. She went up to Robber Mother and scratched at her skirt, and Robber Mother bent down to her and praised her young.

Robber Mother's own youngsters cried out in delight. They stuffed themselves with wild strawberries that hung on the bushes, large as pine cones. One of them played with a litter of young hares; another ran a race with some young crows, which had hopped from their nest; a third caught up an adder from the ground and wound it around his neck and arm.

Robber Father was standing out on a marsh eating raspberries. When he glanced up, a big black bear stood beside him. "Keep to your own ground, you!" Robber Father said. "This is my turf." The huge bear turned around and lumbered off in another direction.

New waves of warmth and light kept coming, and now golden pollen fairly flew in the air. The beehive in a hollow oak was already so full of honey that it dripped down on the trunk of the tree. The loveliest roses climbed up the mountain wall, and from the forest meadow sprang flowers as large as human faces.

Abbot Hans thought of the flower he was to pluck for Bishop Absalon; but each new flower that appeared was more beautiful than the others, and he wanted to choose the most beautiful of all.

Wave upon wave kept coming until the air was so filled with light that it glittered. All the life and beauty and joy of summer smiled on Abbot Hans. He felt a celestial atmosphere enfolding him, and tremblingly he began to anticipate, now that earth's joys had come, the glories of heaven approaching, glories such that the heart wanted to stop beating and the soul longed to soar away into the Eternal. From far in the distance faint harp tones were heard, and celestial song, like a soft murmur, reached him. Abbot Hans clasped his hands and dropped to his knees, his face radiant with bliss.

But in the mind of the lay brother who had accompanied Abbot Hans there were dark thoughts. "This cannot be a true miracle," he thought, "since it is revealed to malefactors. This does not come from God, but has its origin in witchcraft and is sent hither by Satan."

Now Abbot Hans saw the bright forms of the angel throng through the forest branches. The lay brother saw them, too; but back of all this wondrous beauty he saw only some dread evil.

All the while the birds had been circling around the head of Abbot Hans, and they let him take them in his hands. But they were afraid of the lay brother. Yet when a little forest dove saw that the angels were nearing, she plucked up courage and flew down on the lay brother's shoulder and laid her head against his cheek.

Then it appeared to him as if sorcery were come right upon him, to tempt and corrupt him. He struck with his hand at the forest dove and cried in such a loud voice that it rang throughout the forest, "Go thou back to hell, whence thou art come!"

Just then the angels were so near that Abbot Hans felt the feathery touch of their great wings, and he bowed down to earth in reverent greeting.

But when the lay brother's words sounded, their song was hushed and the holy guests turned in flight. At the same time the light and the mild warmth vanished. Darkness sank over the earth, like a coverlet; frost came, all the growths shriveled up; the animals and birds hastened away; the rushing of streams was hushed; the leaves dropped from the trees, rustling like rain.

Abbot Hans felt how his heart, which had but lately swelled with bliss, was now contracting with insufferable agony. "I can never outlive this," thought he, "that the angels from heaven had been so close to me, that they wanted to sing Christmas carols for me and were driven to flight."

Then he remembered the flower he had promised Bishop Absalon, and at the last moment he fumbled among the leaves and moss to try and find a blossom. But he sensed how the ground under his fingers froze and how the white snow came gliding over it. Then his heart caused him ever greater anguish. He could not rise, but fell prostrate on the ground and lay there.

When the robber folk and the lay brother had groped their way back to the cave, they missed Abbot Hans. They took torches with them and went out to search for him. They found him dead upon the coverlet of snow. Then the lay brother began weeping, for he understood that it was he who had killed Abbot Hans because he had dashed from him the cup of happiness.

When Abbot Hans had been carried down to Övid, those who took charge of the dead saw that he held his right hand locked tight around something which he must have grasped at the moment of death. It was a pair of white root bulbs, which he had torn from among the moss and leaves.

When the lay brother saw the bulbs, he took them and planted them in Abbot Hans's herb garden. He guarded them the whole year to see if any flower would spring from them. But in vain he waited through the spring, the summer and the autumn. Finally, when winter had set in and all the leaves and the flowers were dead, he ceased caring for them.

But when Christmas Eve came again, he was so strongly reminded of Abbot Hans that he wandered out into the garden to think of him. And look! as he came to the spot where he had planted the bare root bulbs, he saw that from them had sprung flourishing green stalks, which bore beautiful flowers with silver white leaves.

157

He called out all the monks, and when they saw that this plant bloomed on Christmas Eve, when all the other growths were as if dead, they understood that this flower had in truth been plucked by Abbot Hans from the Christmas garden in Göinge forest. Then the lay brother asked the monks if he might take a few blossoms to Bishop Absalon. When he appeared before the Archbishop, he gave him the flowers and said: "Abbot Hans sends you these. They are the flowers he promised to pick for you from the garden in Göinge forest."

When Bishop Absalon beheld the flowers, which had sprung from the earth in darkest winter, and heard the words, he turned as pale as if he had met a ghost. He sat in silence a moment; thereupon he said, "Abbot Hans has faithfully kept his word and I shall also keep mine." And he ordered that a letter of ransom be drawn up for the outlawed robber.

He handed the letter to the lay brother, who departed at once for the Robbers' Cave. When he stepped in there on Christmas Day, the robber came toward him with axe uplifted. "I'd like to hack you monks into bits, as many as you are!" said he. "It must be your fault that Göinge forest did not last night dress itself in Christmas bloom."

"The fault is mine alone," said the lay brother, "and I will gladly die for it. But first I must deliver a message from Abbot Hans." And he drew forth the Bishop's letter and told the man that he was free. "Hereafter you and your children shall celebrate your Christmas among people, just as Abbot Hans wished to have it," said he.

Then Robber Father stood there pale and speechless, but Robber Mother said in his name, "Abbot Hans has indeed kept his word, and Robber Father will keep his."

When the robber and his wife left the cave, the lay brother moved in and lived alone in the forest, in constant meditation and prayer that his hard-heartedness might be forgiven him.

But Göinge forest never again celebrated the hour of our Saviour's birth; and of all its glory, there lives today only the plant which Abbot Hans had plucked. It has been named CHRISTMAS ROSE. And each year at Christmas-tide she sends forth from the earth her green stalks and white blossoms, as if she never could forget that she had once grown in the great Christmas garden at Göinge forest.

CAROL
by Dorothy L. Sayers

The Ox said to the Ass, said he, all on a Christmas night:
"Do you hear the pipe of the shepherds a-whistling over the hill?
That is the angels' music they play for their delight,
'Glory to God in the highest and peace upon earth, goodwill' . . .
Nowell, nowell, my masters, God lieth low in stall,
And the poor, labouring Ox was here before you all."

The Ass said to the Ox, said he, all on a Christmas day:
"Do you hear the golden bridles come clinking out of the east?
Those are the three wise Magi that ride from far away
To Bethlehem in Jewry to have their lore increased . . .
Nowell, nowell, my masters, God lieth low in stall,
And the poor, foolish Ass was here before you all."

MIRACLE ON 34th STREET

by Valentine Davies

1

If you searched every old folks' home in the country, you couldn't find anyone who looked more like Santa Claus. He was the living, breathing incarnation of the old gent—white beard, pink cheeks, fat tummy and all—and his name was Kris Kringle, too. Whether this was coincidence or design—a sort of stage name he had assumed—his friends at the Maplewood Home for the Aged never knew. Nor did they know exactly how old he was. His white whiskers made him look a good seventy-five, and yet when he laughed or walked you would swear he wasn't a day over fifty. His eyes were quick and happy, and he had a smile to match. Not only did Kris look precisely like Santa Claus, he firmly believed he *was* that jolly old gentleman.

Dr. Pierce, the Maplewood physician, found this delusion innocent and harmless. In fact, the old man's kindly shrewdness in all other respects had won Pierce completely. He often came to visit Kris in his little room at Maplewood, which was littered with toys of all sizes and shapes.

161

One November morning when Dr. Pierce dropped in, Kris was reading an advertisement, his eyes snapping with indignation. A customized shopping service offered to purchase Christmas gifts. "Just send us the names and ages of the people you wish to remember," Kris read aloud. "We will relieve you of the boring necessity of Christmas shopping." Angrily, Kris threw the paper down. "Is this what Christmas has degenerated into—pure commercialism? Is there no true Christmas spirit left in the world?"

Dr. Pierce was afraid not. Christmas had become big business, and the spirit behind it seemed to be lost in the milling crowds that packed the stores.

Kris was not prepared to believe that. "No, Doctor," he said. "Underneath all the hurry and bustle people still believe in Santa Claus and all Christmas stands for." He suddenly smiled and asked the doctor what *he* wanted for Christmas.

"I'll tell you what I want," said Pierce. "An X-ray machine. We've needed one here for years."

"You shall have it," Kris said.

The doctor smiled. "If I get an X-ray machine, I'll *know* you're Santa Claus."

"You just wait, Doctor. You'll see."

But now a frown settled over Dr. Pierce's pleasant face. There was something on his mind and finally he came right out with it. "Kris, you're going to have to leave Maplewood," he said.

"Why?" asked Kris in astonishment.

Well, the doctor explained, he had been fighting the board on this for years, but they had finally overruled him and issued a definite order. "The laws of the state and Maplewood's charter only allow us to keep old people so long as they are in good physical *and* mental health," he said.

"What's the matter with me? I'm in better physical shape than ninety percent of your patients, and I passed all your mental tests." And Kris went through the familiar routines, adding and subtracting and so forth.

"I know," said the doctor quietly. "But it's this Kris Kringle business."

"You mean because I'm Santa Claus? There's nothing wrong with that. It happens to be the truth."

"It's not quite that simple," Pierce replied. "Unfortunately, the board does not believe in Santa Claus, Kris."

"So I'm not sane because the board of directors doesn't believe in Santa Claus!"

"That's one way of putting it."

Kris reflected for a moment. "What happens next?"

Pierce explained that Maplewood had an arrangement with the Mount

Hope Sanatarium, and Kris exploded. "That nut house? Never!" He'd be damned if he'd go to an asylum. Finally Dr. Pierce conceded that it was up to Kris. But how could he fend for himself? He was too old to earn a living and he didn't have much money. Where would he stay?

"The zoo keeper in Central Park is a friend of mine. I'll stay with him," Kris answered.

"Well, you'll have time to think it over. We'll talk about it again," Dr. Pierce said as he moved toward the door.

Kris nodded silently, but there was a look of determination on his face. The moment the doctor had gone, he hauled out a large suitcase from his closet and began to pack.

2

The Central Park Zoo was nearly deserted at this early hour, but in one of the enclosures a keeper, tidying up, eagerly greeted Kris as he approached. "How are you?" he called.

"Fine, Jim! Never better. And how are the boys?"

"Fat and lazy." Jim smiled. "And it's mostly your fault!"

Kris laughed and gave a whistle. From within the shed, a reindeer's head peered shyly out, then another. The old man called again and held out a handful of carrots. In a few minutes half a dozen reindeer were eating out of his hand while Jim watched, smiling. Kris had an uncanny way with the deer. Jim had fussed over them for years and he couldn't get near them.

"Jim, could you put me up for a while?" asked Kris.

"Why, certainly, Kris, as long as you want."

So all was well. Kris started on his way again. He had no special destination, but he loved being outdoors in this crisp cold air. As he approached the western limits of the park, he suddenly stopped and cocked his head to one side, listening. Somewhere just outside the park, a band was playing *Jingle Bells*. Kris turned and made for the nearest exit.

He found that Central Park West and the side streets leading into it were filled with excitement and confusion, for the Macy's Parade was about to start. Sponsored annually by the department store, it was a child's dream of a Christmas parade, or as near as adults could make it. Huge inflated figures blew every which way in the wind: Jack the Giant Killer; a Panda; Sleepy, Grumpy, Dopey, and the other dwarfs. The costumed men who held the guide ropes seemed like frantic Lilliputians. A myriad of storybook characters were climbing aboard their floats and a dozen bands were loudly tuning up.

The person in charge of the whole business was a handsome, well-dressed, businesslike young woman whom Kris heard addressed as Mrs. Walker. Assisting her was a spectacled, bald-headed and harried gentleman named Mr. Shellhammer.

The thing that really fascinated Kris was the last float in the Parade—Santa Claus in his sleigh, pulled by eight realistic wooden reindeer. The Santa Claus was practicing with his whip in a wild, lurching manner as Kris sauntered up. Kris watched as long as he could, then stepped up and with a polite "Allow me, sir," took the whip from his hand. With a single expert flip of the wrist he flicked the long whip. The end crackled smartly one inch over the farthest reindeer's ear. "You see, it's all in the wrist," he said.

But Macy's Santa wasn't impressed, and one whiff of his breath told Kris the reason. Kris was horrified at the idea of a drunk depicting Santa Claus to thousands of children. He started toward Mrs. Walker to protest, but suddenly she was standing next to him, beckoning for the float to move ahead. Before Kris could speak, it lurched forward and the saturated Santa nearly toppled off. It didn't take Mrs. Walker long to size up the situation. She fired the man on the spot.

But now, with the whole parade ready to start, they had no Santa Claus. Mrs. Walker and Shellhammer saw Kris at the same time and pounced on him.

"Would you be Santa Claus?" Mrs. Walker asked.

"Have you had any experience?" Shellhammer inquired.

The question struck the old man's funnybone, and his little round body shook with chuckles. "Yes," he said. "A little."

"Then you've got to help us out. Please!" said Mrs. Walker.

"Madam," Kris replied with quiet dignity, "I am not in the habit of substituting for spurious Santas."

"Mrs. Walker, we can't hold the Parade up any longer. We'll have to do without a Santa Claus," said Mr. Shellhammer.

But Kris looked toward the crowd of excited children lining the streets, and then he realized that he couldn't disappoint those eager faces. "All right," he said, handing his hat and cane to Shellhammer. "Get me the clothes. I'll do it!"

A few minutes later, Kris found himself the central figure of the great Parade, waving and smiling at thousands of children, cracking his whip and having the time of his life.

3

When she had finally managed to get the Parade under way, Doris Walker, exhausted, returned to her apartment on Central Park West. The Parade was

"Madam," Kris replied with quiet dignity, "I am not in the habit of substituting for spurious Santas."

passing by the building, but Doris entered without giving it so much as a glance. She didn't care if she never saw a parade again.

She opened the door to her small, sternly modern apartment and called, "Susan—Susan!" Cleo, the maid, poked her head out of the kitchen and said that Susan was in "Uncle" Fred's apartment watching the Parade. Doris went to her living-room window. It looked directly into the rear windows of the front apartment, across the courtyard. She rapped on the glass and in a moment Fred appeared. They waved and she shouted that she'd be over.

"Uncle" Fred Gayley was no relation at all. Young and attractive, he was a lawyer with one of the city's oldest law firms. He and Susan had become pals and out of this had grown a pleasant, casual friendship between Fred and Doris. It was far more casual than Fred would have liked. But Doris's marriage had ended in divorce and from her avoidance of any reference to it, Fred gathered that it had been a bitter disillusionment. She seemed determined to avoid further entanglement.

From Fred's front windows, he and Susan, a rather serious child of six, had a perfect view of the Parade. The sound of band music and cheering children filled the air, but Fred was filled with much more childlike wonder and excitement than his little companion. As one of the huge inflated figures passed the window, he said eagerly, "That's Jack the Giant Killer! And look, that big fellow is the giant!"

"Of course," said Susan, "there are no giants, really. Some people grow very tall—but that is abnormal. Mommy told me."

Fred couldn't help but feel sorry for the child. She was intelligent, but fun was a stranger to her. There was no gaiety about her. "Maybe your mother's right," he said, "but I believe in giants anyhow!"

When Doris arrived, she launched into an account of her troubles with the Santa, while Fred tried to quiet her with grimaces. Finally, using a cup of coffee as a pretext, he dragged her into his kitchen and begged her not to disillusion Susan. But Doris had very definite ideas about bringing up children. She believed in realism and truth. Susan was *not* going to believe in myths like Santa Claus.

"Why not?" asked Fred. "What harm does it do?"

"When girls grow up considering life a big fairy tale," Doris answered, "they wait subconsciously for Prince Charming to come along. When he does, and turns out to be—"

"Look, Doris," Fred said. "You had a tough break. You trusted and loved someone deeply—and then one day you woke up and found how wrong you'd been. But all men aren't like that, and Susan's not going to be any happier growing up to think so."

Fred's directness found its target. Doris turned away as he went on. "I'm sorry, but I'm right." He moved closer to her. "I only wish you'd give me a chance to prove that I'm not the sort of person he was."

"I burned my fingers once," Doris answered quietly. She turned back toward the living room.

4

Early the next morning, looking very smart and businesslike, Doris Walker entered her office at the huge store on the corner of 34th Street and Broadway. There sat Kris waiting to see her. Doris was Macy's personnel director, and Mr. Shellhammer, head of the toy department, had suggested that Kris be given a permanent job as Macy's Santa Claus. Kris had made a tremendous hit at the Parade and was by far the most authentic Santa they had ever found.

Kris told Doris that he would be very happy to accept the job and Doris hired him instantly. Then she buzzed for her assistant, who took Kris to her office and asked him to fill out an employment card. He did so in a clear, Spencerian hand: *Name:* Kris Kringle *Address:* Maplewood Home, Great Neck, Long Island *Age:* As old as my tongue and a little bit older than my teeth.

He handed the card to the assistant, who glanced at it mechanically and said, "Thank you, Mr. Kringle. Mr. Shellhammer's waiting for you."

Mr. Shellhammer took Kris to change into his Santa Claus outfit. While he dressed, Shellhammer handed him a list of the stock of the toy department. He had checked the items that were to be pushed this year and emphasized that if a child asked for something they did not carry, Kris was to suggest a checked item. Kris nodded grimly. He knew exactly what Mr. Shellhammer meant. As soon as he left, Kris tore the list into very small pieces.

Enthroned on the dais with a long line of eager kids waiting to see him, Kris was in his element. He loved every minute of it and so did the children. Mr. Shellhammer looked out of his office and beamed happily.

"And what do you want for Christmas?" Kris asked, as a little boy climbed up on his ample lap.

"I want a fire engine," the youngster replied, "the kind that's got real hoses that squirt real water."

Behind the boy's back, his mother was gesturing frantically. But Kris paid no attention. "All right, sonny," he said. "I'm sure you're a good boy. You'll get one."

Delighted, the child climbed down. The mother was fuming as she said quietly to Kris, "Why did you tell him that? They're not making that kind of fire engine. I've looked everywhere."

"Oh, but you *can* get them," Kris replied, "at the Acme Toy Company at 246 West 26th Street. They're only eight-fifty."

The woman stared in amazement. Was Macy's Santa Claus sending her to another store? Kris replied that the important thing was to make kids happy, and whether Macy's or Acme sold the toy didn't make any great difference.

And so Kris continued. His only thought was for each boy and girl on his lap to get his wish at Christmas. If the toys seemed too expensive, or Macy's didn't carry them, Kris told the mother just where she could get a less expensive train or find the right doll. The parents were surprised and pleased.

Unfortunately, Mr. Shellhammer overheard Mr. Kringle advising a little boy's mother to go to Gimbels for skates. Gimbels, Macy's main rival! Mr. Shellhammer went into shock, and then started for Mrs. Walker's office to have Kringle fired. But as he proceeded through the store he was stopped by a number of mothers who couldn't thank him enough for this helpful service. It was wonderful, the real Christmas spirit, and they would be regular Macy customers from now on. Mr. Shellhammer began to wonder. Then, in his office, he found many grateful messages and notes. He sat down at his desk to think things over.

"I think it's a wonderful idea!" his secretary said.

"You think so, and the women think so," he said sadly, "but will *Mr. Macy* think so?" He looked beseechingly toward the ceiling, but the answer was not there.

5

Fred had a date to take Susan out that afternoon. Still disturbed by her precociousness, he had hatched a plot. He would take her to see the new Santa at Macy's, who would worm a Christmas wish out of her, and Fred would arrange to have it under the tree. Perhaps then Susan might believe in Santa Claus, or at least have some normal childlike wonder.

But when Mr. Kringle took Susan upon his lap, she refused to ask for anything. Her mother would get her what she needed—if it wasn't too expensive. She told Kris he was merely a gentleman her mother had employed to play the part of Santa Claus.

"You *are* a little better than most," said Susan. "Anyway, your beard looks real."

Mr. Kringle answered that it was real, and *he* was real, too. But he could get nowhere with Susan. Kris was troubled. This was just the sort of thing he feared was happening in the world.

Doris emerged from her office, glanced toward the dais, and stopped dead when she saw her daughter on Santa Claus's lap and Fred standing there looking sheepish. Brusquely, Doris whisked Susan away and planted her in a chair near the office. Then she asked Fred to step inside.

Susan paused for a moment and watched Kris as he took a little girl with golden pigtails upon his lap. Her foster mother explained to Kris that the child had only recently arrived from an orphanage in Holland. She spoke hardly a word of English, but insisted that "Sinterklaas," as she called him, should speak Dutch. Now the girl was confidently talking away to Kris and her foster mother's annoyance was obvious. She started to explain to the child, but Kris raised his hand for silence, and when the child had finished he answered her in fluent Dutch. The sudden light in the little Dutch girl's eyes did a funny thing to Susan. There was something very real about this Santa Claus, and it puzzled her.

Inside her office, Doris told Fred that she appreciated his kindness, but Susan was *her* responsibility, and she insisted that Fred respect her wishes regarding the child. Fred promised to do so if he could go on being friends with Susan. Contritely, he said goodnight to Susan and Doris and departed.

When Susan joined her mother, she began asking questions about Mr. Kringle. Doris carefully explained that he was just an employee of the store, like anyone else.

"I know," said Susan. "But when he spoke Dutch to that little girl—"

"Susan, I speak French," said Doris patiently. "But that doesn't make me Joan of Arc." And in order to clear up any confusion, she sent for Kris.

"You're an employee of this store, aren't you?" she asked. Kris nodded, smiling. "And you're not Santa Claus; because there really is no such person."

"I'm sorry to contradict you, Mrs. Walker," Kris replied. "But there certainly is, and here I stand to prove it!"

Susan's eyes opened wide, and Doris looked annoyed. "I want you to be perfectly honest," she said. "What is your real name?"

"Kris Kringle."

Doris pulled Kris's employment card from the file on her desk and she suddenly stiffened.

"Is there anything more I can tell you?" Kris asked.

But Mrs. Walker was frightened. "No—no—thank you!" she said hastily as she ushered Susan from the room. This man really believed he *was* Santa

Claus! He seemed kindly enough, but he might be dangerous! And he had been with children all day long!

Quietly but firmly she gave Kris his notice, with two weeks' pay. The old man's only reaction seemed to be one of concern for Doris and little Susan—as if Doris were the one to be pitied.

As he walked out the door the phone rang. Mr. Macy wished to see her immediately. Doris entered his office in trepidation: had he found out that she'd hired a nut? And when she saw Mr. Shellhammer there, her heart skipped a beat.

But to her amazement, Mr. Macy congratulated both of them. Because of Mr. Kringle's recommendations, Macy's was being flooded with messages from grateful parents. This was the biggest goodwill idea ever, and Mr. Macy intended to make it policy throughout the store: "The Store with the *Real* Christmas Spirit." They must keep this Santa Claus—find some other work for him after the holidays. Mr. Macy promised both Doris and Shellhammer immediate raises.

Outside Mr. Macy's office, Doris shakily broke the news to Shellhammer that she had just fired Mr. Kringle. Shellhammer exploded: they must get him back *at once!* So after a frantic search, Doris caught Kris in the service elevator and told him he could have the job back. To her dismay, he politely declined. She had indicated her cynical disbelief. That was enough for him.

Frantically Doris explained that his helpfulness and kindness had caused a sensation, and finally she broke down and told him that if he left it would mean her job. His whole attitude changed. In that case, he said, he would certainly stay. He couldn't have her losing her job just before the holidays. "Think what that would mean to your lovely little daughter," he said.

Kris now realized that Doris and Susan were but unhappy products of their times. They presented a test case for him. If he could get them to believe in him—there was still hope. If not, Santa Claus and all he stood for were through.

"You know, Mrs. Walker," he said, "for fifty years or so I've been more and more worried about Christmas. We're all so busy trying to make things go faster and look shinier and cost less that Christmas and I are getting lost in the shuffle."

"But Christmas is still Christmas," said Doris.

"No." Mr. Kringle shook his head. "Christmas isn't just a day. It's a frame of mind. That's what's been changing. That's why I'm glad I'm here. Maybe I can do something about it."

In spite of herself, Doris was impressed. She couldn't help liking the old man, even if he was a little off the beam.

"No." Mr. Kringle shook his head. "Christmas isn't just a day. It's a frame of mind."

6

The next morning, Kris was back on the dais and the line of children was longer than ever, for word of mouth was spreading. But Doris felt a lingering worry. Although he seemed harmless, she had better make sure. On his employment card, his address was Maplewood Home, Great Neck, Long Island. She called the place, but the results were hardly helpful. Yes, a Mr. Kringle had lived there, but he was away. Any questions concerning his mental condition would have to be taken up with Dr. Pierce. He, too, was away that day. Doris left a request for Pierce to call her and hung up.

Reluctantly, she called Albert Sawyer, Macy's expert on vocational guidance, a pompous little man who knew all the answers. Perhaps this was not his field? Doris suggested. But Sawyer assured her he was just the man. Why, he had made quite a study of abnormal psychology! He would be happy to interview this fellow. So Kris was ushered into Mr. Sawyer's presence and Sawyer proceeded to "examine" him. Mr. Kringle had passed mental tests a dozen times, and Sawyer's questions were just like all the rest: Who was the first President of the United States? How much was three times five? Kris answered them all patiently, but Sawyer's self-importance and barking manner rubbed him the wrong way. Finally, Sawyer held up three fingers in front of Kris's nose. "How many fingers do you see?" he asked.

"Three," answered Kris, "and I see that you bite your nails, Mr. Sawyer. Now, nervous habits like yours are often the result of insecurity. Do you sleep well? Are you happy at home?"

This was more than Sawyer could stand. "That will be all, Mr. Kringle," he said coldly. "You may go."

"Thank you," said Kris as he rose, "and take it easy, Mr. Sawyer. Get some exercise. Relax."

Meantime, Dr. Pierce came to see Doris. There was something reassuring in his easy, quiet manner. He was delighted that Mr. Kringle had found this job. There were just a few things, however, that Doris ought to know. Kris had some peculiarities . . .

"Yes!" said Doris. "We found that out."

"But thousands of people lead perfectly normal lives with similar mild delusions," Dr. Pierce assured her. "Mr. Kringle is incapable of harming anyone. He just wants to be helpful." Pierce's only concern was for Kris's welfare. "It would be better if someone would keep an eye on him after working hours," he said. "You know, he is a very old man and I hate to think of his wandering about New York alone."

Grateful and relieved, Doris promised that this would be done.

Mr. Sawyer wore an imposing frown as he entered Doris's office with Shellhammer. "This man has a fixed delusion," Sawyer told her. Doris knew that, she said, but the Maplewood Home doctor had just convinced her that he was harmless. Sawyer was not convinced. "Cases like this often become violent when their delusion is attacked." If Kris were kept on, he could take no responsibility. Doris said *she* would then, and Sawyer rose to leave. "I warn you, Mrs. Walker, if something happens—the responsibility will be entirely yours!"

Afterward, Doris and Shellhammer agreed that all that was necessary was for someone to keep an eye on Mr. Kringle. "And, of course, you're *just* the person to do it, Mrs. Walker!" said Mr. Shellhammer.

Doris shook her head. "I live alone with my daughter."

"Well," said Shellhammer, "my boy's away at school, so we do have an empty room. But I'll have to arrange it with Mrs. Shellhammer, and that will take a little doing. I'll tell you what. If you'll take him home to dinner, I'll call you later."

And so it was agreed.

7

In spite of Dr. Pierce, Doris feared that having Kris to dinner would be quite an ordeal, so she invited Fred as well. He accepted eagerly and even supplied the entrée—a venison steak a friend had given him.

It looked tempting, indeed, but Mr. Kringle wouldn't touch a mouthful. "I'm not a vegetarian," he explained. "But deer meat—I just couldn't!"

As a matter of fact, Kris turned out to be quite a gourmet, expounding on many kinds of choice dishes: he had come by his vast tummy honestly. Dinner went off far better than Doris had expected.

While Fred and Doris helped Cleo with the dishes, Mr. Kringle seized the opportunity to have a talk with Susan. All through dinner he had been studying her solemn, wistful little face. Susan had been studying him, too. She knew her mother was right: Mr. Kringle couldn't be Santa Claus. Yet he was different from anyone she had ever seen, and she secretly wished that he were.

"And what sort of games do you play with the other children?" Mr. Kringle wanted to know.

Susan didn't play with them very much, she told him. The games they played were silly. "Why, today they were playing zoo," said Susan scornfully. "They asked me what kind of an animal I wanted to be. I didn't want to be an animal, so I didn't play."

172

"Why didn't you tell them you were a lion?"

"Because I'm *not* a lion," Susan said flatly. "I'm a girl."

"The other children weren't animals, either. They were just *pretending*."

"That's what makes the game so silly."

"But it's a lot of fun to use your imagination," said Kris. "Do you know what the imagination is, Susan?"

"That's when you see things that aren't really there."

"Well, not exactly," said Kris. "To me the imagination is a very wonderful country. You've heard of the British nation and the French nation?" Susan nodded. "Well, this is the *Imagi*nation. Once you get there you can do almost anything you want. How would you like to be the Statue of Liberty in the morning and fly south with a flock of geese in the afternoon? Or have your own ship that makes daily trips to China and Australia?"

Susan's face broke into a little smile. Perhaps this *was* silly, but it was a lot of fun to think about.

"Well, it's very simple really," Kris said. "All it takes is a little practice. Wouldn't you like to try?"

"Yes," said Susan softly.

"I thought so." Mr. Kringle beamed. "Now let's start with something easy. How would you like to be a monkey in the zoo?"

"I'd like to," said Susan. "But I don't know *how*."

"Sure you do!" said Kris. "Just bend over a little—that's right—then curl your hands in." And in a few minutes, to his delight, Kris found that he had a very apt pupil.

In the kitchen, Doris was wishing out loud that Shellhammer would call and take Kris off her hands. She didn't like his influence over Susan—even for one evening. Fred, on the other hand, was delighted. Kris was just what the doctor ordered for a far too serious six-year-old. Picking up a silver platter, he asked, "Where does this go?"

"In the living room," said Doris, "on the second shelf."

When Fred came into the room, Susan had evolved from a monkey to a fairy queen. With a touch of her wand she was about to render Kris invisible. Fred watched this performance, delighted. A little more contact with the old man might do wonders not only for Susan, but for Doris, too. Suddenly, Fred had a brilliant idea.

"Where are you staying, Mr. Kringle?" he asked.

He was temporarily living with his friend, the zoo keeper, Kris said, but he felt that he was imposing and would have to find some other place. Fred jumped at the chance. He had an extra bed, and he would be delighted to have Mr. Kringle stay with him.

In the kitchen, Doris was talking to Mr. Shellhammer on the phone. He

Fred, on the other hand, was delighted. Kris was just what the doctor ordered for a far too serious six-year-old.

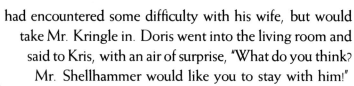

had encountered some difficulty with his wife, but would take Mr. Kringle in. Doris went into the living room and said to Kris, with an air of surprise, "What do you think? Mr. Shellhammer would like you to stay with him!"

When Kris told her he had already accepted Mr. Gayley's invitation, Doris was dumbfounded. So Fred had double-crossed her! With a grim "I see," she went back to the phone to tell Mr. Shellhammer that Kris had made previous arrangements.

So Mr. Kringle moved in with Fred that night. As he was about to turn the light out, Fred looked over at Kris, snug in the other bed. "I'm very glad to have you, Mr. Kringle," he confessed, "because I've always wanted to know something. Does Santa sleep with his whiskers in or out of the blankets?"

"Always sleep with 'em out," said Kris. "The cold air makes 'em grow!"

8

In the next few days Doris found that, whether he was sane or not, Mr. Kringle's influence had spread amazingly. Mr. Macy had advertised the idea, and all Macy's employees now cheerfully recommended other stores to their customers. Not only had Macy's gained many new accounts, but the idea was spreading from coast to coast. It became the subject of articles and editorials, comedians joked about it, and Mr. Kringle was the center, the symbol of it all. In spite of herself, Doris was impressed. She admitted as much to Kris, who smiled happily: it was the first encouraging sign. He seemed to be making progress with Susan, too. On Sunday, he went to the Central Park Zoo with her, and as usual, the reindeer came running up to him and ate out of his hand. Susan was very much impressed, and as they walked on together, the old man broached the subject of her Christmas wish. Though she seemed to have no wishes at all, she must want *something*.

Susan hesitated a long time before she answered. She had only one wish. She wished for a *real* house where she and her mother could live. It would have a big yard with trees and a swing, so she could run out and play any time she wanted instead of having to wait for someone to take her to the park. From inside her little purse she took a worn and folded magazine page and handed it to him. It was an architect's drawing of a charming little Colonial home. Susan explained the floor plan in detail.

Kris gulped. "That's a tall order; but I'll do my best."

"If you're Santa," Susan said, "you can get it for me! If you can't, you're only a nice man with a white beard, like Mother says."

Susan had placed Kris squarely on the spot. He began to worry a little. "Every child can't get every wish," he told her, "but that doesn't mean there isn't a Santa Claus. Some children wish for things they couldn't possibly use. Besides, if every child got what he wanted right away, life wouldn't be half so much fun, would it? Sometimes it's better to keep on wishing, so that when you get your wish you really appreciate it."

"But I've wished for this house a long time," she told him, "and I *will* appreciate it!"

So it was up to Kris now, and he realized that there was only one way he could make Susan's wish come true. Mr. and Mrs. Fred Gayley might live in such a house, but Doris Walker could not swing it alone. That night, he casually questioned Fred about his relationship with Doris. Fred admitted that he was in love with her but could make no headway at all, and he told Kris what her first marriage had done to her.

"We've got to do something!" Kris said with determination.

"You're right, we do," said Fred. "But what?"

Kris was full of ideas. He persuaded Fred to take Doris out to dinner the following evening. She had steadfastly refused up to now. This time, Kris convinced him, things would be different.

The next morning, Kris gave Doris a great sales talk about Fred, and about the need for recreation for someone who worked as hard as she did, and Doris agreed with everything he said. So when Fred appeared in the store at closing time, Kris beamed at him happily. Had Fred come to take Doris to dinner? Fred shook his head. Doris was much too busy for anything but a sandwich and coffee at her desk. So Fred had stopped by for Kris. *They* could go home together.

"Perhaps if I talked to her—" Kris began.

"It's no use," Fred told him. "I've talked myself hoarse."

"I see," Kris mused. "Well, we'll have to think of something."

There was a peculiar glint in Mr. Kringle's eyes as he retired to the locker room to change.

It seemed to Fred that he took a long time there. Finally Fred went to the locker room to find him. The old man had gone some time ago, the porter told him. What *was* Kris up to? Fred went to Doris's office and phoned. Nobody answered in his apartment. Doris called the Maplewood Home, but Kris had not been there.

By now Doris, too, was alarmed, for Kris had left the locker room nearly three hours ago. They checked all the police stations and hospitals, and even called the Bellevue psychiatric wards. Kris was no place to be found. As the evening wore on, Doris's anxiety grew; she had grown much fonder of Mr. Kringle than she had realized.

"I'm frankly amazed," Fred told her. "It's not like you to get so upset about an eccentric old man."

"Kris is not just an eccentric old man, Fred," said Doris. "He's much more than—he's—" Doris couldn't find the words.

Fred was elated. "I know just what you mean," he said.

On the way home, exhausted, Fred and Doris stopped off at the Central Park Zoo, but Jim had not seen Kris. That was the last straw, and to add to Doris's unhappiness, she had lost a brooch, a treasured heirloom, and knew she'd never see it again.

When Fred left Doris at her apartment, she was on the verge of tears. His heart went out to her, but he knew her too well to say anything tender or comforting. The evening had brought them closer than ever before, but any acknowledgment of this he knew would only frighten her right back into her shell again.

He said good night and turned to go, but Doris seemed reluctant to see him leave. "I—I don't know how I could have gone through the evening without you," she said.

Fred smiled. "I'm glad I could be helpful."

"You were more than helpful, Fred," she said. "And—and I'm more than grateful." Tears welled up in her eyes and she took a little step toward him, raising her head. For a fleeting second Fred thought she was going to kiss him. But something caught her and her face froze into a smile as she closed the door.

Fred was smiling to himself as he entered his dark apartment, but cold fear about Kris had begun to grip his heart. Then, as he snapped on the light in his bedroom, he suppressed a bellow—for there in his bed lay Mr. Kringle peacefully asleep. Fred quickly snapped off the light again, but Kris was already sitting up eagerly to ask Fred what had happened.

"We nearly went crazy, that's what happened!" Fred told him. "Why didn't you answer the phone? Doris and I've been looking for you all over town."

"Oh, you have—*together*, eh?" Kris had a twinkle in his eye. "Didn't you enjoy it?" Well, yes—Fred admitted that they had. "And that's what I hoped would happen!" Kris said with satisfaction.

"You ought to be ashamed of yourself," Fred told him. "I'm going over to tell Doris before she spends a sleepless night."

"Yes, do, by all means," said Kris, beaming. "That'll give you a little more time together!"

Doris came to the door in a sheer, ruffled dressing gown, her hair streaming down her back. Fred had never seen her looking so feminine or appealing. She was so relieved by his news that she quite forgot her appearance as she let Fred in. But she couldn't understand why the old man had done it.

Fred tried to explain. "It seems Mr. Kringle is playing Cupid as well as Santa Claus," he said. "He thinks we should spend more time together."

"Oh!" said Doris. But she didn't seem to mind the idea as much as Fred had thought she would. "In that case," she said, "you'd better stay and have a cup of coffee."

Fred enjoyed the next half hour, sitting on the couch with Doris, more than any he could remember. But as he rose to leave there was a terrified cry from Susan's room. He rushed in and caught the child up in his arms, and Doris followed. As Fred comforted her, Susan awoke from her nightmare, and when she saw Fred a smile of happiness broke out on her tear-streaked face. "Oh, Uncle Fred, it's you," she said with great relief and reassurance, and Doris was touched by the scene.

As Fred said good night to Doris he took her tenderly in his arms and kissed her—and neither of them mentioned Kris.

9

Fred entered the imposing portals of Tiffany's the following afternoon to buy Doris a brooch. But none of the very handsome ones the elderly clerk showed him looked like the one Doris had lost. The clerk thought he knew what Fred had in mind. Unfortunately he had nothing like that at the moment. "Why don't you try Cartier's?" he suggested. "They have some lovely things."

Fred stared at the clerk in amazement.

"Cartier's sent me here," he said.

"Oh, yes," remarked the clerk, "Cartier's have sent us a number of customers lately."

Fred left the store still lost in wonder. He had seen news stories heralding the wave of good will that Kris had started; but now he realized how widespread it had become. If Tiffany's were sending people to Cartier's, anything could happen!

After trying many stores, Fred had finally found a brooch like the one Doris had lost, and he entered Macy's in high spirits. To his surprise

everyone in the store seemed to reflect his mood. The doorman beamed at him pleasantly; the elevator boys wore grins as big as his; even the customers who jammed the aisles were jovial.

Fred found Doris in one corner of the toy department where a large crowd had gathered. There, in a special setting in front of a Christmas tree, Mr. Macy was formally presenting Mr. Kringle with a check from the company "in appreciation of the wonderful new spirit which you have brought not only to Macy's but to the entire city as well!"

Mr. Macy jokingly asked Kris what he intended to do with all that money, but Kris knew exactly what he would do. "I'm going to make this a particularly happy Christmas for a doctor who has been very kind to me," he said. "I'm going to give him an X-ray machine."

"We'll get it for you at cost!" said Mr. Macy.

Fred turned to Doris and took a little package from his pocket. "I have a little presentation to make myself," he said.

Doris was touched and delighted by the brooch, and as they walked back toward her office, she slipped her arm through his, right in front of the entire toy department. "It seems to me you're catching the Kringle spirit, too," Fred told her.

Doris smiled. "I'm afraid I am," she said.

10

That evening, Doris saw Susan playing with several other children. She was surprised because up to now Susan had been more or less a lone-wolf cub in the neighborhood. Now here she was, knee-deep in a game of fantasy and obviously liking it. Doris couldn't help but be pleased, for she had never seen Susan enjoying herself so much.

At dinner, Doris, too, seemed a different person, happy, warm, and relaxed. Kris was in the clouds. As he read a story to Susan after dinner, he happily assured the child that she would get her wish for Christmas.

In the kitchen, Doris was regretfully explaining to Fred that she had to leave him for the evening. Mr. Sawyer, the vocational guidance expert, was giving a lecture before a group of personnel executives, and Doris, as chairman of the committee, had arranged for Sawyer to speak and was to introduce him. Due to the nature of the lecture, Doris thought it better not to mention where she was going in front of Kris.

After she had gone, Fred and Kris put Susan to bed. While Fred went next door to get his pipe, Kris's eye caught a mimeographed postcard on Doris's desk. He picked it up and read:

Doris Walker, Chairman

8:30 P.M., Wed., Dec. 18

Neighborhood Center Auditorium, Greenwich Village

Speaker: MR. ALBERT SAWYER

Subject: EXPLODING THE MYTH OF SANTA CLAUS

An open discussion will follow the lecture.

Bristling, Kris picked up his hat and his cane and stalked out.

At the Neighborhood Center, the usher refused to let Kris into the auditorium, since admission was by invitation only. But determined to hear what Sawyer had to say, Kris wandered down a hallway beside the auditorium. Coming to an unlocked door, he opened it quietly and walked up a few steps. He found himself backstage, and could hear Doris saying, ". . . and so it gives me great pleasure to introduce Mr. Albert Sawyer."

After polite applause, Sawyer began by saying that the setting hardly seemed appropriate, since a children's theater was giving its Christmas production on this stage and the set, which contained a large window and a huge fireplace back of the speaker, could not be removed between performances.

"The symbolic figure of Santa Claus," Sawyer said, "is a classic expression of the wishful dreaming of all children. He is the omnipotent giver, the generous father. Mature adults who seek to perpetrate this myth reveal themselves as incomplete personalities, unable to face reality."

At this remark there was a burst of laughter from the audience. Sawyer looked up, disturbed. He did not know that behind him, at the back of the stage, the figure of Kris Kringle was framed in the large cellophane window. Doris had spotted Kris and was in a panic, but though mystified by the laughter, Sawyer continued his lecture. Fathers who felt guilty toward their children often wished to act as Santa, he said, showering them with gifts, and wealthy men who played Santa in their philanthropies covered guilt feelings about their money.

Kris had begun to sputter and shake his cane in anger. Doris tried to quiet him with grimaces and gestures, but as Sawyer went on, Kris's mutterings grew more voluble. He now had but one idea—to get out onto the stage.

Finally he saw a small aperture in the scenery, and as Sawyer declared, "Far from doing good in the world, this vicious myth has done more harm than opium," Mr. Kringle burst out onto the stage while the audience rocked and screamed with laughter.

"Now look here . . . !" Kris began.

"*I* am giving this lecture, Mr. Kringle," Sawyer declared. The name of Kringle brought another laugh.

"There is to be open discussion," replied Kringle, "and who is better qualified than myself to answer your absurd remarks?"

"No discussion until *after* the lecture," said Sawyer.

"Very well," said Kris. He walked to one side of the stage and waited for Sawyer to resume. Completely flustered, poor Mr. Sawyer attempted to do so, but each time he made a remark, Kris's face clearly indicated his reaction. All Kris had to do was raise one eyebrow to bring a roar of laughter.

It was at this point that Fred slipped into the auditorium. After trying to locate Kris in vain, he had found the card on Doris's desk and rushed here to tell her. Grinning when he saw Kris on the platform, he sat down to watch. Struggling to continue, Sawyer began to stutter and to mix words up. His reference to "Clanta Sause" sent the audience into stitches. Finally, one sentence was so garbled that Kris could not resist the temptation. He held up two fingers at Mr. Sawyer.

"How many fingers do you see?" he asked.

This was too much for Sawyer. White with rage, he advanced ominously. "I refuse to continue until this old jackanapes is removed."

"Jackanapes, am I?" Kris said, raising his cane. Sawyer grabbed for it furiously. With a quick tug Kringle pulled it free, but as he did so, the stick grazed Mr. Sawyer's cheek.

"He hit me!" screamed Sawyer, jumping back. "I'm going to call the police!"

"No! No!" cried Doris, quickly stepping between them.

"Very well," said Sawyer, nursing a slightly red spot on his cheek. "I shall not call the police—now. I will see you in Mr. Shellhammer's office tomorrow morning and we shall decide on a course of action." He glared at Kris. "Society has ways of protecting itself against such people!" And he strode from the platform.

11

Early the next morning, Doris found herself facing the combined wrath of Messrs. Sawyer and Shellhammer. Giving a lurid account of Kris's behavior the night before, Sawyer had convinced Shellhammer that Kringle was extremely dangerous. After all the publicity and buildup, Macy's Santa had turned out to be a nut.

"We've got to do something at once!" said Shellhammer.

"He's just a kind old man," Doris said. "He won't ever . . ."

"Oh, but he *will*, Mrs. Walker!" Mr. Sawyer said. "He's evidently entered into a violent phase. The very least that should be done is to have him examined by competent psychiatrists at once."

This seemed sound to Shellhammer. "There's no harm in that. If he's harmless, he can come right back."

Doris was shaken. She knew that Kris had not been violent and she disliked Sawyer intensely, but under the cirumstances, Mr. Shellhammer was right. Anyway, Kris would obviously pass any sanity test with flying colors. She acquiesced with a nod.

Mr. Sawyer said he would be glad to arrange for the examination right away. "The only problem now is how to get him out of the store without creating another—er—situation."

"Mrs. Walker, you'll have to explain it to him," said Shellhammer. "After all, you're his friend. He trusts you."

But Doris flatly refused. She had become far too fond of the old man to bring herself to hurt him.

"Never mind," said Sawyer with a quiet nod to Shellhammer. "I know how we can do it."

Kris was on his dais as usual when Shellhammer approached. They wanted to have his picture taken with the mayor down at City Hall, and a car was waiting.

So Kris left his dais and went with him, and it was not until he entered the limousine and saw Mr. Sawyer in front that he suspected anything.

"Where to?" the driver asked.

"Bellevue," said Sawyer.

Kris started to rise angrily but the two men forced him back into his seat. He sat there stunned as the car moved slowly down the rain-soaked street. Finally he said, "Does Doris Walker know about this?"

"Of course," said Sawyer. "She arranged the whole thing."

From that minute, Kris was a beaten man. If Doris could do this to him, all he had worked for was a hopeless cause. When they arrived, Kris seemed to have lost all interest in what was going on.

12

For Doris, the rest of the afternoon was an ordeal. She kept going to the door to see if Kris had returned, but the dais remained empty. She tried to learn where he had been taken, but all Shellhammer said was that Sawyer had arranged for an examination and gone off with Kris in the car.

Then, near closing time, Doris received a hurried and furious telephone call from Fred. The psychopathic ward at Bellevue had called to ask him to bring down Kris's toilet articles right away. "They said he wouldn't be needing any street clothes for quite a while."

"Bellevue! So that's where Sawyer took him—!" Doris's voice was choked with rage.

"What's this all about anyway?" Fred asked indignantly.

Doris told him that Sawyer had threatened to send for the police, so she had no choice but to consent to an examination. No one had mentioned Bellevue.

"But why did you let them take him *anywhere?*" demanded Fred. Doris tried to explain, but Fred had no time to argue. He had to get to the hospital. "I'll see you later, Doris," he said.

At Bellevue, Mr. Kringle had answered questions in a dull haze of indifference, often saying yes to ridiculous ones because he was paying no attention. He kept thinking, "How could she have done it? How *could* she have done it?"

Taking his Santa Claus costume away and substituting a limp gray dressing gown, they had placed Kris in a long, bare room with a lot of other men in shroudlike dressing gowns. He sat in the chair staring blankly at the wall.

It was there Fred found him: a little, tired old man with a white beard. All the youthful, eager brightness was gone from his eyes. "This is nonsense, Kris," Fred told him. "You're just as sane as anybody and a lot saner than most!" Kris shook his head, and Fred went on. "I'll have you out of here in no time."

But Kris did not want to be released. Doris had deceived him, just when he thought she was beginning to believe in him. "She must have been humoring me all the time," he said sadly. "If that's how sane people behave, I'd rather stay here."

"But Sawyer threatened to send for the police. She thought he was taking you to a private doctor."

"Then why didn't *she* come and explain the whole thing? No—she had doubts about *me*, Fred. And it's not just Doris. It's men like Sawyer—dishonest and vicious. Yet he's out there and I'm in here. Well, if *he's* normal, *I* don't want to be."

"But you can't just think of yourself, Kris," Fred argued. "What happens to you matters to a lot of people. People like me, who believe in you and what you

"*This is nonsense, Kris,*" *Fred told him.* "*You're just as sane as anybody and a lot saner than most!*"

stand for, and people like little Susan who are just beginning to. You can't quit now, Kris. Don't you see?"

As Kris thought this over, the light began to come back into his eyes. "Maybe you're right," he said slowly.

"Of course I am! You wouldn't let us down."

"I should be ashamed of myself!" The ring was back in Kris's voice. "Maybe we won't win, Fred, but we'll go down swinging!"

"Now you're talking!" Fred said jubilantly. "Just sit tight, Kris, and I'll have you out of here in no time."

But it wasn't as easy as Fred had thought. He finally managed to see the chief psychiatrist, Dr. Rogers, a kindly, quiet man who sent for Kris's file. Fred explained that he had lived with Kris, who was as sane as any man. This whole procedure was merely revenge on Sawyer's part. But Dr. Rogers was quietly unconvinced. In the file, every interview, every test had led clearly to this same conclusion: Kris was unbalanced, if not actually dangerous, at least potentially so. On the basis of the reports, they would have to file immediate commitment papers.

It was then that Fred fully realized what had happened. Kris had failed these tests deliberately! But it was hopeless to try to convince Dr. Rogers of this. And Fred had promised Kris his freedom! He thanked Dr. Rogers and left. His job was almost impossible and he knew it.

13

Judge Henry X. Harper was sitting in his chambers reading some routine mail and wondering what to get his wife for Christmas when Finley, his clerk, came in. Mr. Mara, from the state attorney-general's office, was there to see His Honor.

"Show him in—show him in!" said His Honor heartily.

Mr. Mara entered smiling, a folder in his hand. He and the judge were old friends. "Just some routine commitment papers, Your Honor," Mara said, placing them on the desk. Harper started to leaf through the thick file, and Mara said, "You'll find everything in order, Judge. The lunacy report from Bellevue is attached."

"I suppose I ought to read all this," sighed Harper.

"Take my word for it, Judge—it's cut and dried. This fellow thinks he's Santa Claus!"

"Oh, oh." Harper chuckled and reached for his pen.

Finley entered again. "A Mr. Gayley to see you, an attorney. It's about this Santa Claus case."

"Show him in." The judge sighed and put his pen down again.

Fred was polite but emphatic. His client, Mr. Kringle, was being railroaded, and he requested a proper hearing, with witnesses. "If Your Honor signs the commitment papers," said Fred, "I shall bring in a habeas corpus in the morning."

"That won't be necessary," said the judge. "We'll have a hearing. Ten o'clock Monday morning."

Outside, in Harper's anteroom, Mr. Sawyer sat nervously waiting to see Mr. Mara. Mr. Macy's words when he learned of Kris's absence were still ringing in Sawyer's ears: If Sawyer didn't get Kris released immediately, his career at Macy's was ended. As Sawyer waited, trying not to bite his nails, Fred left with a nod to Finley.

"Who—who was that?" asked Sawyer anxiously.

"Mr. Kringle's lawyer," Finley told him.

Sawyer didn't like the sound of that at all. "I'd like to drop the whole case right now," he said when Mara finally appeared. But Mara shook his head. A committal had to go through the regular routine. There would be a hearing Monday morning. "But don't worry!" Mara went on. "Gayley's just a young lawyer trying to get himself a little free publicity."

Publicity! The worst thing that could *possibly* happen. Sawyer dashed down the hall and caught Fred just as he was getting in the elevator. He introduced himself, and told Fred that Mr. Macy was very anxious to avoid any publicity. If Gayley would cooperate, Mr. Macy would find some very generous way of expressing his appreciation.

Fred laughed, for Macy had nothing to do with this, he knew. Sawyer was in the frying pan and squirming to get out. "I'm glad you mentioned publicity," said Fred. "I'm going to need all the publicity I can get to win this case." And he walked away into the court reporters' room.

The next morning, front-page stories appeared in the New York papers, for a celebrity, a nationwide symbol of good will, had been charged with lunacy. A radio commentator summed it up: "Kris Kringle, the simple, kindly old man responsible for the wave of good will sweeping this city, will appear before Judge Henry X. Harper on Monday morning, charged with, of all things, *lunacy*. Incredible! If bringing back the true Christmas spirit is a form of insanity, then these are very strange times indeed!"

At his home, Judge Harper heard this and beamed. His name was on the air! But Charlie Halloran, listening with him, wasn't pleased at all. Charlie was a power behind many political thrones and a lifelong friend and advisor of Harper's.

"Henry," he said thoughtfully, "I think you ought to take a few weeks off.

184

Go fishing—go hunting—go anywhere. This case is dynamite, and you've got to let some other judge handle it—someone who isn't coming up for re-election next year. You'd be every little kid's villain, and their parents would hate you, too."

Harper laughed. "Nonsense," he said, wondering why Charlie was upset.

But at that moment, Mrs. Harper came into the room, calling her grandchildren to come and say good night. They scampered in and gave their granny a big hug and a good-night kiss, but walked coldly past Harper and up to bed.

The judge was dumbfounded, but Mrs. Harper said, "I don't blame them! Any man who'll put Santa Claus on trial for lunacy—!"

"You see what I mean," said Charlie drily.

14

The courtroom was packed with reporters, photographers, and a large slice of the general public. Mr. Mara slouched in his chair, sorry that he had ever been handed the case. It would be one of those dragged-out affairs, for Kringle would now deny he had ever said he was Santa Claus.

The bailiff chanted his "Hear ye—Hear ye," the judge entered, and Mara rose to call his first witness, Mr. Kringle. Kris rose and entered the witness box, and Harper studied the old man. He certainly didn't fit the description in the report.

"Good morning, Your Honor!" said Mr. Kringle, beaming brightly. In spite of himself, the judge smiled and nodded in return.

"What is your name?" asked Mara.

"Kris Kringle."

"Where do you live?"

"That's what this hearing will decide." This brought a chuckle from the courtroom.

"A very sound answer, Mr. Kringle," said His Honor.

"So you believe that you are Santa Claus?"

"Of course!" said Mr. Kringle.

A stunned silence fell over the courtroom. Judge Harper's face fell. Why, the old man was admitting his insanity!

"The state rests, Your Honor," Mara said, and sat down. Kris left the stand, but Fred was on his feet now, and he seemed not a bit perturbed.

"The state declares," he began, "that this man is not sane because he believes himself to be Santa Claus."

"I'm afraid that's reasonable and logical," said Harper.

"Not necessarily," said Fred quietly. "You believe yourself to be Judge Harper, and nobody questions your sanity, Your Honor, because you *are* Judge Harper. If Mr. Kringle is the person he believes himself to be, then he is just as sane as you are."

"Of course," said the judge. "But he isn't Santa Claus."

"Your Honor, I intend to prove that he *is*."

There was bedlam in the room. This was crazy, but it was good copy. Flash bulbs exploded. Reporters dashed for phones as Judge Harper banged his gavel and adjourned the court.

Doris read the stories in the papers on her way home. She was worried. Fred was making a fool of himself and jeopardizing his job, and when he came over that evening she told him so. But Fred was confident. Public sympathy was behind Kris, he said. As for his job, Doris was right. Old Haislip, the senior partner, had called him in that afternoon. They were an old established firm, and they couldn't have a junior partner making a spectacle of himself. Unless he dropped the case at once they would drop him.

"Then you'll have to give it up," said Doris.

"I can't, Doris," Fred said. "Kris needs me, and I can't let him down. I told old Mr. Haislip so and that was that!"

Now Doris was really upset. How could Fred be so quixotic? "How could you do a crazy thing like this! I thought you were sensible, not a—a star gazer."

"I guess I am a star gazer—and a darn good lawyer, too. I'll make out all right. What it boils down to is this: you don't have faith in me."

"Of course I do, but—"

"No, you don't," Fred interrupted. "Faith is believing in things when common sense tells you not to, and you've just got too much common sense."

"It's a good thing one of us has," said Doris heatedly.

"Can't you get over being afraid?" Fred pleaded. "Can't you let yourself believe in people like Kris—in fun, joy, love?"

Doris stiffened almost imperceptibly. "You can't pay the rent with intangibles," she said.

"And you can't live a life without them," Fred answered. "I thought Kris and I had changed you, Doris. I hoped you'd be ready to string along with me, but—I guess you're not." Fred gave a hopeless shrug. "Well, I can see there's no use talking. It's just no go."

"No, I suppose not," Doris said slowly with a bitter little smile. "It's funny," she added, "but with all my common sense, I thought it was really going to work out this time."

"So did I," said Fred. He picked up his hat and coat, hesitated, then said "Good night" and left.

15

The next day at the hearing, most of the packed courtroom was rooting for Kris. The rest were there to see what that crazy young lawyer was going to do.

Fred's first witness was Mr. Macy, who seemed rather uneasy as he took the oath. He identified Kringle as his employee, and said that he believed him to be sane and truthful.

Mr. Mara jumped up. "Mr. Macy, you are under oath," he warned. "Do you honestly believe that this man is Santa Claus?"

Macy hesitated, but this was Macy's Santa; he had no choice. "Yes!" he said in a loud, defiant voice.

"That is all," said Fred.

On his way back to his seat, Macy's eye caught Sawyer seated in the third row. He glared. "You're fired!" he said.

Dr. Pierce was the next to take the stand. The physician at the Maplewood Home had known Kris for many years. Did he, too, believe him to be Santa Claus? "I do," said Dr. Pierce quietly.

Again Mara was on his feet. Had the doctor any scientific reason for this opinion?

"Yes," said Dr. Pierce, "I have."

Mr. Mara sat down, and Fred said, "Did you express a Christmas wish to Mr. Kringle?"

"Yes," Dr. Pierce said. "I wanted an X-ray machine for Maplewood but I knew it was too expensive. Then yesterday an X-ray machine arrived with a card that said 'Merry Christmas from Kris Kringle.' "

Next Fred put the zoo keeper on the stand, and Jim testified that reindeer ate right out of Kris's hand. This was too much for Mr. Mara. The whole line of testimony was ridiculous, irrelevant, and immaterial. There was no Santa Claus and everybody knew it. This brought a murmur of disagreement in the courtroom. Could Mr. Mara, Fred said, offer any proof that there was no Santa Claus?

No, of course Mr. Mara couldn't! They were wasting the court's time, he said hotly, with childish nonsense. Was there or was there not a Santa Claus? He asked the judge for an immediate ruling.

Judge Harper looked unhappy indeed, for officially there was only one decision. But then he saw Charlie Halloran shaking his head and gesturing toward the judge's chambers. "The court will take a short recess to consider the matter," Harper announced.

"Look," said Charlie when they were alone, "if you go back and rule that there's no Santa Claus, you might as well start looking for a chicken farm right now. We couldn't even put you up for the primaries."

"But I can't say there *is* a Santa Claus. I'm a judge. They'd try *me* for insanity."

"Henry, I'm telling you—if you rule that there's no Santa Claus you can count on getting just three votes—yours, mine, and that fellow Mara's."

His Honor shook his head and raised two fingers. "We're Democrats. Mara's a Republican." He returned to the bench and called the court to order. "Many people firmly believe in Santa Claus," he said. "Others do not. The tradition of American justice demands a broad and unprejudiced view. So this court will hear any evidence on either side."

Suppressed cheers greeted this announcement, but Mr. Mara said scornfully, could Mr. Gayley produce any such evidence? Yes, he could. Would Mr. Thomas Mara, Junior, please take the stand?

A seven-year-old boy dashed down the aisle. Completely bewildered at the appearance of his son, Mr. Mara glared at his wife, standing near an aisle seat. She held up a subpoena and shook her head helplessly.

"Do you believe in Santa Claus?" Fred asked Tommy.

"Sure I do. He gave me a sled last year!"

"And what does he look like, Tommy?"

Tommy pointed at Kris. "There he is, right there!"

"Tell me, Tommy, why are you so sure there is a Santa Claus?"

"Because my Daddy told me so!" said Thomas, Jr. "And he wouldn't tell me a thing that wasn't so!" There was a roar of laughter, and even the judge grinned as he rapped for order.

"Thank you, Tommy," said Fred quietly, and sat down.

Tommy scrambled down from the witness box. On the way to his mother, he passed close to Mr. Kringle, leaned over and said, "Don't forget! An official football helmet!"

"You shall have it, Tommy," Kris said, and Tommy ran happily back to his mother.

"Your Honor," Mr. Mara said slowly, "the State of New York concedes the existence of Santa Claus."

"This court concurs." Harper beamed at Charlie Halloran in the crowd. He had gotten out of that one nicely.

But Fred still had a major hurdle ahead of him, and Mara knew it. "Having so conceded, Your Honor," he was saying, "we ask that Mr. Gayley submit *proof* that Mr. Kringle is *the one and only Santa Claus!*"

"Your point is well taken, Mr. Mara," the judge said. Was Mr. Gayley prepared to show this? Fred was not prepared to do so at this time. He asked for an adjournment.

"This hearing stands adjourned till tomorrow afternoon at three," Harper announced.

Fred left the courtroom with a heavy heart. What "competent authority" could he possibly produce?

16

That evening at supper, Susan asked her mother, "Is Mr. Kringle coming over tonight? He hasn't been here for so long."

"Susan, Mr. Kringle may never be able to come here again." And Doris tried to explain. "You see, it's because he says he's Santa Claus, and some people don't believe that. So they're having a sort of trial."

"But he *must* be Santa Claus, he's so sweet and kind and jolly. Nobody could be like Mr. Kringle *except* Santa Claus."

"I think perhaps you're right," said Doris slowly.

"Is Mr. Kringle unhappy, Mother?"

"I'm afraid he is, dear," Doris answered.

"Then I'm going to write him right away, to cheer him up."

After supper, Doris helped her address the letter: To Mr. Kris Kringle, New York County Court House, Center and Pearl Streets, New York City. Doris promised to mail the letter right away. When Susan went off to play, she read it over, smiling:

Dear Mr. Kringle,
    I miss you very much and I hope I will see you soon. I know it will come out all right. I believe you are Santa Claus and I hope you are not sad.

Susan Walker

Doris added a footnote: "I believe in you, too," and signed it "Doris." She sealed the envelope, put on a special delivery stamp, and dropped it in the mail chute in the hall.

Late that night, down at the main post office, Al Golden was scowling as he sorted the mail. Christmas mail was a pain in the neck. It wasn't only the extra packages—it was those letters to Santa Claus; literally thousands of them. They had to be kept for thirty days, too—some crazy law.

Suddenly Al stopped sorting and held out a letter. "Here's a new one!" he said. "I've seen 'em write to Santa Claus at the North Pole, but this kid writes to Mr. Kris Kringle, New York County Court House! Can you beat that?"

"The kid's right: that's where he is," said Lou Spoletti. "They got him on trial down there. Claims he's Santa Claus. A lot of folks think he is, but some D.A. claims he's nuts."

Al looked thoughtful as he threw Susan's letter into the special delivery bag. "You mean there's a guy who really might be Santa Claus? This might be the answer to our prayers!"

"Why didn't I think of that!" said Lou.

"Order a special big truck—order a couple of 'em," said Al. "All the Santa Claus mail we got goes to Mr. Kris Kringle, down at the court house!"

17

In the judge's chambers the following afternoon, Charlie Halloran was at Harper again. "Today is Christmas Eve, Henry. If you sentence Santa Claus to a padded cell on Christmas Eve, you're liable to be mobbed—or murdered!"

The judge was really nervous now. If Gayley could find the slightest pretext of "competent authority," Harper would give him every break. Kris seemed to be only a kindly old man, but unless something miraculous happened, Harper would have to have him put away.

Fred was deeply worried as the judge came in. The courtroom was tense, as if all realized that the finale was at hand. In a few hours, Santa would be starting his annual ride over the rooftops. Fred had wired the mayor, the governor, and many other officials to obtain competent authority—all to no avail.

Mr. Mara was reading out reports from various mental institutions. One had four men who thought they were Napoleon, two who thought they were Caruso, one who thought he was Tarzan. Judge Harper's face grew long and everyone looked glum except Kris, who was even merrier than usual because Susan's letter had been delivered just as court reconvened. No matter how this hearing ended, his efforts had not been in vain!

Meantime, Fred was feeling desperate when there was a tap on his shoulder. He looked up in surprise as a court attendant whispered to him. Looking puzzled, Fred followed the man out of the courtroom. Mara was still droning on as Fred returned, his manner suddenly changed, and he sneaked a confident wink at Kris.

Finally Mara finished and the judge turned to Fred. "Have you further evidence to submit, Mr. Gayley?" he asked, in the tone of one who knew the answer.

"I have, Your Honor," said Fred, rising. He held a *World Almanac* in his hand. "It concerns the Post Office Department, an official agency of the U.S. government, created in July 1776 by the Second Continental Congress, and now one of the largest government organizations in the United States. Last year it did a gross business of $1,112,877,174.48."

Mr. Mara's patience was wearing thin. "It is gratifying to know that the Post Office is doing so nicely," he said, "but it hardly has any bearing on this case."

"It has a great deal of bearing, Your Honor," said Fred. "If I may be allowed to proceed—"

"By all means," said Harper, grasping at any straw.

"U.S. postal laws make it a *prison offense* to deliver mail to the wrong party," Fred went on. He listed a number of safeguards used by the department to assure the correct delivery of mail.

Mr. Mara rose. "Your Honor," he said irritably, "we are ready to concede that the U.S. Post Office is a most authoritative organization! Anything to get on with this hearing."

Fred then introduced three letters as evidence. "Mark them Exhibits A, B, and C," he told the clerk. "These letters," said Fred, "addressed to 'Santa Claus, U.S.A.,' have just been delivered to Mr. Kringle, here in this building, by the Post Office. I submit, Your Honor, that this is positive

proof that a competent federal authority recognizes Mr. Kringle to be the one and only Santa Claus."

The judge took the letters and glanced at them, impressed, but Mara said, "Three letters are hardly positive proof."

"I have further exhibits," Fred replied, "but I hesitate to produce them."

Judge Harper was impatient. "Just bring them in, young man! Put them right here on the bench."

"But Your Honor—" Fred began again.

"I said put them right here!" ordered the judge.

"Yes, we'd all like to see them, I'm sure," added Mara sarcastically.

"Very well." Fred nodded toward a door, and a line of attendants came in wheeling hand trucks loaded with bags of mail. One by one, they dumped them before the judge's bench until it was almost overwhelmed in an avalanche of letters. "Your Honor," said Fred, "every one of these is simply addressed: *Santa Claus.*"

Harper looked up from the pile and banged his gavel. "The United States of America believes this man is Santa Claus. This court will not dispute it— case dismissed!"

Kris stood up. He was smiling, but there were tears in his eyes as he dashed up to the bench. "Thank you, Your Honor," he said. "And Merry Christmas!"

Judge Harper was beaming broadly. "Merry Christmas to you, Mr. Kringle!" he said, extending his hand. He cast a quick glance at Charlie Halloran, who gave him a happy wink.

In the excitement that followed, Fred was surrounded by admirers, photographed, slapped on the back and congratulated—but he could not find Kris. The reporters also wanted pictures of the one and only Santa Claus, but Kris had disappeared.

"Well," said one of the reporters, "it's five o'clock on Christmas Eve. I'll bet the old boy is hitching up the reindeer now!"

"And it's just beginning to snow, too," said another.

In the back of the courtroom Doris rose, started for the door—then hesitated. Perhaps she ought to congratulate Fred. As she stood there a couple of reporters passed her. "You've got to hand it to Gayley," one reporter was saying. "He believed in the old man from the start—and before he was finished, he had everybody else believing in him, too."

The point hit home, and Doris left the courtroom silently. By now everybody was headed for the door except the clerk, who was trying to extricate himself from the mountain of letters—letters that were there only because a little girl believed in Kris Kringle and wrote to tell him so.

On his way out Mr. Mara mused over what had happened. He knew he should be angry, but actually he felt rather cheerful. Suddenly he glanced at his wristwatch. "Good Lord," he said anxiously. "I've got to get that football helmet!"

18

Early Christmas morning, Susan tiptoed into the living room to see the presents under the tree. There were lots of exciting-looking packages, but not *the* present Kris had promised her. She hadn't expected to find a house under the tree, but she did expect some sign to show that her wish was answered. Doris came in to find Susan in tears: Mr. Kringle wasn't Santa Claus after all! Her mother was right. There *was* no Santa Claus, Susan said. The whole business was a lot of silly nonsense. As she listened, Doris could almost hear herself—and it wasn't pleasant.

"But I was wrong when I said that. You *must* believe in Mr. Kringle, and keep on believing," Doris said, taking Susan in her arms. And she added, echoing Fred's words as much to herself as to Susan, "Faith is believing in things when common sense tells you not to. If you don't believe, you never get the things you really want." Doris had learned that, to her bitter sorrow. "Anyone can have faith when everything is fine. But real faith means *believing*, rain or shine."

Susan thought that over. Then she began murmuring with conviction: "I believe, I believe, I believe . . . "

The annual Christmas morning breakfast at the Maplewood Home was to have been especially festive this year for Mr. Kringle was coming back!— legally sane and therefore eligible to return. But Kris had failed to make his appearance. Dr. Pierce phoned Jim at the zoo. No sign of Kris, said Jim, looking out in the yard. What was worse—no sign of the reindeer either!

When he hung up, Jim dashed to the reindeers' shed, then stopped in amazement. There were his reindeer, sitting down in pairs, panting, their bodies covered with sweat and lather. Jim shook his head.

A few minutes later Kris came walking briskly into Maplewood, looking tired but full of good cheer. The greetings were effusive: they had been waiting for him to officiate by the Christmas tree, as he had for so many years. But before he could do so, Kris said, he had to make a call to invite some special guests—if that was all right.

Then Kris called Fred and asked him as a special favor to get Doris and Susan and bring them to Maplewood. He outlined the route for them to

take. The evening snowstorm had been quite severe—Fred had better follow Kris's instructions.

"Well," said Fred, "you know how things are, Kris."

"I know," said Kris, "but on Christmas morning—" So of course Fred agreed.

With some embarrassment Fred rang Doris's doorbell and explained what Kris had called about. Were they willing to go with him? Doris's manner was somewhat strained, but she said they would be glad to go.

It was a beautiful Christmas morning and the countryside glistened under the new layer of snow. The rather roundabout way Kris had recommended led through pleasant suburbs, each house with a gay Christmas wreath on the door. Suddenly Susan gave a cry and nearly jumped through the car window. There was *her* house—her Christmas present! It was exactly like the picture she had given Mr. Kringle! They must stop at once. Fred and Doris looked at each other in bewilderment as he stopped the car.

Susan was beside herself with excitement as she ran up the walk, opened the door, and went inside. Fred and Doris followed her past a small "For Sale" sign on the lawn.

The house was empty and gave evidence of recently departed tenants. A broken umbrella, some old overshoes, and a few boxes were scattered about. By now, Susan had seen the second floor. She came dashing down the stairs blazing with excitement. She told them of her Christmas wish to Mr. Kringle. It had come true! Each room was exactly as she had known it would be from the plan in the magazine.

"Mother, you were right about believing. See! I kept on believing, and you were right!" And she ran off to the back yard.

Fred looked at Doris. "Did you really tell Susan that?" he asked. Doris nodded silently, on the verge of tears. And then they were in each other's arms.

"Well, everybody believes in Mr. Kringle now," Fred said happily, and Doris nodded, still unable to speak. "This house made Susan believe in him," said Fred, "and it seems to be for sale. We can't let Kris down now, can we?"

Doris shook her head, smiling, and finally found her voice. "I never really doubted you in my heart," she said. "It was just my silly common sense."

"Well—it even makes sense to believe in me now," said Fred. "After all, I must be a pretty good lawyer. I legally proved to the world that a little old man from an old folks' home was Santa Claus!"

Then something caught Fred's eye. Standing in the corner near the fireplace was a cane, a common, ordinary cane just like the one Mr. Kringle always carried. Doris saw it, too.

"Oh, no!" she said. "It couldn't be!"

Fred scratched his head and gave her a wry smile. "But on the other hand, maybe I didn't do anything so wonderful after all!"

THE LORD OF MISRULE
by Norah Lofts

'Tis the Twelve Days of Christmas,
   a time to be merry.
Be carefree, be joyous
   but also be wary
Of he who is chosen
   to reign o'er the Yule—
Not the Steward, the Priest,
   not the Knight nor the Fool—
But the sovereign of mischief,
   the Lord of Misrule.

One of the most democratic bodies in Christendom was about to hold its annual meeting in the Steward's room at Soneborough Castle.

There were twelve of them. Twelve was not a magic number, like seven, but it had significance. There had been twelve Apostles, twelve men constituted a jury, and it was the Twelve Days of Christmas which they had met to discuss.

The Priest represented the Church—and all the spiritual aspects of the festival; the Knight would speak for the resident knights; the Jester for those who entertained; the Steward would guard the interests of his master and mistress. There were three freemen who ploughed their own acres, three

serfs who tilled their lord's, three indoor servants. Each man's vote was as good as the next.

The Steward took charge of the meeting and started the brown ale jug on its way. Pompously, and quite unnecessarily, he said, "You know the purpose of this meeting. It is to choose the Lord of Misrule, who will take charge of the revels from Christmas Eve until Twelfth Night."

The Priest gave a small silent sigh. He deplored the whole business; it had nothing to do with the birth of Our Lord; much of it was pagan in origin; it was noisy, unruly, sometimes downright disgusting, but it was custom and must, he supposed, be observed.

The Knight glanced at the time-keeping candle; the white section above each of the colored rings burned roughly for an hour. He hoped the meeting would end before the next marker was reached. It was his duty to be here—and he was a man mindful of his duty—but he preferred the company of his fellows and wine to ale.

"May your Christmas be merry," the Steward said, raising his cup. "We will now begin. . . ."

Upstairs in the solar the ladies were stitching, putting the final touches to gowns and headdresses for the festive season. They were aware of the meeting taking place in the Steward's room, and presently the Countess herself spoke of it. "It is to be hoped that they do not choose another coarse fellow. Last year was a misery." For the benefit of those who had not been present last year, she explained. "The oaf ordered *all* headgear to be removed. That included my barbe."

The ladies made noises of sympathy, genuine or feigned. They knew what *that* meant. Ladies getting on in years forsook the decorative, provocative headdresses—the steeples, the butterflies—and took to the barbe, a merciful device, not unlike a nun's wimple. Fitting close, it concealed the

furrowed forehead, the sagging jowls, the wrinkled chin. It even hid a shriveled neck and a bosom of which one could no longer be proud, for its lower half consisted of a pleated frill, stiffly starched and reaching halfway to the waist.

"To be old," the Countess said, "is no shame. It is hardship." She had been a great beauty in her youth, and as her looks faded, she had taken pains to hide the damage Time had inflicted. Her husband had not, for some years, seen her without her barbe by day, or, if he came—rarely now—to say good night, a cloud of gauze wrapped round her.

She looked at her ladies, most of them young, and said, "It will come to you, too, should you live long enough."

And she thought—Yes, even to little Felicity there, quiet in her corner, her lute beside her, ready to play a pleasant tune when asked to do so. A very meek child and quite pretty, not a penny of dowry, of course. And nothing to be done about that. If one undertook to provide a dowry, however modest, for every young kinswoman, however remote, there would be no end to it: one would be ruined. The Countess had offered what she could: a place in her household, bed and board, a chance for the child to be seen, to offer her wares—youth, the prettiness that was so different from beauty, and an amiable nature—on one of the most active, if not the largest, marriage markets in England. She'd come at Michaelmas, and for a short time it had looked as though she had attracted the attention of the senior resident knight; nearing forty, due for retirement, Sir Baldwin was not without means. What could be more suitable?

Something had gone wrong. Possibly, despite his means and his age, Sir Baldwin had been put off when he learned that the girl had no dowry. Or perhaps he had considered that she was too young, too ignorant to rule even such a comparatively modest household as he would retire to. For whatever reason, somewhere around Allhallows Eve the small attentions which a man offered as proof of intentions had ceased.

The girl, Felicity, sat quiet in her corner, listening to the chatter which the Countess's reference to last year's revels had evoked. She had never kept Christmas in any style at all. She'd lived all her years with her grandfather—a splendid knight in his time, if his stories were to be believed, but old, still inclined to talk about the Battle of Crecy, and poor now. His house was, literally, falling down over his head. He and she and two old servants had moved about as the thatch and then even the beams sagged under the thrash of the rain, the more insidious but more deadly threat of melting snow. But she had been happy. And free.

In the summer her grandfather had suddenly become concerned about her future, had decided that she needed a husband and that the best place to find one was at Soneborough Castle where the Countess, a distant relative, would doubtless do her best for her.

At Soneborough Felicity had been happy, too, despite the realization that her clothes were poor, her manners and speech on the rustic side, her prospects of marriage rather remote. She had been grateful for, and slightly flattered by Sir Baldwin's attentions and in all probability would have married him, thinking herself fortunate, had not a strolling minstrel arrived shortly after All Souls' Day. He had simply walked in, as was the way of minnesingers and other entertainers, and could have been back on the road next morning, but he had a store of merry songs, handled his lute well and had been invited to stay over Christmas.

Love—hitherto just a thing of song and story—had become real to her. Hopeless, of course. She had acquired enough worldly knowledge to understand that girls of good family, however poor, could not possibly marry minstrels.

In this swarming place she had not even been near him, always the length of the great hall between them—she as a member of the family, however humble, on the dais, he on a platform at the far end, near the kitchen screens. But once, changing his tune from merry to wistful, he had sung a poignant love song, and he'd seemed to look only at her as he sang.

Little enough, but her life before she came to Soneborough had been largely concerned with making much of little. His name was Martin and she loved him. So she had cruelly snubbed Sir Baldwin, and now, listening to the pranks which the Lord of Misrule could order—everything turned topsy-turvy for twelve days—hearing about the kisses demanded as forfeits, she thought—Let it happen, dear God, that we come together, one kiss, one embrace, and I shall live content forever. Even as a nun if that's to be my fate.

Downstairs the meeting was not going well. Her ladyship had had a secret word with the Steward. "Let it not be as last year. Choose a decent man." Part of the trouble was that many of those present had thoroughly enjoyed last year's performance and would have liked to see it repeated. Another trouble was that of decent men, most had had their turn. The Priest had supported every opposition, cherishing the forlorn hope that the whole thing might come to a deadlock and be done away with. But the Knight, eager only to have it over and done with, supported all suggestions.

The Jester said, "How about me?" That was a joke and as such acknowl-

edged, except by the Steward, who said coldly, "Hood, you know as well as I do that no one on the Choosing Council is eligible. You waste our time."

"Waste. Waist. Where's the difference? I'll tell you. One goes out. The other goes up, or down." Not a bad quip, he thought, waists having risen at least four inches in three months.

"I wish you would be serious," the Steward said.

"I will. I am." The Jester owed some of his success and permanent employment to his glib tongue, some to his gift of mimicry. In two seconds he was the spitting image of the Steward, saying with the Steward's voice, "I propose young Martin."

Somebody said, "But he's a foreigner," meaning one not born and bred at Soneborough.

"Maybe. But you go on and on about representing this, that and the other. We, the people who *entertain* you, never have been represented as far back as I remember. And that is back to when Adam met Eve."

The Priest said, in a tone of rebuke, "That comes near blasphemy, Fool. Nonetheless, I agree. A wise choice."

The Knight, his eye on the candle, said that he agreed, too. And since the jug was empty and the fire dying down, there were no objections. But the ritual demanded a show of hands. The workers' palms were toil-hardened, the Knight's almost as coarse; only the Priest, the Steward and the Jester raised hands as white as a lady's.

"Good," said the Steward. "I do not need to remind you that the choice is secret until the bringing in of the Yule Log. And that leads to the next matter. Whose oxen? Whose labor?"

Bringing in the log was heavy work, since the tree trunk chosen must be substantial enough to burn from Christmas Eve until Twelfth Night, and still leave a sufficient portion to be carefully stored and used to kindle its successor. Had the meeting not lasted so long, had the ale not run out, had there been any sign of replenishment, there would have been more wrangling; as it was, the freemen hastened to offer their oxen, and the serfs their own hands—or those of their sons—to carry the log from door to hearth.

The Priest knew that he was breaking a rule, but it was a rule concerning something of which he did not approve, and good might come of it. He went straight to Martin and after swearing him to secrecy, told him that he had been chosen. The young man, who had seen various Lords of Misrule in action, turned pale.

"Sir Priest, I could not do it. I have no talent for inventing absurdities. Besides, it would mean not playing my lute. The Lord of Misrule cannot *do.*

He can only command others to do. Sir, you must go back and tell them to choose again. Please."

"Now that is absurdity indeed," the Priest said testily. "How could I go back and tell them that I had revealed their secret? Now this is what I have in mind. I have noted you, a pious youth, regular at Mass, also a song-maker of considerable talent. . . . There are Christmas songs in plenty—but they are wrong in *spirit*. Too much concerned with the holly and the ivy, the beef and the boar's head, the wine and the ale. Merry, I grant you. But would it not be possible to make a song, to a merry tune, which acknowledged the simple truth—that Christmas celebrates the Birth of Our Lord? Simple words to an easy tune."

"I could do *that*, of course. But I . . ."

"As Lord of Misrule you can order it to be sung."

"And who would make the music?"

"The Lady Felicity. I have noted her, too. She has a true ear and a good hand. Also she is untainted by worldliness—yet." It would come, of course, the Priest thought with sadness. By this time next year she'd be like the rest of them, concerned only with dresses and hair styles and paint for the face, and quarrels, and men.

To practice whatever it was that they were about—a secret for Christmas, they said, and the Priest seemed to know about it, which made it all in order—Felicity and Martin had been allotted a little side room. With Christmas only three days distant, intense practice was needed. The room had no hearth, and the weather was cold.

Seen close to, Felicity was even lovelier than he had thought her when he looked at her across the length of the hall and lost his heart. He was wrong, of course, seeing only what he wished to see and ignoring the fact that she was not unlike—especially in moments of concentration—a pretty young bulldog. Seen close to, Martin was even more handsome than he had seemed at a distance. She, too, saw what she wished to see and could ignore the fact that his nose was too large and too beaky.

They had both behaved perfectly, mindful of reality. A glance, suddenly betraying and yearning, hastily diverted. Alone together, yet each as firmly entrapped in the feudal hierarchy as flies in amber.

Until Felicity struck three wrong notes in succession and had to apologize.

"I am sorry. . . ." Dare she say "Martin?" Why not, everybody else called him by his name—except the lord who said, "Boy! Boy, for the love of God, gives us a cheerful tune."

"I am sorry, Martin." And the use of his given name betrayed her. "My hands are so cold."

She began to rub them together. He reached out and took them in his, warm despite the weather. A practical act, he thought, and she thought that it meant no more than the meeting of hands in a formal dance.

Both wrong.

Both undone.

Murmurs like those of doves in summer trees.

"Martin, I loved you from the first moment."

"Sweeting, I have nothing to offer, except my heart and my songs."

"I have nothing but myself." And that was more than it might seem to be; she could cook as well as play the lute, patch as well as embroider. She was accustomed to hardship and careless of comfort, and now that her feelings were stirred, unmindful of rank. Unmindful, too, of his protests.

"Darling, I have no home but the open road. No roof but the sky. It is unthinkable!"

"Yet, I have thought it. As for a roof! The sky itself could not be leakier than the roof I slept under until I came here."

"It would never be permitted," he said.

"Permission will not be sought. It is not as though I owned anything and the transfer of property were involved. My grandfather sent me here to find a husband, and that I have done. Unless you are stubborn. In which case I shall have no husband. I shall go to Lamarsh. To the convent there. And die of grief." She waited a moment to allow *that* to be understood, and then said, a gentle touch of the spur, "And then, maybe, you will make another sad song about that!"

That was a challenge and he rose to meet it. He could make plans as well as songs.

As the Yule Log was being brought in the first flakes fell, hesitant at first, then thickening. "Ah," everybody said, "a good omen for the year. A green Christmas makes the graveyard fat. A white one starves it." It was a common belief with nothing to support it, yet even the aged and the ailing took heart, hopeful of seeing another year through.

The Day itself. The Lord of Misrule in the lord's place at the high table, empowered to command anything except the permanent transfer of goods; even through the Twelve Days, property was sacrosanct. So far—and it was now time for the boar's head to be brought in—his rule had been mild, concerned mainly with conciliation. There was some amusement to be gained from seeing two ladies who had not spoken a civil word to each other

for a year giving the kiss of peace; in seeing a knight who had kicked his squire—unjustly—being kicked in return. But it was not uproarious as it had been the year before. The lord blamed himself for ill-judgment. The Boy had arrived with a handful of merry songs, soon changed to piteous ones, all about love, a thing to which the lord had given no thought for some years.

With the boar's head, rendered by the cook's art to a startling verisimilitude of the defiant agony in which it had died—white almond nuts for teeth, preserved cherries for eyes—sizzling on the table, alongside all the other meats, the Lord of Misrule issued another order.

"You will all stand." He stood himself. "Now we will sing. You will take the words from me, then the tune from the Lady Felicity. Then you will sing."

He had chosen his moment well, the Priest thought. With the food waiting, learning would be quick.

> Our Lady into Bethlehem rode
> and found no place for her abode.
> Her Babe was born in a stable.
>
> Dark was the night; the wind was chill;
> the shepherds saw beyond the hill,
> The Star shone over the stable,
> When Christ was born in a stable.
>
> We honor on His day of birth,
> the Child born to bring peace on earth.
> The God who was born in a stable.

Exactly right, the Priest thought; a reminder that Christmas is not merely greenery and gluttony, yet with so catchy a tune that yardmen would be whistling it as they groomed horses and fed pigs; kitchen scullions would hum it as they scoured pots.

Martin was less content with his work, but he had not had much time. He was breaking new ground in setting a religious song to a riotous tune, and most of the time his thoughts had been elsewhere. They were still wandering as the eating and drinking proceeded and the more usual entertainments followed one another. The short day began to darken and he issued another, typical order. "The Knights will now bring in the candles." The Knights rose obediently to perform this menial task, and some were not too steady on

their feet. "I give warning," said the Lord of Misrule with suitable and acceptable arrogance, "I shall exact a forfeit for every drop of tallow spilt."

With the bringing in of the candles the twilight outside seemed to deepen. And now even the most voracious appetite appeared to be satisfied.

"We will now play a game," Martin said. "An old one but with something new about it. You will all go into hiding—not singly, but in couples. No hiding place is forbidden, and no light allowed. A prize awaits the couple last to be found."

The Countess thought—How absolutely disgusting! Worse even than last year! And I told Steward to see that a *decent* man was chosen. I shall have something to say to *him*, presently. Meanwhile she looked around for her lord and failed to find him, for the confusion was absolute. Nobody noticed that Felicity had slipped away; nobody expected the Lord of Misrule to participate in his own game. All he was supposed to do was to sit and wait in the lighted hall while the seekers unearthed their quarry, from nooks and corners, cupboards and chests, from behind wall hangings, from under beds.

Alone in the hall Martin moved quickly, quenching two candles at a time, one by blowing, one by a twist of the wick between a moistened thumb and forefinger. The darkness would cause further confusion and delay. Then he ran out to where Felicity waited, with her lute and his snug in their sailcloth covers. She had another bundle, too. "Food for four days, if we are sparing," she said.

The drawbridge was down, for even in time of war, Christmas was a season of amnesty. Once across it, they took to the woods, making for none of the obvious places where runaway lovers—one a minstrel—might be sought.

Martin said, "Since I neglected to name any seekers, that game could go on till morning."

"And doubtless will. And then there are the eleven days during which nobody is willing to bestir himself to raise a hue and cry. Why should they bother? I do not think they will."

Yet they were missed, in a way, and by, of all people, the lord himself. The second day of Christmas was always somewhat flat after the excesses of eating and drinking; this year there were other excesses to be paid for in one way or another. And the Lord of Misrule's chair empty. Why? How? No time to go into that.

"You, Hood, hop up there and take charge," the lord, restored unexpectedly to power, said. "And let us, for God's sake, be merry."

The Jester was apt at inventing absurdities. But something nagged at the back of his lordship's mind. That unforgettable tune. He had not cared for

the words—too solemn—but the tune had caught his ear. Set his toes twitching as for a dance. Made all other tunes sound dull. Finally, he crooked a finger at the Priest and said, "That song, yesterday, Sir Priest, can you recall it?"

The Priest knew that he would never forget it—despite the fact that the Minstrel, having done what was asked of him, absconded. The song held out a glimmer of hope for the future; a hundred years from now the whole nonsense might be done away with.

In the meantime, miss no opportunity, however small. The biggest oak in the forest had grown from an acorn.

"My lord, I remember it well. My disability is—I believe it not uncommon—I can only carry a tune when it is linked to words. And," he added this hastily, "I cannot sing alone. For one thing my voice is weak—and it would smack too much of my being a mere entertainer."

"Then we will all sing," the lord said. His voice was peevish, for he had not liked the words.

"But, my lord—I ask you pardon. In the present situation only Hood the Jester can give orders."

"Nonsense! He was not *elected*. He was *appointed*. Until next Christmas when, if I have any say in the matter, things will be done *very* differently, I am in command here." To prove it, fantastic as it was, just at this season, the lord stood up and roared, "Everybody sing."

Snug in the shelter of a hollow tree, two lovers eating sparingly, thinking only of the future . . . London, perhaps even Westminster.

In the castle, miles behind them now and quite forgotten, people stood singing, "Our Lady into Bethlehem rode. . . ."

NATIVITY
from WEST AFRICAN MELODIES

by Gladys May Casely Hayford

Within a native hut, ere stirred the dawn,
Unto the Pure One was an Infant born;
Wrapped in blue lappah that His mother dyed,
Laid on His father's home-tanned deerskin hide,
The Babe still slept, by all things glorified.
Spirits of black bards burst their bonds and sang
"Peace upon earth" until the heavens rang.
All the black babies who from earth had fled
Peeped through the clouds, then gathered round His head.
Telling of things a baby needs to do,
When first he opens his eyes on wonders new;
Telling Him that to sleep was sweeter rest,
All comfort came from his black mother's breast.
Their gifts were of Love, caught from the springing sod,
Whilst tears and laughter were the gifts of God.
Then all the Wise Men of the past stood forth,
Filling the air East, West, and South and North;
And told Him of the joys that wisdom brings
To mortals in their earthly wanderings.
The children of the past shook down each bough,
Wreathed frangipani blossoms for His brow;
They put pink lilies in His mother's hand,
And heaped for both the first fruits of the land.
His father cut some palm fronds, that the air
Be coaxed to zephyrs while He rested there.
Birds trilled their hallelujahs; and the dew
Trembled with laughter, till the Babe laughed too.
All the black women brought their love so wise,
And kissed their motherhood into His mother's eyes.

MR. EDWARDS MEETS
SANTA CLAUS
by Laura Ingalls Wilder

The days were short and cold, the wind whistled sharply, but there was no snow. Cold rains were falling. Day after day the rain fell, pattering on the roof and pouring from the eaves.

Mary and Laura stayed close by the fire, sewing their nine-patch quilt blocks, or cutting paper dolls from scraps of wrapping-paper, and hearing the wet sound of the rain. Every night was so cold that they expected to see snow next morning, but in the morning they saw only sad, wet grass.

They pressed their noses against the squares of glass in the windows that Pa had made, and they were glad they could see out. But they wished they could see snow.

Laura was anxious because Christmas was near, and Santa Claus and his reindeer could not travel without snow. Mary was afraid that, even if it snowed, Santa Claus could not find them, so far away in Indian Territory. When they asked Ma about this, she said she didn't know.

"What day is it?" they asked her, anxiously. "How many more days till Christmas?" And they counted off the days on their fingers, till there was only one more day left.

Rain was still falling that morning. There was not one crack in the gray sky. They felt almost sure there would be no Christmas. Still, they kept hoping.

Just before noon the light changed. The clouds broke and drifted apart, shining white in a clear blue sky. The sun shone, birds sang, and thousands

of drops of water sparkled on the grasses. But when Ma opened the door to let in the fresh, cold air, they heard the creek roaring.

They had not thought about the creek. Now they knew they would have no Christmas, because Santa Claus could not cross that roaring creek.

Pa came in, bringing a big fat turkey. If it weighed less than twenty pounds, he said, he'd eat it, feathers and all. He asked Laura, "How's that for a Christmas dinner? Think you can manage one of those drumsticks?"

She said, yes, she could. But she was sober. Then Mary asked him if the creek was going down, and he said it was still rising.

Ma said it was too bad. She hated to think of Mr. Edwards eating his bachelor cooking all alone on Christmas day. Mr. Edwards had been asked to eat Christmas dinner with them, but Pa shook his head and said a man would risk his neck, trying to cross that creek now.

"No," he said. "That current's too strong. We'll just have to make up our minds that Edwards won't be here tomorrow."

Of course that meant that Santa Claus could not come, either.

Laura and Mary tried not to mind too much. They watched Ma dress the wild turkey, and it was a very fat turkey. They were lucky little girls, to have a good house to live in, and a warm fire to sit by, and such a turkey for their Christmas dinner. Ma said so, and it was true. Ma said it was too bad that Santa Claus couldn't come this year, but they were such good girls that he hadn't forgotten them; he would surely come next year.

Still, they were not happy.

After supper that night they washed their hands and faces, buttoned their red-flannel nightgowns, tied their night-cap strings, and soberly said their prayers. They lay down in bed and pulled the covers up. It did not seem at all like Christmas time.

Pa and Ma sat silent by the fire. After a while Ma asked why Pa didn't play the fiddle, and he said, "I don't seem to have the heart to, Caroline."

After a longer while, Ma suddenly stood up.

"I'm going to hang up your stockings, girls," she said. "Maybe something will happen."

Laura's heart jumped. But then she thought again of the creek and she knew nothing could happen.

Ma took one of Mary's clean stockings and one of Laura's, and she hung them from the mantel-shelf, on either side of the fireplace. Laura and Mary watched her over the edge of their bed-covers.

"Now go to sleep," Ma said, kissing them good night. "Morning will come quicker if you're asleep."

She sat down again by the fire and Laura almost went to sleep. She woke

up a little when she heard Pa say, "You've only made it worse, Caroline."
And she thought she heard Ma say: "No, Charles. There's the white sugar."
But perhaps she was dreaming.

Then she heard Jack growl savagely. The door-latch rattled and some one
said, "Ingalls! Ingalls!" Pa was stirring up the fire, and when he opened the
door Laura saw that it was morning. The outdoors was gray.

"Great fishhooks, Edwards! Come in, man! What's happened?" Pa exclaimed.

Laura saw the stockings limply dangling, and she scrooged her shut eyes
into the pillow. She heard Pa piling wood on the fire, and she heard Mr.
Edwards say he had carried his clothes on his head when he swam the creek.
His teeth rattled and his voice shivered. He would be all right, he said, as
soon as he got warm.

"It was too big a risk, Edwards," Pa said. "We're glad you're here, but that
was too big a risk for a Christmas dinner."

"Your little ones had to have a Christmas," Mr. Edwards replied. "No
creek could stop me, after I fetched them their gifts from Independence."

Laura sat straight up in bed. "Did you see Santa Claus?" she shouted.

"I sure did," Mr. Edwards said.

"Where? When? What did he look like? What did he say? Did he really
give you something for us?" Mary and Laura cried.

"Wait, wait a minute!" Mr. Edwards laughed. And Ma said she would put the presents in the stockings, as Santa Claus intended. She said they mustn't look.

Mr. Edwards came and sat on the floor by their bed, and he answered every question they asked him. They honestly tried not to look at Ma, and they didn't quite see what she was doing.

When he saw the creek rising, Mr. Edwards said, he had known that Santa Claus could not get across it. ("But you crossed it," Laura said. "Yes," Mr. Edwards replied, "but Santa Claus is too old and fat. He couldn't make it, where a long, lean razor-back like me could do so.") And Mr. Edwards reasoned that if Santa Claus couldn't cross the creek, likely he would come no farther south than Independence. Why should he come forty miles across the prairie, only to be turned back? Of course he wouldn't do that!

So Mr. Edwards had walked to Independence. ("In the rain?" Mary asked. Mr. Edwards said he wore his rubber coat.) And there, coming down the street in Independence, he had met Santa Claus. ("In the daytime?" Laura asked. She hadn't thought that anyone could see Santa Claus in the daytime. No, Mr. Edwards said; it was night, but light shone out across the street from the saloons.)

Well, the first thing Santa Claus said was, "Hello, Edwards!" ("Did he know you?" Mary asked, and Laura asked, "How did you know he was really Santa Claus?" Mr. Edwards said that Santa Claus knew everybody. And he had recognized Santa at once by his whiskers. Santa Claus had the longest, thickest, whitest set of whiskers west of the Mississippi.)

So Santa Claus said, "Hello, Edwards! Last time I saw you you were sleeping on a corn-shuck bed in Tennessee." And Mr. Edwards well remembered the little pair of red-yarn mittens that Santa Claus had left for him that time.

Then Santa Claus said: "I understand you're living now down along the Verdigris River. Have you ever met up, down yonder, with two little young girls named Mary and Laura?"

"I surely am acquainted with them," Mr. Edwards replied.

"It rests heavy on my mind," said Santa Claus. "They are both of them sweet, pretty, good little young things, and I know they are expecting me. I surely do hate to disappoint two good little girls like them. Yet with the water up the way it is, I can't ever make it across that creek. I can figure no way whatsoever to get to their cabin this year. Edwards," Santa Claus said. "Would you do me the favor to fetch them their gifts this one time?"

"I'll do that, and with pleasure," Mr. Edwards told him.

Then Santa Claus and Mr. Edwards stepped across the street to the hitching-posts where the pack-mule was tied. ("Didn't he have his reindeer?" Laura asked. "You know he couldn't," Mary said. "There isn't any snow." Exactly, said Mr. Edwards. Santa Claus traveled with a pack-mule in the southwest.)

And Santa Claus uncinched the pack and looked through it, and he took out the presents for Mary and Laura.

"Oh, what are they?" Laura cried; but Mary asked, "Then what did he do?"

Then he shook hands with Mr. Edwards, and he swung up on his fine bay horse. Santa Claus rode well, for a man of his weight and build. And he tucked his long, white whiskers under his bandana. "So long, Edwards," he said, and he rode away on the Fort Dodge trail, leading his pack-mule and whistling.

Laura and Mary were silent an instant, thinking of that.

Then Ma said, "You may look now, girls."

Something was shining bright in the top of Laura's stocking. She squealed and jumped out of bed. So did Mary, but Laura beat her to the fireplace. And the shining thing was a glittering new tin cup.

Mary had one exactly like it.

These new tin cups were their very own. Now they each had a cup to drink out of. Laura jumped up and down and shouted and laughed, but Mary stood still and looked with shining eyes at her own tin cup.

Then they plunged their hands into the stockings again. And they pulled out two long, long sticks of candy. It was peppermint candy, striped red and white. They looked and looked at that beautiful candy, and Laura licked her stick, just one lick. But Mary was not so greedy. She didn't take even one lick of her stick.

Those stockings weren't empty yet. Mary and Laura pulled out two small packages. They unwrapped them, and each found a little heart-shaped cake. Over their delicate brown tops was sprinkled white sugar. The sparkling grains lay like tiny drifts of snow.

The cakes were too pretty to eat. Mary and Laura just looked at them. But at last Laura turned hers over, and she nibbled a tiny nibble from underneath, where it wouldn't show. And the inside of that little cake was white!

It had been made of pure white flour, and sweetened with white sugar.

Laura and Mary never would have looked in their stockings again. The cups and the cakes and the candy were almost too much. They were too happy to speak. But Ma asked if they were sure the stockings were empty.

Then they put their arms down inside them, to make sure.

And in the very toe of each stocking was a shining bright, new penny!

They had never even thought of such a thing as having a penny. Think of having a whole penny for your very own. Think of having a cup and a cake and a stick of candy *and* a penny.

There never had been such a Christmas.

Now of course, right away, Laura and Mary should have thanked Mr. Edwards for bringing those lovely presents all the way from Independence. But they had forgotten all about Mr. Edwards. They had even forgotten Santa Claus. In a minute they would have remembered, but before they did, Ma said, gently, "Aren't you going to thank Mr. Edwards?"

"Oh, thank you, Mr. Edwards! Thank you!" they said, and they meant it with all their hearts. Pa shook Mr. Edwards' hand, too, and shook it again. Pa and Ma and Mr. Edwards acted as if they were almost crying, Laura didn't know why. So she gazed again at her beautiful presents.

She looked up again when Ma gasped. And Mr. Edwards was taking sweet potatoes out of his pockets. He said they had helped to balance the package on his head when he swam across the creek. He thought Pa and Ma might like them, with the Christmas turkey.

There were nine sweet potatoes. Mr. Edwards had brought them all the way from town, too. It was just too much. Pa said so. "It's too much, Edwards," he said. They never could thank him enough.

Mary and Laura were too much excited to eat breakfast. They drank the milk from their shining new cups, but they could not swallow the rabbit stew and the cornmeal mush.

"Don't make them, Charles," Ma said. "It will soon be dinner-time."

For Christmas dinner there was the tender, juicy, roasted turkey. There were the sweet potatoes, baked in the ashes and carefully wiped so that you could eat the good skins, too. There was a loaf of salt-rising bread made from the last of the white flour.

And after all that there were stewed dried blackberries and little cakes. But these little cakes were made with brown sugar and they did not have white sugar sprinkled over their tops.

Then Pa and Ma and Mr. Edwards sat by the fire and talked about Christmas times back in Tennessee and up north in the Big Woods. But Mary and Laura looked at their beautiful cakes and played with their pennies and drank water out of their new cups. And little by little they licked and sucked their sticks of candy, till each stick was sharp-pointed on one end.

That was a happy Christmas.

THE JOY OF GIVING
attributed to John Greenleaf Whittier

Somehow not only for Christmas
    But all the long year through,
The joy that you give to others
    Is the joy that comes back to you.
And the more you spend in blessing
    The poor and lonely and sad,
The more of your heart's possessing
    Returns to make you glad.

CHRISTMAS DAY
IN THE MORNING

by Pearl S. Buck

He woke suddenly and completely. It was four o'clock, the hour at which his father had always called him to get up and help with the milking. Strange how the habits of his youth clung to him still! Fifty years ago, and his father had been dead for thirty years, and yet he waked at four o'clock in the morning. He had trained himself to turn over and go to sleep, but this morning, because it was Christmas, he did not try to sleep.

Yet what was the magic of Christmas now? His childhood and youth were

long past, and his own children had grown up and gone. Some of them lived only a few miles away but they had their own families, and though they would come in as usual toward the end of the day, they had explained with infinite gentleness that they wanted their children to build Christmas memories about *their* houses, not his. He was left alone with his wife.

Yesterday she had said, "It isn't worthwhile, perhaps—"

And he had said, "Oh, yes, Alice, even if there are only the two of us, let's have a Christmas of our own."

Then she had said, "Let's not trim the tree until tomorrow, Robert—just so it's ready when the children come. I'm tired."

He had agreed, and the tree was still out in the back entry.

He lay in his big bed in his room. The door to her room was shut because she was a light sleeper, and sometimes he had restless nights. Years ago they had decided to use separate rooms. It meant nothing, they said, except that neither of them slept as well as they once had. They had been married so long that nothing could separate them, actually.

Why did he feel so awake tonight? For it was still night, a clear and starry night. No moon, of course, but the stars were extraordinary! Now that he thought of it, the stars seemed always large and clear before the dawn of Christmas Day. There was one star now that was certainly larger and brighter than any of the others. He could even imagine it moving, as it had seemed to him to move one night long ago.

He slipped back in time, as he did so easily nowadays. He was fifteen years old and still on his father's farm. He loved his father. He had not known it until one day a few days before Christmas, when he had overheard what his father was saying to his mother.

"Mary, I hate to call Rob in the mornings. He's growing so fast and he needs his sleep. If you could see how he sleeps when I go in to wake him up! I wish I could manage alone."

"Well, you can't, Adam." His mother's voice was brisk. "Besides, he isn't a child anymore. It's time he took his turn."

"Yes," his father said slowly. "But I sure do hate to wake him."

When he heard these words, something in him woke: his father loved him! He had never thought of it before, taking for granted the tie of their blood. Neither his father nor his mother talked about loving their children—they had no time for such things. There was always so much to do on a farm.

Now that he knew his father loved him, there would be no more loitering in the mornings and having to be called again. He got up after that, stumbling blind with sleep, and pulled on his clothes, his eyes tight shut, but he got up.

And then on the night before Christmas, that year when he was fifteen, he lay for a few minutes thinking about the next day. They were poor, and most of the excitement was in the turkey they had raised themselves and in the mince pies his mother made. His sisters sewed presents and his mother and father always bought something he needed, not only a warm jacket, maybe, but something more, such as a book. And he saved and bought them each something, too.

He wished, that Christmas he was fifteen, he had a better present for his father. As usual he had gone to the ten-cent store and bought a tie. It had seemed nice enough until he lay thinking the night before Christmas, and then he wished that he had heard his father and mother talking in time for him to save for something better.

He lay on his side, his head supported by his elbow, and looked out of his attic window. The stars were bright, much brighter than he ever remembered seeing them, and one star in particular was so bright that he wondered if it were really the Star of Bethlehem.

"Dad," he had once asked when he was a little boy, "what is a stable?"

"It's just a barn," his father had replied, "like ours."

Then Jesus had been born in a barn, and to a barn the shepherds and the Wise Men had come, bringing their Christmas gifts!

The thought struck him like a silver dagger. Why should he not give his father a special gift too, out there in the barn? He could get up early, earlier than four o'clock, and he could creep into the barn and get all the milking done. He'd do it alone, milk and clean up, and then when his father went in to start the milking, he'd see it all done. And he would know who had done it.

He laughed to himself as he gazed at the stars. It was what he would do, and he mustn't sleep too sound.

He must have waked twenty times, scratching a match each time to look at his old watch—midnight, and half past one, and then two o'clock.

At a quarter to three he got up and put on his clothes. He crept downstairs, careful of the creaky boards, and let himself out. The big star hung lower over the barn roof, a reddish gold. The cows looked at him, sleepy and surprised. It was early for them, too.

"So, boss," he whispered. They accepted him placidly, and he fetched some hay for each cow and then got the milking pail and the big milk cans.

He had never milked all alone before, but it seemed almost easy. He kept thinking about his father's surprise. His father would come in and call him, saying that he would get things started while Rob was getting dressed. He'd go to the barn, open the door, and then he'd go to get the two big empty milk cans. But they wouldn't be waiting or empty; they'd be standing in the milkhouse, filled.

"What the—" he could hear his father exclaiming.

He smiled and milked steadily, two strong streams rushing into the pail, frothing and fragrant. The cows were still surprised but acquiescent. For once they were behaving well, as though they knew it was Christmas.

The task went more easily than he had ever known it to before. Milking for once was not a chore. It was something else, a gift to his father who loved him. He finished, the two milk cans were full, and he covered them and closed the milkhouse door carefully, making sure of the latch. He put the stool in its place by the door and hung up the clean milk pail. Then he went out of the barn and barred the door behind him.

Back in his room he had only a minute to pull off his clothes in the darkness and jump into bed, for he heard his father up. He put the covers over his head to silence his quick breathing. The door opened.

"Rob!" his father called. "We have to get up, son, even if it is Christmas."

"Aw-right," he said sleepily.

"I'll go on out," his father said. "I'll get things started."

The door closed and he lay still, laughing to himself. In just a few minutes his father would know. His dancing heart was ready to jump from his body.

The minutes were endless—ten, fifteen, he did not know how many—and he heard his father's footsteps again. The door opened and he lay still.

"Rob!"

"Yes, Dad—"

"You son of a—" His father was laughing, a queer sobbing sort of a laugh. "Thought you'd fool me, did you?" His father was standing beside his bed, feeling for him, pulling away the cover.

"It's for Christmas, Dad!"

He found his father and clutched him in a great hug. He felt his father's arms go around him. It was dark and they could not see each other's faces.

"Son, I thank you. Nobody ever did a nicer thing—"

"Oh, Dad, I want you to know—I do want to be good!" The words broke from him of their own will. He did not know what to say. His heart was bursting with love.

"Well, I reckon I can go back to bed and sleep," his father said after a moment. "No, hark—the little ones are waked up. Come to think of it, son, I've never seen you children when you first saw the Christmas tree. I was always in the barn. Come on!"

He got up and pulled on his clothes again and they went down to the Christmas tree, and soon the sun was creeping up to where the star had been. Oh, what a Christmas, and how his heart had nearly burst again with shyness and pride as his father told his mother and made the younger children listen about how he, Rob, had got up all by himself.

220

"The best Christmas gift I ever had, and I'll remember it, son, every year on Christmas morning, so long as I live."

They had both remembered it, and now that his father was dead he remembered it alone: that blessed Christmas dawn when, alone with the cows in the barn, he had made his first gift of true love.

Outside the window now the great star slowly sank. He got up out of bed and put on his slippers and bathrobe and went softly upstairs to the attic and found the box of Christmas-tree decorations. He took them downstairs into the living room. Then he brought in the tree. It was a little one—they had not had a big tree since the children went away—but he set it in the holder and put it in the middle of the long table under the window. Then carefully he began to trim it. It was done very soon, the time passing as quickly as it had that morning long ago in the barn.

He went to his library and fetched the little box that contained his special gift to his wife, a star of diamonds, not large but dainty in design. He had written the card for it the day before. He tied the gift on the tree and then stood back. It was pretty, very pretty, and she would be surprised.

But he was not satisfied. He wanted to tell her—to tell her how much he loved her. It had been a long time since he had really told her, although he loved her in a very special way, much more than he ever had when they were young.

He had been fortunate that she had loved him—and how fortunate that he had been able to love! Ah, that was the true joy of life, the ability to love! For he was quite sure that some people were genuinely unable to love anyone. But love was alive in him, it still was.

It occurred to him suddenly that it was alive because long ago it had been born in him when he knew his father loved him. That was it: love alone could waken love.

And he could give the gift again and again. This morning, this blessed Christmas morning, he would give it to his beloved wife. He could write it down in a letter for her to read and keep forever. He went to his desk and began his love letter to his wife: *My dearest love . . .*

When it was finished he sealed it and tied it on the tree where she would see it the first thing when she came into the room. She would read it, surprised and then moved, and realize how very much he loved her.

He put out the light and went tiptoeing up the stairs. The star in the sky was gone, and the first rays of the sun were gleaming the sky. Such a happy, happy Christmas!

Once there was this little child

You know her I believe

Here's who she is me ELOISE

And it is Christmas Eve

KAY THOMPSON'S

ELOISE
AT
CHRISTMASTIME

DRAWINGS BY HILARY KNIGHT

It's Christmas Eve
with a blizzard outside
And four below zero
or more

But inside the Plaza
we're cozy and warm
in our rooms
on the tippy top floor

Oooooooooooooooooooooo!

We're Skipperdee who is my turtle and Weenie who is my dog

Nanny my mostly companion and ME and the blazing Yuletide log

Our face is absolutely aglow

Then it's dash away jingle
to hear Nanny say
"Do mind the tree my dear
I'd rawther you didn't
come into this closet
I'm hiding the presents
in here"

You can hear Nanny say
"Oh trinkles
my dear
Oh drinkles and sklinkles of fun
It's Christmas
Christmas
Christmas Eve
Oh my
there's a lot to be done"

I agree with her

So I put on my Christmas jingle bells
and jingle around or so
Into this Christmas closet
for my halo of mistletoe

It is absolutely sweet

While Nanny is filling the stockings
I shout out loud and clear
"I must go down
to the lobby
to spread some Christmas cheer"

And Nanny says
"Of course
of course
of course
you must my dear"

Then I jingle out to the elevator

All of the cars are full
to the brim
because of the holiday
God rest ye merry gentlemen
Let nothing you dismay

It is rawther crowded

𝄞 Fa la la la fa la la la lolly ting tingledy here and there. Blow music of trinkles and drinkles of glass it's Christmas everywhere

And you should see the lobby

You absolutely can't get near it

There are all these people

roaming around

Filled with the Christmas spirit

I usually wear a star or so

in case there is this package

that doesn't know where it's going

Fa la la la la fa la la la lolly ting tingledy here and there. Blow music of trinkles and drinkles of glass there's Christmas everywhere

Then it's zippity jingle and dash away ping
Hang holly and berries in all the halls
Tie tassels on all the thermostats and
Write Merry Christmas on all of the walls

I go to as many holiday parties as I possibly can
They are rawther festive

Oh zippity jingle and dash away tingle

to shout out loud and clear

Oh come All Ye Faithful

It's me ELOISE Nanny dear

You can hear Nanny say
"Put the peppermint sticks
over there
with the cookies and fruities
and do
oh do
oh do
get on
with all of your Christmas duties

Now
who who who
in the whole wide world
Could be sending American Beauties?"

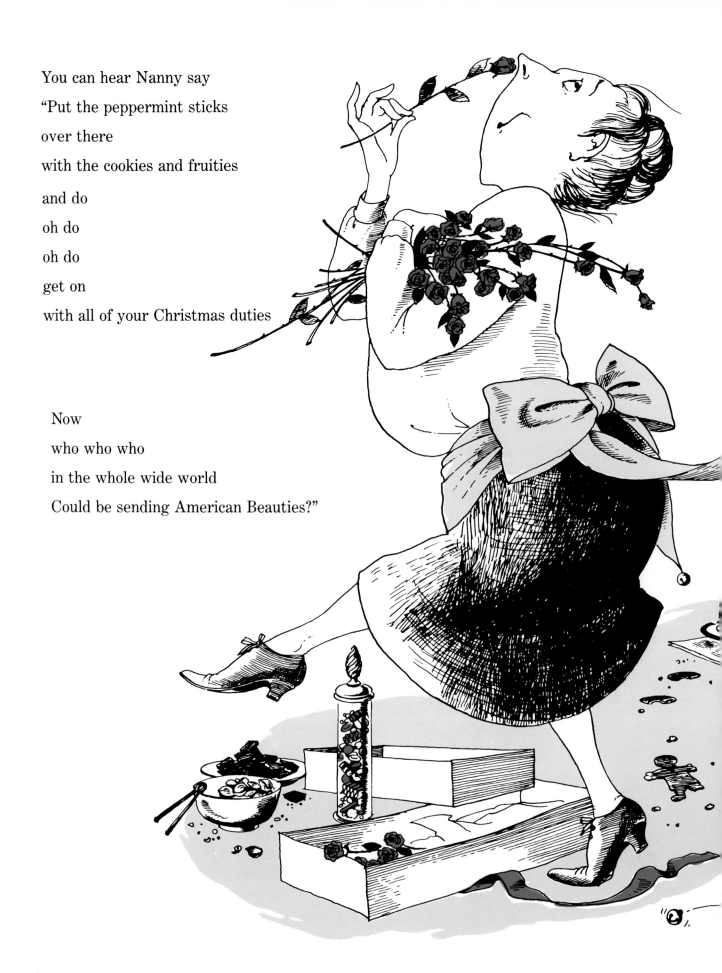

Oh candy the apples
Oh shell the nuts
Oh crackledy crack yum yum
Trink trinkle around the taffy box
Oh yum gulp gulp and yum

Weenie usually helps me
But this year he will not budge
unless he has two of peppermint puffs
and one and a half of fudge

I usually have two of peppermint puffs
and three or four of fudge

Skipperdee dislikes peppermint puffs
and won't even smell the fudge

I have to do quite a bit
of trimming
for it's Christmas Eve tonight
trim trinkles and drinkles
and sklinkles of glass
Trim everything in sight

Jingle here jingle there jingle Christmas everywhere

We hang everything
on our Christmas tree
Ornaments big and bright
and all of these
sparkling icicles
and twirling balls of white

I always hang a star on top
With angels in between

Here's how many lights we have—
Thirty-seven and sixteen

I am giving the bellboys earmuffs
The waiters baseball socks
Thomas is getting a vest with a bib
Room Service a music box

And for my friend Vincent the barber
this rawther unusual brush
with rawther unusual bristles
that got caught in the Christmas rush

But wrap it oh wrap it oh holly oh Christmas
in tinsel and ribbon and paste
Then stick with a sticker a seal and a card
TO THE BARBER SHOP POSTHASTE

I'm giving Mr. Harris in catering
a pair of woolen gloves
and a piece of fruit cake from Japan
which he absolutely loves

For the 59th Street doorman
a bottle of Guinness Stout
to keep him warm on the inside
when there's a blizzard on the out

And for that darling carriage horse
who stands across the street
a blanket with his initials on it
and a Christmas boiled sweet

I sent a folding Christmas card
to the ducks in Central Park
Skipperdee thought he had captured a bug
but it was only a yuletide spark

The special delivery postman arrived
at absolutely hawlf pawst ten
It was a zippy bag from my mother's lawyer
so I wrapped it back up again

I got a present for Nanny for Nanny for Nanny
but don't tell her
It's a little silver thimble full of
frankincense and myrrh

For Weenie a roastbeef bone deluxe
For Skipperdee raisin milk
I'm giving the valet a beehive of course
made of safety pins and silk

And when my gifts are delivered and wrapped
and put under the tree tree tree
I have to trim this children's one
for Weenie and Skipperdee

If anyone remembers
the porter needs suspenders

Sometimes there is so much to do that
I get sort of a headache around the sides and partially under it

Give a Christmas stocking at Christmas time

and here's the thing of it

It doesn't matter if it has a hole or not

put a poinsettia

in it in it

or a nut

if that

doesn't

fit

But you absolutely <u>have</u> to put

a present inside of it of it

It's Christmas Eve so hurry fa lo oh my there's a lot to be done. Oh gather your presents with a tinkle and quick and deliver them on the run

♪ Oh trinkles oh trinkles sing fa la la la lolly ring tinkle bells here and there. Blow music of trinkles and drinkles of glass there's Christmas everywhere

Then I must lie down
and smell the pine
and gaze at the Christmas star
Perchance to feel in these piney pine needles
just where
my presents are

For when you are a child of six
it's difficult to know
if you deserve a present or not
at Christmas time
or so

So if no one remembers me
and no presents can I find
I'll know I don't deserve them
It doesn't matter
I don't mind

Fa la la la fa la la la lolly ting tingles of angel hair. Blow music of trinkles and drinkles of glass there's Christmas everywhere

Put a candle in the window

This glistening Christmas light

For a lonely stranger passing by

to come in and out of the night

Fa la la la fa la la lolly ting tingles of angel hair. Blow music of trinkles and drinkles of glass there's Christmas everywhere

My favorite carol

is trinkles and drinkles

and Nanny's absolute choice

is We Three Kings of Orient Are

She has a rawther unusual voice

Whenever we sing

"Oh still the night

'Ere lo 'ere lo

Comes o'er"

Emily and Weenie and

Skipperdee shout

Encore Encore Encore

Then we all shout bravo

And it's zippety jingle and dashaway ping ting tingles of angel hair. Blow music of trinkles and drinkles cof glass there's Christmas everywhere

I'm rawther fond of caroling

Fa la on every floor

Fa la la la to catering

Fa la from door to door

Fa la la la fa la la la lolly ting tingles of angel hair. Blow music of trinkles and drinkles of glass there's Christmas everywhere

We sang Noel for 506

Silent Night for 507

We didn't sing for 509
at the request of 511

But ho ho ho and jiggeldy ping
We were not dismayed
We skibbled into the exit sign
and sang

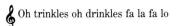
𝄞 Oh trinkles oh drinkles fa la fa lo

for Lily
the nightmaid

Skipperdee lost a tooth
singing Good King Wenceslaus
But we found it behind
this azalea plant
hiding under this moss

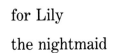

My mother called
long distance
from the Mediterranean
I believe
We talked for an hour and
charged it
like we did last Christmas Eve

She was sunburned on her legs
and sent me this absolutely
sweet cartwheel hat
with these earpuffs on it

I think it looks absolutely darling on me

Emily wasn't feeling well
It's rawther sad to mention
Nanny said "Oh pooh pooh pooh
it's Christmas indigestion"

But she looked like she had a fever or so
especially around the face
So I put this Christmas basket
out on the flagpole
for her
just in case

I usually walk around quite a bit or so thinking of a way to stay up hawlf the night

Oh trinkles oh trinkles sing fa la la la lolly ring tinkle bells here and there. Blow music of trinkles and drinkles of glass there's Christmas everywhere

Then Nanny stretched and yawned out loud
and cheerily inquired
"What <u>are</u> we doing
up up up
when we're so tired tired tired?"

"Let's jingle to bed

Now there's a girl

Let's have no tears of sorrow

Let's close our eyes

and sleep sleep sleep

so we can carry on tomorrow"

I always hang a two legged Christmas stocking just in case

Some us were rawther tired

Then some of us sort of closed some of our eyes
to have this Christmas dream

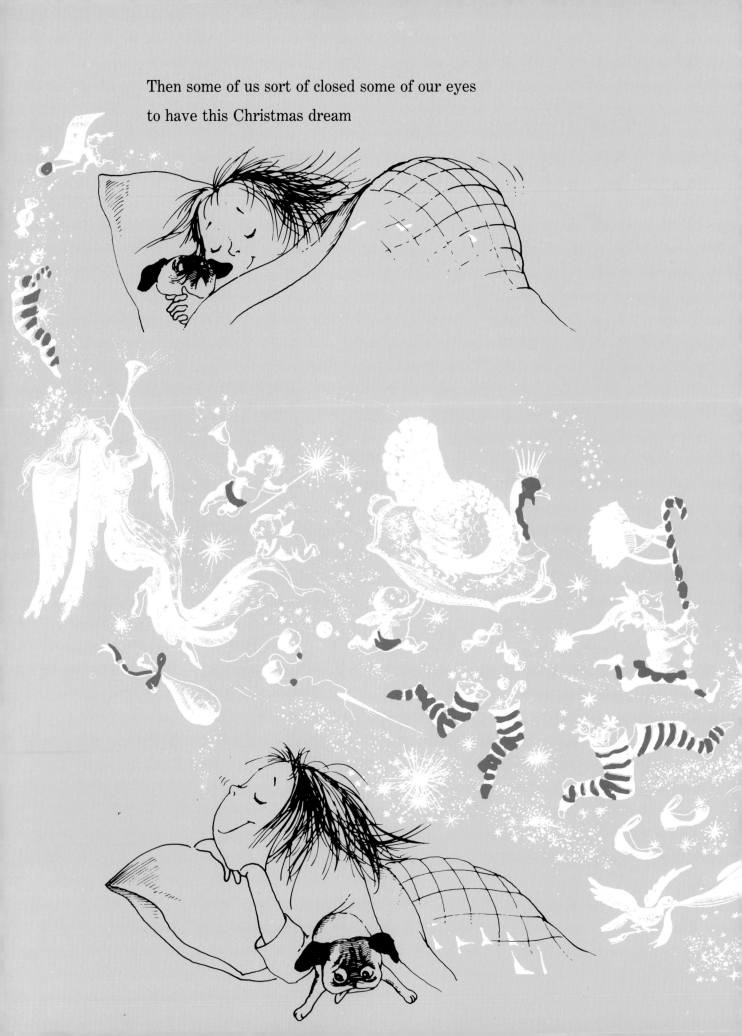

of some steaming hot plum pudding

with extra cream cream cream

Of reindeers with sunglasses on
ice-skating on the stars
with mittens on their antlers
and mufflers made in Mars

And Santa chuckled and said "Dash on to the Plaza my lovely boys
We'll have Christmas punch with Nanny and give Eloise her toys"

I thought he looked terribly well

And when we awakened
he'd come and gone
and in all of this midnight and dark
we could see these reindeers zimbering
through the trees in Central Park

We could even see this tail-light
on Santa Claus' sleigh

and Emily had a baby pigeon
on absolutely Christmas day

Of course she named it Raphael,
because it was born in this big hotel

"Bleh-ess you dear Emily"
Nanny then said
"Now what time can it possibly be?"
We said
"It's absolutely Christmas
and time to sklinkle off to the tree"
"Of course" she yawned "of course of course
Sing trinkles and follow me"

And we did

And we lawghed and dawnced in our Christmas barefeet ting ting to the Christmas tree

Then oh oh oh absolutely oh oh
Oh trinkles and sklinkles of glee
Oh look oh look oh <u>will</u> you look
at the presents under the tree

And in all of this
everly Christmas excitement
we could hardly wait to see

What Nanny gave Weenie

What Weenie gave Emily

What Nanny gave Emily

What Weenie gave Nanny

What Emily gave Nanny

What Emily gave Weenie

What Skipperdee gave

Weenie and Emily and Nanny

What Nanny and Emily and Weenie gave Skipperdee

And of course what they all
gave me

And everyone shouted and yelled oh oh oh
and unwrapped this Christmas surprise
And some of us couldn't believe what
we saw
with some of our Christmas eyes

Weenie was digging
as he usually does
around this Christmas tree
and under this light
to the left of this bough
we found this present for me

And this dear little angel
with snow on her head
Said
"What can this possibly be?"

Then Nanny said
"Little Miss Christmas
Miss Christmas
Miss Christmas
that one is from me"
"Oh Nanny how darling!
What is it?" I said
She said
"Open it up and see"

And there it was
and it sparkled at me
A diamond necklace of trinkles and glue
"Oh trinkles" I said
"Nanny dear I love you
I absolutely do"

Here is who my absolutely best friend
in this whole wide world is
Nanny

Then it's up and it's oh
to the telephone go
"Hello there Room Service dear
Send Christmas breakfast
on Christmas trays
to these four Christmas children
up here

"And if you'd like
to nibble on something
like some Christmas
cinnamon trees
Simply tell the chef
to bake some at once
and charge it to me
ELOISE"

They're absolutely delicious

It's absolutely Christmas
so come to the top floor please
come all of my friends where ever you are
For a trinkle with
ME
ELOISE

Jingle

here

jingle

there

jingle

Christmas

everywhere

Oooooooooooooooooooooooooo! I absolutely love Christmas

OLD APPLEJOY'S GHOST

by Frank R. Stockton

The large and commodious apartments in the upper part of the old Applejoy mansion were occupied exclusively, at the time of our story, by the ghost of the grandfather of the present owner of the estate.

For many years old Applejoy's ghost had wandered freely about the grand old house and the fine estate of which he had once been the lord and master. But early in that spring a change had come over the household of his grandson, John Applejoy, an elderly man, a bachelor, and—for the later portion of his life—almost a recluse. His young niece, Bertha, had come to live with him, and it was since her arrival that old Applejoy's ghost had confined himself to the upper portions of the house.

This secluded existence, so different from his ordinary habits, was adopted entirely on account of the kindness of his heart. During the lives of two generations of his descendants he knew that he had frequently been seen by members of the family, but this did not disturb him, for in life he had been a man who had liked to assert his position, and the disposition to do so had not left him now. His skeptical grandson John had seen him and spoken with him, but declared that these ghostly interviews were only dreams or hallucinations. As to other people, it might be a very good thing if they believed that the house was haunted. People with uneasy consciences would not care to live in such a place.

But when this fresh young girl came upon the scene the case was entirely different. She was not twenty yet, and if anything should happen which would lead her to suspect that the house was haunted she might not be willing to live there. If that should come to pass, it would be a great shock to the ghost.

For a long time the venerable mansion had been a quiet, darkened, melancholy house. A few rooms only were occupied by John Applejoy and his housekeeper, Mrs. Dipperton, who for years had needed little space in which to pass the monotonous days of their lives. Bertha sang; she danced by herself on the broad piazza; she brought flowers into the house from the gardens, and, sometimes, it almost might have been imagined that the days which were gone had come back again.

One winter evening, when the light of the full moon entered softly through every unshaded window of the house, old Applejoy's ghost sat in a high-backed chair, which on account of an accident to one of its legs had been banished to the garret. Throwing one shadowy leg over the other, he clasped the long fingers of his hazy hands and gazed thoughtfully out the window.

"Winter has come," he said to himself. "And in two days it will be Christmas!" Suddenly he started to his feet. "Can it be," he exclaimed, "that my close-fisted grandson John does not intend to celebrate Christmas! It has been years since he has done so, but now that Bertha is in the house, will he dare to pass over it as though it were but a common day? It is almost incredible that such a thing could happen, but so far there have been no signs of any preparations. I have seen nothing, heard nothing, smelt nothing. I will go this moment and investigate."

Clapping his misty old cocked hat on his head and tucking the shade of his faithful cane under his arm, he descended to the lower part of the house. Glancing into the great parlors dimly lit by the moonlight, he saw that all the furniture was shrouded in ancient linen covers.

"Humph!" ejaculated old Applejoy's ghost. "He expects no company here!" Forthwith he passed through the dining room and entered the kitchen and pantry. There were no signs that anything extraordinary in the way of cooking had been done, or was contemplated. "Two days before Christmas," he groaned, "and a kitchen thus! How widely different from the olden time when I gave orders for the holidays! Let me see what the old curmudgeon has provided for Christmas."

So saying, old Applejoy's ghost went around the spacious pantry, looking upon shelves and tables. "Emptiness! Emptiness! Emptiness!" he exclaimed. "A cold leg of mutton, a ham half gone, and cold boiled potatoes—it makes me shiver to look at them! Pies? there ought to be rows and rows of them, and there is not one! And Christmas two days off!

"What is this? Is it possible? A chicken not full grown! Oh, John, how you have fallen! A small-sized fowl for Christmas day! And cider? No trace of it! Here is vinegar—that suits John, no doubt," and then forgetting his present condition, he said to himself, "It makes my very blood run cold to look upon a pantry furnished out like this!" And with bowed head he passed out into the great hall.

If it were possible to prevent the desecration of his old home during the sojourn of the young and joyous Bertha, the ghost of old Applejoy was determined to do it, but to do anything he must put himself into communication with some living being. Still rapt in reverie he passed up the stairs and into the chamber where his grandson slept. There lay the old man, his eyelids as tightly closed as if there had been money underneath them. The ghost of old Applejoy stood by his bedside.

"I can make him wake up and look at me," he thought, "so that I might tell him what I think of him, but what impression could I expect my words to make upon a one-chicken man like John? Moreover, if I should be able to speak to him, he would persuade himself that he had been dreaming, and my words would be of no avail!"

Old Applejoy's ghost turned away from the bedside of his descendant, crossed the hall, and passed into the room of Mrs. Dipperton, the elderly housekeeper. There she lay fast asleep. The kindhearted ghost shook his head as he looked down upon her.

"It would be of no use," he said. "She would never be able to induce old John to turn one inch aside from his parsimonious path. More than that, if she were to see me she would probably scream—die, for all I know—and that would be a pretty preparation for Christmas!"

Out he went, and getting more and more anxious in his mind, the ghost passed to the front of the house and entered the chamber occupied by young Bertha. Once inside the door, he stopped reverently and removed his cocked hat.

The head of the bed was near the uncurtained window, and the bright light of the moon shone upon a face more beautiful in slumber than in the sunny hours of day. She slept lightly, her delicate eyelids trembled now and then as if they would open, and sometimes her lips moved, as if she would whisper something about her dreams.

Old Applejoy's ghost drew nearer and bent slightly over her. If he could hear a few words he might find out where her mind wandered, what she would like him to do for her.

At last, faintly whispered and scarcely audible, he heard one word, "Tom!"

Old Applejoy's ghost stepped back from the bedside, "She wants Tom! I like that! But I wish she would say something else. She can't have Tom for Christmas—at least, not Tom alone. There is a great deal else necessary before this can be made a place suitable for Tom!"

Again he drew near to Bertha and listened, but instead of speaking, she suddenly opened her eyes. The ghost of old Applejoy drew back, and made a low, respectful bow. The maiden did not move, but fixed her lovely blue eyes upon the apparition, who trembled for fear that she might scream or faint.

"Am I asleep?" she murmured, and then, after turning her head from side to side to assure herself that she was in her own room, she looked full into the face of old Applejoy's ghost, and boldly spoke to him. "Are you a spirit?" said she.

If a flush of joy could redden the countenance of a ghost, his face would have glowed like a sunlit rose. "Dear child," he exclaimed, "I am the ghost of your uncle's grandfather. His younger sister, Maria, was your mother, and, therefore, I am the ghost of your great-grandfather."

Bertha could not refrain from a smile. "It would be funny to help a ghost," she said.

"Then you must be the original Applejoy," said Bertha, "and I think it very wonderful that I am not afraid of you. You look as if you would not hurt anybody in this world, especially me!"

"There you have it, my dear!" he exclaimed, bringing his cane down upon the floor with a violence which had it been the cane it used to be would have wakened everybody in the house. "I vow to you there is not a person in the world for whom I have such an affection as I feel for you. You have brought into this house something of the old life. I wish I could tell you how happy I have been since the bright spring day that brought you here."

"I did not suppose I would make anyone happy by coming here," said Bertha. "Uncle John does not seem to care much about me, and I did not know about you."

"No, indeed," exclaimed the good ghost, "you did not know about me, but you will. First, however, we must get down to business. I came here to-night with a special object. It is about Christmas. Your uncle does not mean to have any Christmas in this house, but I intend, if I can possibly do so, to prevent him from disgracing himself. Still, I cannot do anything without help, and there is nobody to help me but you. Will you do it?"

Bertha could not refrain from a smile. "It would be funny to help a ghost," she said, "but if I can assist you I shall be very glad."

"I want you to go into the lower part of the house," said he. "I have something to show you. I shall go down and wait for you. Dress yourself as warmly as you can, and have you some soft slippers that will make no noise?"

"Oh, yes," said Bertha, her eyes twinkling with delight. "I shall be dressed and with you in no time."

"Do not hurry yourself," said the good ghost as he left the room. "We have most of the night before us."

When the young girl had descended the great staircase almost as noise-lessly as the ghost, she found her venerable companion waiting for her. "Do you see the lantern on the table?" said he. "John uses it when he goes his round of the house at bedtime. There are matches hanging above it. Please light it. You may be sure I would not put you to this trouble if I were able to do it myself."

When she had lighted the brass lantern, the ghost invited her to enter the study. "Now," said he as he led the way to the large desk with the cabinet above it, "will you be so good as to open that glass door and put your hand into the front corner of that middle shelf? You will feel a key hanging upon a little hook."

"But this is my uncle's cabinet," Bertha said, "and I have no right to meddle with his keys and things!"

The ghost drew himself up to the six feet two inches which had been his stature in life. "This was my cabinet," he said, "and I have never surrendered it to your uncle John! With my own hands I screwed the little hook into that dark corner and hung the key upon it! Now I beg you to take down that key and unlock that little drawer at the bottom."

Without a moment's hesitation Bertha took the key from the hook, unlocked and opened the drawer. "It is full of old keys all tied together in a bunch!" she said.

"Yes," said the ghost. "Now, my dear, I want you to understand that what we are going to do is strictly correct and proper. This was once my house—everything in it I planned and arranged. I am now going to take you into the cellars of my old mansion. They are wonderful cellars; they were my pride and glory! Are you afraid," he said, "to descend with me into these subterranean regions?"

"Not a bit!" exclaimed Bertha. "I think it will be the jolliest thing in the world to go with my great-grandfather into the cellars which he built himself, and of which he was so proud."

This speech so charmed the ghost of old Applejoy that he would instantly have kissed his great-granddaughter had it not been that he was afraid of giving her a cold.

"You are a girl to my liking!" he exclaimed. "I wish you had been living at the time I was alive and master of this house. We should have had gay times together!"

"I wish you were alive now, dear Great-grandpapa," said she. "Let us go on—I am all impatience!"

They then descended into the cellars, which, until the present owner came into possession of the estate, had been famous throughout the neighborhood. "This way," said old Applejoy's ghost. "Do you see that row of old casks nearly covered with cobwebs and dust? They contain some of the choicest spirits ever brought into this country, rum from Jamaica, brandy from France, port and Madeira.

"Come into this little room. Now, then, hold up your lantern. Notice that row of glass jars on the shelf. They are filled with the finest mincemeat ever made and just as good as it ever was! And there are a lot more jars and cans, all tightly sealed. I do not know what good things are in them, but I am sure their contents are just what will be wanted to fill out a Christmas table.

"Now, my dear, I want to show you the grandest thing in these cellars. Behold that wooden box! Inside it is an airtight box made of tin. Inside that is a great plum cake put into that box by me! I intended it to stay there for a long time, for plum cake gets better and better the longer it is kept. The people who eat that cake, my dear Bertha, will be blessed above all their fellow mortals!

"And now I think you have seen enough to understand thoroughly that these cellars are the abode of many good things to eat and to drink. It is their abode, but if John could have his way it would be their sepulchre!"

"But why did you bring me here, Great-grandpapa?" said Bertha. "Do you want me to come down here and have my Christmas dinner with you?"

"No, indeed," said old Applejoy's ghost. "Come upstairs, and let us go into the study." Once they were there, Bertha sat down before the fireplace and warmed her fingers over the few embers it contained.

"Bertha," said the spirit of her great-grandfather, "it is wicked not to celebrate Christmas, especially when one is able to do so in the most hospitable and generous way. For years John has taken no notice of Christmas, and it is our duty to reform him if we can! There is not much time before Christmas Day, but there is time enough to do everything that has to be done, if you and I go to work and set other people to work."

"And how are we to do that?" asked Bertha.

"The straightforward thing to do," said the ghost, "is for me to appear to your uncle, tell him his duty, and urge him to perform it, but I know what will be the result. He would call the interview a dream. But there is nothing dreamlike about you, my dear. If anyone hears you talking he will know he is awake."

"Do you want me to talk to Uncle?" said Bertha, smiling.

"Yes," said old Applejoy's ghost. "I want you to go to him immediately after breakfast tomorrow morning and tell him exactly what has happened this night; about the casks of spirits, the jars of mincemeat, and the wooden box nailed fast and tight with the tin box inside holding the plum cake. John knows all about that cake, and he knows all about me, too."

"And what is the message?" asked Bertha.

"It is simply this," said the ghost. "When you have told him all the events of this night, and when he sees that they must have happened, I want you to tell him that it is the wish and desire of his grandfather, to whom he owes everything, that there shall be worthy festivities in this house on Christmas Day and Night. Tell him to open his cellars and spend his money. Tell him to send for at least a dozen good friends and relatives to attend the great holiday celebration that is to be held in this house.

"Now, my dear," said old Applejoy's ghost, drawing near to the young girl, "I want to ask you—a private, personal question. Who is Tom?"

At these words a sudden blush rushed into the cheeks of Bertha. "Tom?" she said. "What Tom?"

"I am sure you know a young man named Tom, and I want you to tell me who he is. My name was Tom, and I am very fond of Toms. Is he a nice young fellow? Do you like him very much?"

"Yes," said Bertha, meaning the answer to cover both questions.

"And does he like you?"

"I think so," said Bertha.

"That means you are in love with each other!" exclaimed old Applejoy's ghost. "And now, my dear, tell me his last name. Out with it!"

"Mr. Burcham," said Bertha, her cheeks now a little pale.

"Son of Thomas Burcham of the Meadows?"

"Yes, sir," said Bertha.

The ghost of old Applejoy gazed down upon his great-granddaughter with pride and admiration. "My dear Bertha," he exclaimed, "I congratulate you! I have seen young Tom. He is a fine-looking fellow, and if you love him I know he is a good one. Now, I'll tell you what we will do, Bertha. We will have Tom here on Christmas."

"Oh, Great-grandfather, I can't ask Uncle to invite him!" she exclaimed.

"We will have a bigger party than we thought we would," said the beaming ghost. "All the invited guests will be asked to bring their families. When a big dinner is given at this house, Thomas Burcham, Sr., must not be left out, and he is bound to bring Tom. Now skip back to your bed, and immediately after breakfast come here to your uncle and tell him everything I have told you to tell him."

Bertha hesitated. "Great-grandfather," she said, "if Uncle does allow us to celebrate Christmas, will you be with us?"

"Yes, indeed, my dear," said he. "And you need not be afraid of my frightening anybody. I shall be everywhere and I shall hear everything, but I shall be visible only to the loveliest woman who ever graced this mansion. And now be off to bed without another word."

"If she hadn't gone," said old Applejoy's ghost to himself, "I couldn't have helped giving her a good-night kiss."

The next morning, as Bertha told the story of her night's adventures to her uncle, the face of John Applejoy grew paler and paler. He was a hard-headed man, but a superstitious one, and when Bertha told him of his grandfather's plum cake, the existence of which he had believed was not known to anyone but himself, he felt it was impossible for the girl to have dreamed these things. With all the power of his will he opposed this belief, but it was too much for him, and he surrendered. But he was a proud man and would not admit to his niece that he put any faith in the existence of ghosts.

"I shall be everywhere and I shall hear everything, but I shall be visible only to the loveliest woman who ever graced this mansion."

271

"My dear," said he, rising, his face still pale, but his expression under good control, "although there is nothing of weight in what you have told me—for traditions about my cellars have been afloat in the family—still your pretty little story suggests something to me. This is Christmastime and I had almost overlooked it. You are young and lively and accustomed to the celebration of holidays. Therefore, I have determined, my dear, to have a grand Christmas dinner and invite our friends and their families. I know there must be good things in the cellars, although I had almost forgotten them, and they shall be brought up and spread out and enjoyed. Now go and send Mrs. Dipperton to me, and when we have finished our consultation, you and I will make out a list of guests."

When she had gone, John Applejoy sat down in his big chair and looked fixedly into the fire. He would not have dared to go to bed that night if he had disregarded the message from his grandfather.

Never had there been such a glorious Christmastime within the walls of the old house. The news that old Mr. Applejoy was sending out invitations to a Christmas dinner spread like wildfire through the neighborhood. The idea of inviting people by families was considered a grand one, worthy indeed of the times of old Mr. Tom Applejoy, the grandfather of the present owner, who had been the most hospitable man in the whole country.

For the first time in nearly a century all the leaves of the great dining table were put into use, and the table had as much as it could do to stand up under its burdens brought from cellar, barn, and surrounding country. In the very middle of everything was the wonderful plum cake which had been put away by the famous grandfather of the host.

But the cake was not cut. "My friends," said Mr. John Applejoy, "we may all look at this cake but we will not eat it! We will keep it just as it is until a marriage shall occur in this family. Then you are all invited to come and enjoy it!"

At the conclusion of this little speech old Applejoy's ghost patted his grandson upon the head. "You don't feel that, John," he said to himself, "but it is approbation, and this is the first time I have ever approved of you!"

Late in the evening there was a grand dance in the great hall, which opened with an old-fashioned minuet, and when the merry guests were forming on the floor, a young man named Tom came forward and asked the hand of Bertha.

"No," said she, "not this time. I am going to dance this first dance with— well, we will say by myself!"

At these words the most thoroughly gratified ghost in all space stepped up to the side of the lovely girl, and with his cocked hat folded flat under his left arm, he made a low bow and held out his hand. With his long waistcoat trimmed with lace, his tightly drawn stockings and his buckled shoes, there was not such a gallant figure in the whole company.

Bertha put out her hand and touched the shadowy fingers of her partner, and then, side by side, she and the ghost of her great-grandfather opened the ball. With all the grace of fresh young beauty and ancient courtliness they danced the minuet.

"What a strange young girl," said some of the guests, "to go through that dance all by herself, but how beautifully she did it!"

"Very eccentric, my dear!" said Mr. John Applejoy when the dance was over. "But I could not help thinking as I looked at you that there was nobody in this room that was worthy to be your partner."

"You are wrong there, old fellow!" was the simultaneous mental ejaculation of young Tom Burcham and of old Applejoy's ghost.

THE BALLAD OF THE HARP-WEAVER
by Edna St. Vincent Millay

"Son," said my mother,
    When I was knee-high,
"You've need of clothes to cover you,
    And not a rag have I.

"There's nothing in the house
    To make a boy breeches,
Nor shears to cut a cloth with,
    Nor thread to take stitches.

"There's nothing in the house
    But a loaf-end of rye,
And a harp with a woman's head
    Nobody will buy,"
    And she began to cry.

That was in the early fall.
    When came the late fall,
"Son," she said, "the sight of you
    Makes your mother's blood crawl,—

"Little skinny shoulder-blades
    Sticking through your clothes!
And where you'll get a jacket from
    God above knows.

"It's lucky for me, lad,
    Your daddy's in the ground,
And can't see the way I let
    His son go around!"
    And she made a queer sound.

That was in the late fall.
    When the winter came,
I'd not a pair of breeches
    Nor a shirt to my name.

I couldn't go to school,
    Or out of doors to play.
And all the other little boys
    Passed our way.

"Son," said my mother,
    "Come, climb into my lap,
And I'll chafe your little bones
    While you take a nap."

And, oh, but we were silly
    For half an hour or more,
Me with my long legs
    Dragging on the floor,

A-rock-rock-rocking
    To a mother-goose rhyme!
Oh, but we were happy
    For half an hour's time!

But there was I, a great boy,
    And what would folks say
To hear my mother singing me
    To sleep all day,
    In such a daft way?

Men say the winter
    Was bad that year;
Fuel was scarce,
    And food was dear.

A wind with a wolf's head
    Howled about our door,
And we burned up the chairs
    And sat upon the floor.

All that was left us
    Was a chair we couldn't break,
And the harp with a woman's head
    Nobody would take,
    For song or pity's sake.

The night before Christmas
    I cried with the cold,
I cried myself to sleep
    Like a two-year-old.

And in the deep night
    I felt my mother rise,
And stare down upon me
    With love in her eyes.

I saw my mother sitting
    On the one good chair,
A light falling on her
    From I couldn't tell where,

Looking nineteen,
    And not a day older,
And the harp with a woman's head
    Leaned against her shoulder.

Her thin fingers, moving
    In the thin, tall strings,
Were weav-weav-weaving
    Wonderful things.

Many bright threads,
    From where I couldn't see,
Were running through the harp-strings
    Rapidly,

And gold threads whistling
    Through my mother's hand.
I saw the web grow,
    And the pattern expand.

She wove a child's jacket,
    And when it was done
She laid it on the floor
    And wove another one.

She wove a red cloak
    So regal to see,
"She's made it for a king's son,"
    I said, "and not for me."
    But I knew it was for me.

She wove a pair of breeches
    Quicker than that!
She wove a pair of boots
    And a little cocked hat.

She wove a pair of mittens,
    She wove a little blouse,
She wove all night
    In the still, cold house.

She sang as she worked,
    And the harp-strings spoke;
Her voice never faltered,
    And the thread never broke.
    And when I awoke,—

There sat my mother
    With the harp against her shoulder,
Looking nineteen,
    And not a day older,

A smile about her lips,
    And a light about her head,
And her hands in the harp-strings
    Frozen dead.

And piled up beside her
    And toppling to the skies,
Were the clothes of a king's son,
    Just my size.

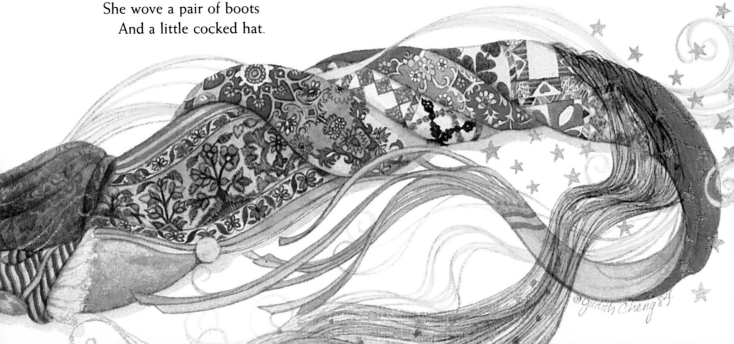

CHRISTMAS EVERY DAY

by William Dean Howells

The little girl came into her papa's study, as she always did Saturday morning before breakfast, and asked for a story. He tried to beg off that morning, for he was very busy, but she would not let him. So he began:

"Well, once there was a little pig—"

She stopped him at the word. She said she had heard little pig-stories till she was perfectly sick of them.

"Well, what kind of story *shall* I tell, then?"

"About Christmas. It's getting to be the season."

"Well!" Her papa roused himself. "Then I'll tell you about the little girl that wanted it Christmas every day in the year. How would you like that?"

"First-rate!" said the little girl; and she nestled into comfortable shape in his lap, ready for listening.

"Very well, then, this little pig— Oh, what are you pounding me for?"

"Because you said little pig instead of little girl."

"I should like to know what's the difference between a little pig and a little girl that wanted it Christmas every day!"

"Papa!" said the little girl warningly. At this her papa began to tell the story.

278

Once there was a little girl who liked Christmas so much that she wanted it to be Christmas every day in the year; and as soon as Thanksgiving was over she began to send postcards to the old Christmas Fairy to ask if she mightn't have it. But the old Fairy never answered, and after a while the little girl found out that the Fairy wouldn't notice anything but real letters sealed outside with a monogram—or your initial, anyway. So, then, she began to send letters; and just the day before Christmas, she got a letter from the Fairy, saying she might have it Christmas every day for a year, and then they would see about having it longer.

The little girl was excited already, preparing for the old-fashioned, once-a-year Christmas that was coming the next day. So she resolved to keep the Fairy's promise to herself and surprise everybody with it as it kept coming true, but then it slipped out of her mind altogether.

She had a splendid Christmas. She went to bed early, so as to let Santa Claus fill the stockings, and in the morning she was up the first of anybody and found hers all lumpy with packages of candy, and oranges and grapes, and rubber balls, and all kinds of small presents. Then she waited until the rest of the family was up, and she burst into the library to look at the large presents laid out on the library table—books, and boxes of stationery, and dolls, and little stoves, and dozens of handkerchiefs, and inkstands, and skates, and photograph frames, and boxes of watercolors, and dolls' houses—and the big Christmas tree, lighted and standing in the middle.

She had a splendid Christmas all day. She ate so much candy that she did not want any breakfast; and the whole forenoon the presents kept pouring in that had not been delivered the night before; and she went round giving the presents she had got for other people, and came home and ate turkey and cranberry for dinner, and plum pudding and nuts and raisins and oranges, and then went out and coasted, and came in with a stomachache, crying; and her papa said he would see if his house was turned into that sort of fool's paradise another year; and they had a light supper, and pretty early everybody went to bed cross.

The little girl slept very heavily and very late, but she was wakened at last by the other children dancing around her bed with their stockings full of presents in their hands. "Christmas! Christmas! Christmas!" they all shouted.

"Nonsense! It was Christmas yesterday," said the little girl, rubbing her eyes sleepily.

Her brothers and sisters just laughed. "We don't know about that. It's Christmas today, anyway. You come into the library and see."

Then all at once it flashed on the little girl that the Fairy was keeping her promise, and her year of Christmases was beginning. She was dreadfully sleepy, but she sprang up and darted into the library. There it was again! Books, and boxes of stationery, and dolls, and so on.

There was the Christmas tree blazing away, and the family picking out their presents, and her father looking perfectly puzzled, and her mother ready to cry. "I'm sure I don't see how I'm to dispose of all these things," said her mother, and her father said it seemed to him they had had something just like it the day before, but he supposed he must have dreamed it. This struck the little girl as the best kind of a joke; and so she ate so much candy she didn't want any breakfast, and went round carrying presents, and had turkey and cranberry for dinner, and then went out and coasted, and came in with a stomachache, crying.

Now, the next day, it was the same thing over again, but everybody getting crosser; and at the end of a week's time so many people had lost their tempers that you could pick up lost tempers anywhere; they perfectly strewed the ground. Even when people tried to recover their tempers they usually got somebody else's, and it made the most dreadful mix.

The little girl began to get frightened, keeping the secret all to herself; she wanted to tell her mother, but she didn't dare to; and she was ashamed to ask the Fairy to take back her gift, it seemed ungrateful and ill-bred. So it went on and on, and it was Christmas on St. Valentine's Day and Washington's Birthday, just the same as any day, and it didn't skip even the First of April, though everything was counterfeit that day, and that was some *little* relief.

After a while turkeys got to be awfully scarce, selling for about a thousand dollars apiece. They got to passing off almost anything for turkeys—even half-grown hummingbirds. And cranberries—well they asked a diamond apiece for cranberries. All the woods and orchards were cut down for Christmas trees. After a while they had to make Christmas trees out of rags. But there were plenty of rags, because people got so poor, buying presents for one another, that they couldn't get any new clothes, and they just wore their old ones to tatters. They got so poor that everybody had to go to the poorhouse, except the confectioners, and the storekeepers, and the booksellers; and *they* all got so rich and proud that they would hardly wait upon a person when he came to buy. It was perfectly shameful!

After it had gone on about three or four months, the little girl, whenever she came into the room in the morning and saw those great ugly, lumpy stockings dangling at the fireplace, and the disgusting presents around everywhere, used to sit down and burst out crying. In six months she was perfectly exhausted; she couldn't even cry anymore.

And how it was on the Fourth of July! On the Fourth of July, the first boy in the United States woke up and found out that his firecrackers and toy pistol and two-dollar collection of fireworks were nothing but sugar and candy painted up to look like fireworks. Before ten o'clock every boy in the United States discovered that his July Fourth things had turned into Christmas things and was so mad. The Fourth of July orations all turned into Christmas carols, and when anybody tried to read the Declaration of Independence, instead of saying, "When in the course of human events it becomes necessary," he was sure to sing, "God rest you merry gentlemen." It was perfectly awful.

About the beginning of October the little girl took to sitting down on dolls wherever she found them—she hated the sight of them so; and by Thanksgiving she just slammed her presents across the room. By that time people didn't carry presents around nicely anymore. They flung them over the fence or through the window; and, instead of taking great pains to write "For dear Papa," or "Mama," or "Brother," or "Sister," they used to write, "Take it, you horrid old thing!" and then go and bang it against the front door.

Nearly everybody had built barns to hold their presents, but pretty soon the barns overflowed, and then they used to let them lie out in the rain, or anywhere. Sometimes the police used to come and tell them to shovel their presents off the sidewalk or they would arrest them.

Before Thanksgiving came it had leaked out who had caused all these Christmases. The little girl had suffered so much that she had talked about it in her sleep; and after that hardly anybody would play with her, because if it had not been for her greediness it wouldn't have happened. And now, when it came Thanksgiving, and she wanted them to go to church, and have turkey, and show their gratitude, they said that all the turkeys had been eaten for her old Christmas dinners, and if she would stop the Christmases, they would see about the gratitude. And the very next day the little girl began sending letters to the Christmas Fairy, and then telegrams, to stop it. But it didn't do any good; and then she got to calling at the Fairy's house, but the girl that came to the door always said, "Not at home," or "Engaged," or something like that; and so it went on till it came to the old once-a-year Christmas Eve. The little girl fell asleep, and when she woke up in the morning—

"She found it was all nothing but a dream," suggested the little girl.

"No, indeed!" said her papa. "It was all every bit true!"

"What *did* she find out, then?"

"Why, that it wasn't Christmas at last, and wasn't ever going to be, anymore. Now it's time for breakfast."

The little girl held her papa fast around the neck.

"You shan't go if you're going to leave it *so!*"

"How do you want it left?"

"Christmas once a year."

"All right," said her papa; and he went on again.

283

Well, with no Christmas ever again, there was the greatest rejoicing all over the country. People met together everywhere and kissed and cried for joy. Carts went around and gathered up all the candy and raisins and nuts, and dumped them into the river; and it made the fish perfectly sick. And the whole United States, as far out as Alaska, was one blaze of bonfires, where the children were burning up their presents of all kinds. They had the greatest *time!*

The little girl went to thank the old Fairy because she had stopped its being Christmas, and she said she hoped the Fairy would keep her promise and see that Christmas never, never came again. Then the Fairy frowned, and said that now the little girl was behaving just as greedily as ever, and she'd better look out. This made the little girl think it all over carefully again, and she said she would be willing to have it Christmas about once in a thousand years; and then she said a hundred, and then she said ten, and at last she got down to one. Then the Fairy said that was the good old way that had pleased people ever since Christmas began, and she was agreed. Then the little girl said, "What're your shoes made of?" And the Fairy said, "Leather." And the little girl said, "Bargain's done forever," and skipped off, and hippity-hopped the whole way home, she was so glad.

"How will that do?" asked the papa.

"First-rate!" said the little girl; but she hated to have the story stop, and was rather sober. However, her mama put her head in at the door and asked her papa:

"Are you never coming to breakfast? What have you been telling that child?"

"Oh, just a tale with a moral."

The little girl caught him around the neck again.

"*We* know! Don't you tell *what*, papa! Don't you tell *what!*"

A CAROL FOR CHILDREN
by Ogden Nash

God rest you, merry Innocents,
Let nothing you dismay,
Let nothing wound an eager heart
Upon this Christmas day.

Yours be the genial holly wreaths,
The stockings and the tree;
An aged world to you bequeaths
Its own forgotten glee.

Soon, soon enough come crueler gifts,
The anger and the tears;
Between you now there sparsely drifts
A handful yet of years.

Oh dimly, dimly glows the star
Through the electric throng;
The bidding in temple and bazaar
Drowns out the silver song.

The ancient altars smoke afresh,
The ancient idols stir;
Faint in the reek of burning flesh
Sink frankincense and myrrh.

Gaspar, Balthazar, Melchior!
Where are your offerings now?
What greetings to the Prince of War,
His darkly branded brow?

Two ultimate laws alone we know,
The ledger and the sword—
So far away, so long ago,
We lost the infant Lord.

Only the children clasp his hand;
His voice speaks low to them,
And still for them the shining band
Wings over Bethlehem.

God rest you, merry Innocents,
While innocence endures.
A sweeter Christmas than we to ours
May you bequeath to yours.

CONVERSATION ABOUT CHRISTMAS
by Dylan Thomas

S*mall Boy*. Years and years ago, when you were a boy . . .

Self. When there were wolves in Wales, and birds the colour of red-flannel petticoats whisked past the harp-shaped hills, when we sang and wallowed all night and day in caves that smelt like Sunday afternoons in damp front farmhouse parlours, and chased, with the jawbones of deacons, the English and the bears . . .

Small Boy. You are not so old as Mr. Benyon Number Twenty-Two who can remember when there were no motors. Years and years ago, when you were a boy . . .

Self. Oh, before the motor even, before the wheel, before the duchess-faced horse, when we rode the daft and happy hills bare-back . . .

Small Boy. You're not so daft as Mrs. Griffiths up the street, who says she puts her ear under the water in the reservoir and listens to the fish talk Welsh. When you were a boy, what was Christmas like?

Self. It snowed.

Small Boy. It snowed last year, too. I made a snowman and my brother knocked it down and I knocked my brother down and then we had tea.

Self. But that was not the same snow. Our snow was not only shaken in whitewash buckets down the sky, I think it came shawling out of the ground and swam and drifted out of the arms and hands and bodies of the trees; snow grew overnight on the roofs of the houses like a pure and grandfather moss, minutely ivied the walls, and settled on the postman, opening the gate, like a dumb, numb thunderstorm of white torn Christmas cards.

Small Boy. Were there postmen, then, too?

Self. With sprinkling eyes and wind-cherried noses, on spread, frozen feet they crunched up to the doors and mittened on them manfully. But all that the children could hear was a ringing of bells.

Small Boy. You mean that the postman went rat-a-tat-tat and the doors rang?

Self. The bells that the children could hear were inside them.

Small Boy. I only hear thunder sometimes, never bells.

Self. There were church bells, too.

Small Boy. Inside them?

Self. No, no, no, in the bat-black, snow-white belfries, tugged by bishops and storks. And they rang their tidings over the bandaged town, over the frozen foam of the powder and ice-cream hills, over the crackling sea. It seemed that all the churches boomed, for joy, under my window; and the weathercocks crew for Christmas, on our fence.

Small Boy. Get back to the postmen.

Self. They were just ordinary postmen, fond of walking, and dogs, and Christmas, and the snow. They knocked on the doors with blue knuckles . . .

Small Boy. Ours has got a black knocker . . .

Self. And then they stood on the white welcome mat in the little, drifted porches, and clapped their hands together, and huffed and puffed, making ghosts with their breath, and jogged from foot to foot like small boys wanting to go out.

Small Boy. And then the Presents?

Self. And then the Presents, after the Christmas box. And the cold postman, with a rose on his button-nose, tingled down the teatray-slithered run of the chilly glinting hill. He went in his ice-bound boots like a man on fishmonger's slabs. He wagged his bag like a frozen camel's hump, dizzily turned the corner on one foot, and, by God, he was gone.

Small Boy. Get back to the Presents.

Self. There were the Useful Presents: engulfing mufflers of the old coach days, and mittens made for giant sloths; zebra scarves of a substance like silky gum that could be tug-o'-warred down to the goloshes; blinding tam-o'-shanters like patchwork tea-cosies, and bunny-scutted busbies and balaclavas for victims of head-shrinking tribes; from aunts who always wore wool next to the skin, there were moustached and rasping vests that made you wonder why the aunties had any skin left at all; and once I had a little crocheted nose-bag from an aunt now, alas, no longer whinnying with us. And pictureless books in which small boys, though warned, with quotations, not to, *would* skate on Farmer Garge's pond, and did, and drowned; and books that told me everything about the wasp, except why.

Small Boy. Get on to the Useless Presents.

Self. On Christmas Eve I hung at the foot of my bed Bessie Bunter's black stocking, and always, I said, I would stay awake all the moonlit, snowlit night to hear the roof-alighting reindeer and see the hollied boot descend through soot. But soon the sand of the snow drifted into my eyes, and, though I stared towards the fireplace and around the flickering room where the black sack-like stocking hung, I was asleep before the chimney trembled and the room was red and white with Christmas. But in the morning, though no snow melted on the bedroom floor, the stocking bulged and brimmed: press it, it squeaked like a mouse-in-a-box; it smelt of tangerine; a furry arm lolled over, like the arm of a kangaroo out of its mother's belly; squeeze it hard in the middle, and something squelched; squeeze it again—squelch again. Look out of the frost-scribbled window: on the great loneliness of the small hill, a blackbird was silent in the snow.

Small Boy. Were there any sweets?

Self. Of course there were sweets. It was the marshmallows that squelched. Hardboileds, toffee, fudge and allsorts, crunches, cracknels, humbugs, glaciers, and marzipan and butterwelsh for the Welsh. And troops of bright tin soldiers who, if they would not fight, could always run. And Snakes-and-Families and Happy Ladders. And Easy Hobbi-Games for Little Engineers, complete with Instructions. Oh, easy for Leonardo! And a whistle to make the dogs bark to wake up the old man next door to make him beat on the wall with his stick to shake our picture off the wall. And a packet of cigarettes: you put one in your mouth and you stood at the corner of the street and you waited for hours, in vain, for an old lady to scold you for smoking a cigarette and then, with a smirk, you ate it. And, last of all, in the toe of the stocking, sixpence like a silver corn. And then downstairs for breakfast under the balloons!

Small Boy. Were there Uncles, like in our house?

Self. There are always Uncles at Christmas. The same Uncles. And on Christmas mornings, with dog-disturbing whistle and sugar fags, I would scour the swathed town for the news of the little world, and find always a dead bird by the white Bank or by the deserted swings; perhaps a robin, all but one of his fires out, and that fire still burning on his breast. Men and women wading and scooping back from church or chapel, with taproom noses and wind-smacked cheeks, all albinos, huddled their stiff black jarring feathers against the irreligious snow. Mistletoe hung from the gas in all the front parlours; there was sherry and walnuts and bottled beer and crackers by the dessertspoons; and cats in their fur-abouts watched the fires; and the high-heaped fires crackled and spat, all ready for the chestnuts and the mulling pokers. Some few large men sat in the front parlours, without their collars, Uncles almost certainly, trying their new cigars, holding them out judiciously at arm's-length, returning them to their mouths, coughing, then holding them out again as though waiting for the explosion; and some few small aunts, not wanted in the kitchen, nor anywhere else for that matter, sat on the very edges of their chairs, poised and brittle, afraid to break, like faded cups and saucers. Not many those mornings trod the piling streets: an old man always, fawn-bowlered, yellow-gloved, and, at this time of year, with spats of snow, would take his constitutional to the white bowling-green, and back, as he would take it wet or fine on Christmas Day or Doomsday; sometimes two hale young men, with big pipes blazing, no overcoats, and windblown scarves, would trudge, unspeaking, down to the forlorn sea, to work up an appetite, to blow away the fumes, who knows, to walk into the waves until nothing of them was left but the two curling smoke clouds of their inextinguishable briars.

Small Boy. Why didn't you go home for Christmas dinner?

Self. Oh, but I did, I always did. I would be slap-dashing home, the gravy smell of the dinners of others, the bird smell, the brandy, the pudding and mince, weaving up my nostrils, when out of a snow-clogged side-lane would come a boy the spit of myself, with a pink-tipped cigarette and the violet past of a black eye, cocky as a bullfinch, leering all to himself. I hated him on sight and sound, and would be about to put my dog-whistle to my lips and blow him off the face of Christmas when suddenly he, with a violet wink, put *his* whistle to *his* lips and blew so stridently, so high, so exquisitely loud, that gobbling faces, their cheeks bulged with goose, would press against their tinselled windows, the whole length of the white echoing street.

Small Boy. What did you have for Dinner?

Self. Turkey, and blazing pudding.

Small Boy. Was it nice?

Self. It was not made on earth.

Small Boy. What did you do after dinner?

Self. The Uncles sat in front of the fire, took off their collars, loosened all buttons, put their large moist hands over their watch-chains, groaned a little, and slept. Mothers, aunts, and sisters scuttled to and fro, bearing tureens. The dog was sick. Auntie Beattie had to have three aspirins, but Auntie Hannah, who liked port, stood in the middle of the snowbound back-yard, singing like a big-bosomed thrush. I would blow up balloons to see how big they would blow up to; and, when they burst, which they all did, the Uncles jumped and rumbled. In the rich and heavy afternoon, the Uncles breathing like dolphins and the snow descending, I would sit in the front room, among festoons and Chinese lanterns, and nibble at dates, and try to make a model man-o'-war, following the Instructions for Little Engineers, and produce what might be mistaken for a sea-going tram. And then, at Christmas tea, the recovered Uncles would be jolly over their mince-pies; and the great iced cake loomed in the centre of the table like a marble grave. Auntie Hannah laced her tea with rum, because it was only once a year. And in the evening, there was Music. An uncle played the fiddle, a cousin sang "Cherry Ripe," and another uncle sang "Drake's Drum." It was very warm in the little house. Auntie Hannah, who had got on to the parsnip wine, sang a song about Rejected Love, and Bleeding Hearts, and Death, and then another in which she said that her Heart was like a Bird's Nest; and then everybody laughed again, and then I went to bed. Looking through my bedroom window, out into the moonlight and the flying, unending, smoke-coloured snow, I could see the lights in the windows of all the other houses on our hill, and hear the music rising from them up the long, steadily falling night. I turned the gas down, I got into bed. I said some words to the close and holy darkness, and then I slept.

Small Boy. But it all sounds like an ordinary Christmas.

Self. It was.

Small Boy. But Christmas when you were a boy wasn't any different to Christmas now.

Self. It was, it was.

Small Boy. Why was Christmas different then?

Self. I mustn't tell you.

Small Boy. Why mustn't you tell me? Why is Christmas different for me?

Self. I mustn't tell you.

Small Boy. Why can't Christmas be the same for me as it was for you when you were a boy?

Self. I mustn't tell you. I mustn't tell you because it is Christmas now.

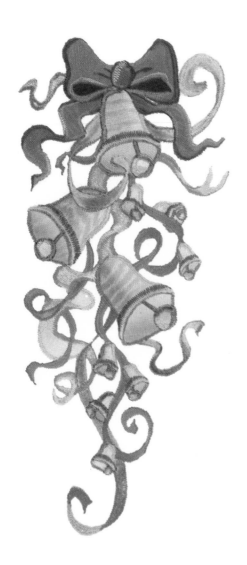

NEW YEAR'S BELLS
by Alfred Lord Tennyson

Ring out, wild bells, to the wild sky,
   The flying cloud, the frosty light:
   The year is dying in the night;
Ring out, wild bells, and let him die.

Ring out the old, ring in the new,
   Ring, happy bells, across the snow:
   The year is going, let him go;
Ring out the false, ring in the true.

Ring out the grief that saps the mind,
   For those that here we see no more;
   Ring out the feud of rich and poor,
Ring in redress to all mankind.

Ring out a slowly dying cause,
   And ancient forms of party strife;
   Ring in the nobler modes of life,
With sweeter manners, purer laws.

Ring out the want, the care, the sin,
   The faithless coldness of the times;
   Ring out, ring out my mournful rhymes,
But ring the fuller minstrel in.

Ring out false pride in place and blood,
   The civic slander and the spite;
   Ring in the love of truth and right,
Ring in the common love of good.

Ring out old shapes of foul disease;
   Ring out the narrowing lust of gold;
   Ring out the thousand wars of old,
Ring in the thousand years of peace.

Ring in the valiant man and free,
   The larger heart, the kindlier hand;
   Ring out the darkness of the land,
Ring in the Christ that is to be.

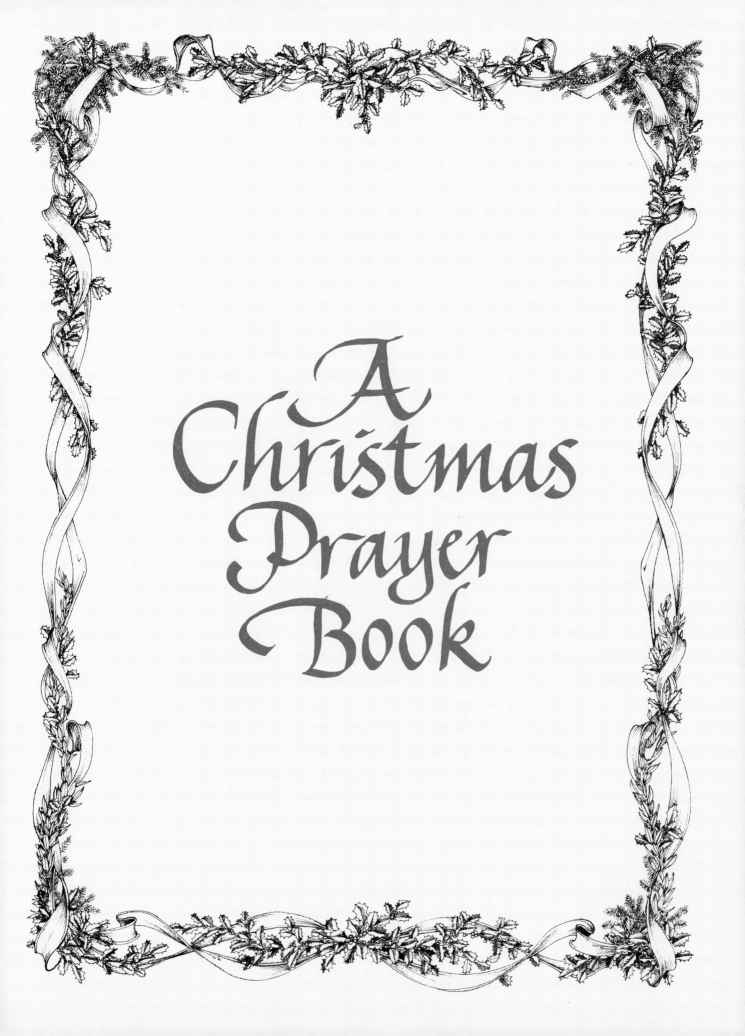

A Christmas Prayer Book

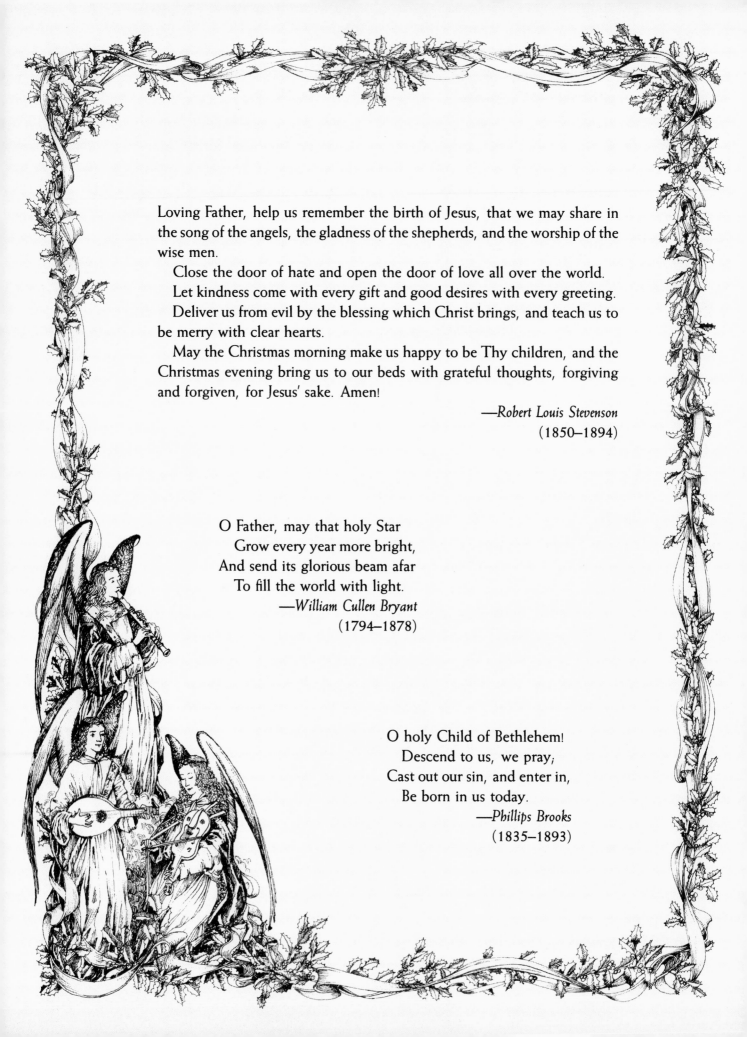

Loving Father, help us remember the birth of Jesus, that we may share in the song of the angels, the gladness of the shepherds, and the worship of the wise men.

Close the door of hate and open the door of love all over the world.

Let kindness come with every gift and good desires with every greeting.

Deliver us from evil by the blessing which Christ brings, and teach us to be merry with clear hearts.

May the Christmas morning make us happy to be Thy children, and the Christmas evening bring us to our beds with grateful thoughts, forgiving and forgiven, for Jesus' sake. Amen!

—Robert Louis Stevenson
(1850–1894)

O Father, may that holy Star
   Grow every year more bright,
And send its glorious beam afar
   To fill the world with light.
—William Cullen Bryant
(1794–1878)

O holy Child of Bethlehem!
   Descend to us, we pray;
Cast out our sin, and enter in,
   Be born in us today.
—Phillips Brooks
(1835–1893)

Little Jesus, wast Thou shy
Once, and just so small as I?
And what did it feel like to be
Out of Heaven, and just like me?

Hadst Thou ever any toys,
Like us little girls and boys?
And didst Thou play in Heaven with all
The angels that were not too tall,
With stars for marbles? Did the things
Play *Can you see me?* through their wings?

Didst Thou kneel at night to pray,
And didst Thou join Thy hands, this way?
And dost Thou like it best, that we
Should join our hands to pray to Thee?
I used to think, before I knew,
The prayer not said unless we do.

And did Thy Mother at the night
Kiss Thee, and fold the clothes in right?
And didst Thou feel quite good in bed,
Kissed, and sweet, and Thy prayers said?

Thou canst not have forgotten all
That it feels like to be small.
To Thy Father show my prayer
(He will look, Thou art so fair),
And say: "O Father, I, Thy Son,
Bring the prayer of a little one."

And He will smile, that children's tongue
Has not changed since Thou wast young!
—*Francis Thompson*
(1859–1907)

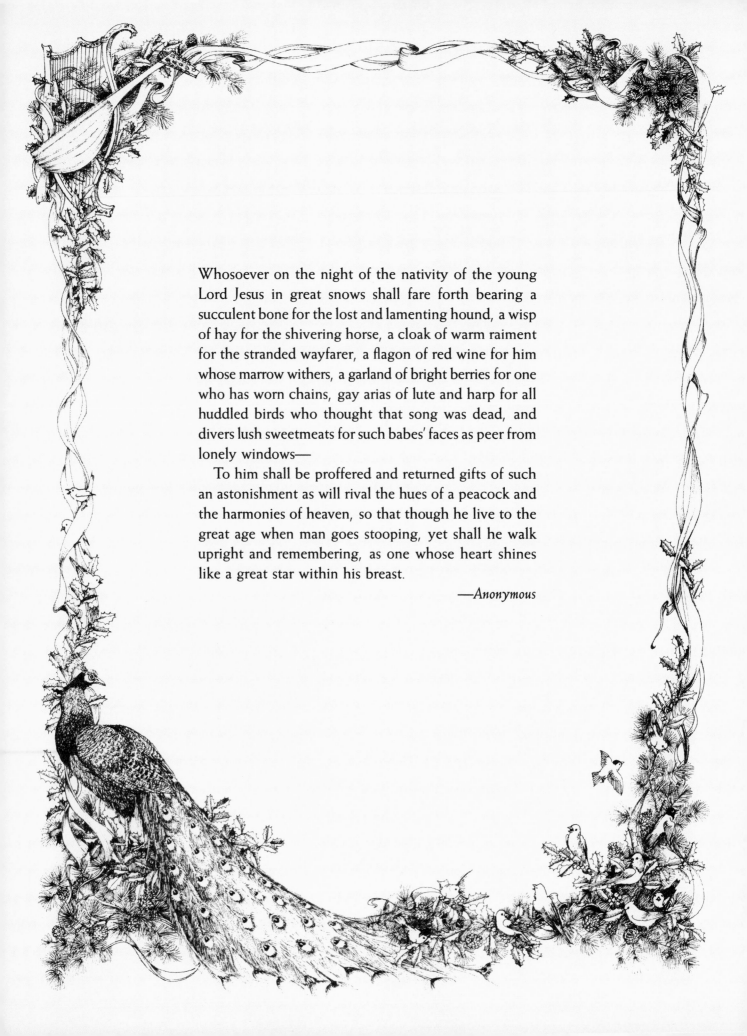

Whosoever on the night of the nativity of the young Lord Jesus in great snows shall fare forth bearing a succulent bone for the lost and lamenting hound, a wisp of hay for the shivering horse, a cloak of warm raiment for the stranded wayfarer, a flagon of red wine for him whose marrow withers, a garland of bright berries for one who has worn chains, gay arias of lute and harp for all huddled birds who thought that song was dead, and divers lush sweetmeats for such babes' faces as peer from lonely windows—

To him shall be proffered and returned gifts of such an astonishment as will rival the hues of a peacock and the harmonies of heaven, so that though he live to the great age when man goes stooping, yet shall he walk upright and remembering, as one whose heart shines like a great star within his breast.

—*Anonymous*

For this day of the dear Christ's birth, for its hours of home gladness and world gladness, for the love within these walls, which binds us together as a family, for our food on this table, for our surroundings in a land of freedom, we bring to Thee, our Father, our heartfelt gratitude. Bless all these, Thy favors, to our good, in Jesus' name. Amen.

—*H. B. Milward*

Dear Lord, we thank you today for all these good things to eat and drink, and especially for those dear friends and family members [names] who have come to be with us. May the happiness we share together on this Christmas day shine in all our hearts forever. Amen.

—*Anonymous*

Little Jesus of the Crib,
Give us the virtues of those who surround you.
Make us philosophical as the fisherman,
Carefree as the drummer,
Merry in exploring the world as the troubadour,
Eager for work as the bugler,
Patient as the spinner,
Kind as the ass,
Strong as the ox which keeps you warm.
Give us the sacred leisure of the hunter.
Give us also the desire of the shepherd for earthly things,
The pride of the trade of the knife grinder and the weaver,
The song of the miller.
Grant us the knowledge of the Magi,
The cheerfulness of the pigeon,
The impulsiveness of the cock,
The discretion of the snail,
The meekness of the lamb.
Give us the goodness of bread,
The tenderness of the wild boar,
The salt of the haddock,
The good humor of old wine,
The ardor of the candle,
The purity of the star.
                    —*The Prayer of the Children of Provence*

In a world that seems not only to be changing, but even to be
dissolving, there are some tens of millions of us who want
Christmas to be the same . . .
    with the same old greeting "Merry Christmas" and no other.

We long for the abiding love among men of good will which the
season brings . . .
believing in this ancient miracle of Christmas with its softening,
sweetening influence to tug at our heart strings once again.

We want to hold on to the old customs and traditions because
they strengthen our family ties,
        bind us to our friends,
    make us one with all mankind
for whom the Child was born,
and bring us back again to the God Who gave His only begotten
Son, that "whosoever believeth in Him should not perish, but
have everlasting life."

So we will not "spend" Christmas . . .
    nor "observe" Christmas.
We will "keep" Christmas—keep it as it is . . .
    in all the loveliness of its ancient traditions.

May we keep it in our hearts,
that we may be kept in its hope.

                                    —*Peter Marshall*
                                     (1902–1949)

ACKNOWLEDGMENTS

TEXT CREDITS

Pages 16–25: essay by John R. Roberson. Page 24: lines from "Tradition Time" by Helen Lowrie Marshall from *Starlight and Candleglow*, copyright © 1971 by Helen Lowrie Marshall, reprinted by permission of John Stanley Marshall. Pages 30–35: essay by James J. Menick. Pages 40–45: essay by Herbert Lieberman. Pages 48–55: essay by Carol D. Tarlow. Pages 62–69: essay by Raymond D. Sipherd. Page 65: "Lines for December 26th" by Richard Armour, copyright 1946, renewed © 1974 by The Curtis Publishing Co., is reprinted from *The Saturday Evening Post* by permission of The Curtis Publishing Co. Pages 74–79: essay by Raymond D. Sipherd. Page 79: "Mistletoe," copyright © 1913 by Walter de la Mare, is reprinted by permission of the Literary Trustees of Walter de la Mare and The Society of Authors as their representative. Pages 84–92: essay by Herbert Lieberman. Page 85: quote from "Santa Claus Is Comin' To Town" by J. Fred Coots and Haven Gillespie, copyright 1934, renewed © 1962 by Leo Feist Inc., is reprinted by permission of Columbia Pictures Publications. Pages 128–133: cookie recipes courtesy of Lorna B. Harris. Pages 140–146: "A Miserable, Merry Christmas" is from *The Autobiography of Lincoln Steffens*, copyright 1931 by Harcourt Brace Jovanovich, Inc., renewed © 1958 by Peter Steffens, reprinted by permission of Harcourt Brace Jovanovich, Inc. Page 159: "Carol," copyright © 1918 by Dorothy L. Sayers, is reprinted by permission of David Higham Associates Ltd. Pages 160–195: *Miracle on 34th Street* by Valentine Davies, copyright 1947 by Harcourt Brace Jovanovich, Inc., renewed © 1975 by Elizabeth S. Davies, is reprinted by permission of Harcourt Brace Jovanovich, Inc. Pages 196–206: "The Lord of Misrule," copyright © 1974 by Norah Lofts, is reprinted by permission of Curtis Brown Ltd., London, on behalf of the Estate of Norah Lofts. Page 207: "Nativity" by Gladys May Casely Hayford, copyright 1927, renewed © 1956 by The Atlantic Monthly Company, is reprinted by permission of The Atlantic Monthly Company. Pages 208–215: "Mr. Edwards Meets Santa Claus" is from *Little House on the Prairie*, text copyright 1935 by Laura Ingalls Wilder, renewed © 1963 by Roger Lea MacBride, reprinted by permission of Harper & Row, Publishers, Inc. and Methuen Children's Books. Pages 216–221: "Christmas Day in the Morning," copyright 1955 by Pearl S. Buck, renewed © 1983 by Janice C. Walsh, Richard S. Walsh, John S. Walsh, Henriette C. Walsh, Mrs. Chieko Singer, Carol Buck, Edgar Walsh, and Mrs. Jean C. Lippincott, is reprinted by permission of Harold Ober Associates, Inc. Pages 222–263: *Eloise at Christmastime* by Kay Thompson, illustrated by Hilary Knight, copyright © 1958 by Kay Thompson, is reprinted by permission of Random House, Inc. Pages 274–277: "The Ballad of the Harp Weaver," copyright 1923 by Edna St. Vincent Millay, renewed © 1951 by Norma Millay Ellis, is reprinted by permission of Norma Millay Ellis, Literary Executor of the Estate. Page 285: "A Carol for Children," copyright 1934, renewed © 1962 by Ogden Nash, is reprinted by permission of Little, Brown & Co. and André Deutsch Ltd. Pages 286–291: "Conversation About Christmas" by Dylan Thomas, copyright 1954 by New Directions Publishing Corp., renewed © 1982 by Caitlin Thomas, Llewelyn Edouard Thomas, Aeronwy Bryn Thomas–Ellis, and Colum Garn Thomas, is reprinted by permission of New Directions Publishing Corp. and David Higham Associates Ltd. Page 299: from "Let's Keep Christmas" by Peter Marshall, copyright 1952, 1953, renewed © 1981 by Catherine Marshall, taken from *The Best of Peter Marshall*, reprinted by permission of Chosen Books.

Additional thanks to the following: Virginia Colton and James L. Forsht, crafts copy writing; Katherine G. Ness and Linda A. Massie, copy editing; Mary Lyn Maiscott, research; Carol D. Tarlow, Charlene H. Roberson, Judith Lieberman, and Lorna B. Harris, recipe testing; Sydney Wolfe Cohen, index; Ruth L. Tedder and Polly Turnesa, rights clearance; Dolores J. MacCarthy and Doris B. Cypher, administrative assistants.

ILLUSTRATION CREDITS

Dust jacket, front cover: *Hoosick Falls in Winter* by Grandma Moses, copyright © 1979, Grandma Moses Properties, New York; Abby Aldrich Rockefeller Folk Art Center, Williamsburg, Virginia. Back cover: by Norman Rockwell; © 1933 The Curtis Publishing Company; *The Saturday Evening Post* cover, December 16, 1933. Front flap (top): reproduced from *Greetings from Christmas Past* by Bevis Hillier, The Herbert Press, London; distributed by Universe Books, New York. Front flap (bottom), back flap (top): photos by St. John Studios, Inc. Back flap (bottom): by Richard Williams.
Pages 8, 13: photos courtesy of Jessamyn West. Pages 16–17:

INDEX

Page numbers in bold refer to illustrations.

303